Y0-BCD-040

The Mixing of Peoples: Problems of Identity and Ethnicity

The Mixing of Peoples: Problems of Identity and Ethnicity

Edited by
Robert I. Rotberg

082155 6

Copyright© 1978 by Greylock, Inc.

No part of this book may be reproduced by any mechanical, photographic, or electronic process, or in the form of a phonographic recording, nor may it be stored in a retrieval system, transmitted, or otherwise copied for public or private use without written permission of the publisher.

Printed in the United States of America.
Library of Congress Catalog Card Number: 78-58529.
ISBN: 0-89223-006-1 (hard cover).

for Harold and Viola Isaacs

Contents

0821556   47230

Preface

For nearly 50 years, Harold Isaacs has been exploring dimensions of ethnicity. He has been concerned with the ways in which men and women dealt with their differences and similiarities—with realities like language, religion, pigmentation. He has been closely involved with the emergence of new nations in Asia and Africa. He is no stranger to the emotions of idealism and disillusionment. He has observed, participated in, and studied and taught the subjects brought together in this book. The new essays are by his associates, colleagues, students, and friends. Each is unpublished, as is one by himself. Together they comprise a dedication to him and to his interests.

In addition to the individual authors, Cecilia Dohrman, Rhoda Fischer, Donna Rogers, and Nancy Simkin contributed in significant ways to this book's final content and style.

R.I.R.
January, 1976

The Authors

AI-LI S. CHIN is a member of the faculty of College III, the University of Massachusetts at Boston. She is the author of "Family Relations in Modern Chinese Fiction," in Maurice Freedman (ed.), *Family and Kinship in Chinese Society* (Stanford, 1970) and (with Robert Chin), *Psychological Research in Communist China* (Cambridge, Mass., 1969). Chin's writing and research interests include women in modern China and Chinese-American identity.

CHAI HON-CHAN, a visiting fellow at the Harvard Institute for International Development during 1975-76, is professor of sociological studies in education at the University of Malaya, where he was dean of the faculty of education from 1971-74. He is a consultant to the Southeast Asian Ministers of Education Organization and is the author of *The Development of British Malaya, 1896-1909* (Kuala Lumpur, 1964), and *Planning Education for a Plural Society* (Paris, 1971).

ARNOLD R. ISAACS is Far East correspondent for *The Baltimore Sun*.

MICHIO NAGAI is Japan's Minister of Education, Science, and Culture. He is the author of *Higher Education in Japan* (Tokyo, 1971), and *An Owl Before Dusk* (Berkeley, 1975). He has taught in universities in Japan, the United States, Mexico, and Hong Kong and was an editorial writer for the *Asahi Shimbun*. The present article was written before he was appointed as minister.

ITHIEL DE SOLA POOL is Arthur and Ruth Sloan Professor of political science, Massachusetts Institute of Technology. His major interests are public opinion and communications. He is the author or editor of numerous books, among them *Handbook of Communications* (Chicago, 1973); *Talking Back: Citizen Feedback and Cable Technology* (Cambridge, Mass., 1973); *Prestige Press: A Comparative Study of Political Symbols* (Cambridge, Mass., 1970); (with Robert P. Abelson and Samuel L. Popkin), *Candidates, Issues and Strategies: A Computer Simulation of the 1960 Presidential Election* (Cambridge, Mass., 1964); (with R.A. Bauer and L.A. Dexter), *American Business and Public Policy* (New York, 1963), for which he received the Woodrow Wilson Award for the best political science book of that year; and *Trends in Content Analysis* (Urbana, Ill., 1959).

LUCIAN W. PYE is Ford Professor of political science, Massachusetts Institute of Technology. He has done extensive field research in Asia, and his special interest is political psychology. His principal works include *Mao Tse-tung: The Man in the Leader* (New York, 1976); *China: An Introduction* (Boston, 1972); *Political Culture and Political Development* (ed.), (Princeton, 1965); and *Politics, Personality, and Nation Building* (New Haven, 1962). He is Director of the Council on Foreign Relations and a member of the Board of Governors of the East-West Center.

ROBERT I. ROTBERG is a professor of history and political science, the Massachusetts Institute of Technology, and a research associate of the Center for International Affairs, Harvard University, and the African Studies Program, Boston University. He is the author or editor of a number of books, including *Joseph Thomson and the Exploration of Africa* (London, 1971), *Haiti: The Politics of Squalor* (Boston, 1971), *Protest and Power in Black Africa* (New York, 1970), *Africa and its Explorers* (Cambridge, Mass., 1970), *A Political History of Tropical Africa* (New York, 1965), *The Rise of Nationalism in Central Africa* (Cambridge, Mass., 1965), *The Family in History* (New York, 1971), and *East Africa and the Orient* (New York, 1975). He edits *The Journal of Interdisciplinary History*.

ROBERT SHAPLEN is Far East Correspondent for *The New Yorker*. He is the author of *A Corner of the World* (New York, 1949); *Free Love and Heavenly Sinners* (New York, 1954); *A Forest of Tigers* (New York, 1956); *Krueger: Genius and Swindler* (New York, 1960); *Toward the Wellbeing of Mankind—The Story of the Rockefeller Foundation* (New York, 1962); *The Lost Revolution* (New York, 1965), for which he received a Columbia School of Journalism award and a National Book Award nomination; *Time Out of Hand—Revolution and Reaction in Southeast Asia* (New York, 1969); and *The Road from War* (New York, 1970); *The Face of Asia* (New York, 1972); as well as numerous articles and TV documentaries. He has won five Overseas Press Club awards for magazine or book writing.

HIROSHI WAGATSUMA is professor of anthropology at the University of California, Los Angeles. Specializing in psychological anthropology, his particular interests include culture and personality in Japan, psychological characteristics among the Asian Americans, cross-cultural studies of minority relations, and problems of identity formation. He is the co-author, with George A. DeVos, of *Japan's Invisible Race: Cast in Culture and Personality* (Berkeley, 1966), as well as the author of numerous books in Japanese.

MYRON WEINER is Chairman of the Department of Political Science, Massachusetts Institute of Technology. Most recently, he was the co-author of *Policy Sciences and Population* (Lexington, Mass., 1975). His many books on India include *Electoral Politics in the Indian States* (co-author and co-editor), (New Delhi, 1975), 4v., and *Party Building in a New Nation: The Indian National Congress* (Chicago, 1967).

I

Harold R. Isaacs and The Mixing of Peoples

by Robert I. Rotberg*

When Harold Robert Isaacs entered life on 13 September 1910 he added measurably to the sum of human curiosity. His father Robert had been born in New York in 1883, son of the hard-driving Joseph Isaacs who had come to America in 1879, part of the earliest wave of the great migration of Eastern European Jews from Poland and Russia. Joseph opened a grocery store, expanded into real estate, and Robert made good the business his father founded. His mother Sophie was the gentle daughter of a gentle improvident religious scholar who had travelled the same route from Russian Poland. Something out of the mix of these origins and personalities, out of the immigrant encounter with American life, out of growing up and going to school in New York City in those years of his boyhood and youth—something about his own unique discovery of his world set Isaacs, boy and youth, on a path quite his own. The young Isaacs was moved from the beginning to question received information thoroughly, to care deeply about others of different and less fortunate circumstances, and to see for himself how the peoples of the world lived, worked, worshipped, and solved problems in their own settings. This was the boy who later took as his motto Victor Serge's line: "The world is always new if your nerves are strong enough,"[1] and proceeded to write about its inhabitants in what has become a shelf of books and a thick file of other published writings.

A poem from Harold's eighth year was long preserved in his father's wallet. It expressed a yearning for far off places, including China. There must have been much more, either prose or poetry, in the same genre, but it has not survived. In the archives of Manhattan's George Washington High School, however, there are the issues of the prize-winning magazine that the young Isaacs edited. In the fall of 1926, the week of his sixteenth birthday, he entered Columbia College. He was not the first but the second of his family to go there, his father's brother Samuel, a lawyer, being of the Class of 1904.

At Columbia the study of philosophy, history, and politics, widened his horizons. In philosophy, he sat in a class of the great John Dewey. The humanistic approach of Irwin Edman, who taught philosophy of religion and art, proved particularly influential. In history he was exposed to Parker T. Moon, who wrote on imperialism and lectured on the Chinese past. Peter Odegard, a young professor of politics who later became president of Reed College and chairman of the political science department of the University of California, Berkeley, introduced Isaacs to political thought and, in another way, to humility. When Isaacs submitted a critique to him of Lenin's *State and Revolution* it was entitled "Bombs, Bolsheviks, and Bombast." Odegard appended a subtitle: "Being a Brief Bit of Balderdash by Barold Bobert Bisaacs." This exchange began a lifelong friendship.

A selectively serious student with a mind of his own, Isaacs followed his bent in nonacademic areas, too. He rowed on the freshman lightweight crew and joined the staff of the Columbia *Spectator*. There he served his apprenticeship as a newspaperman while, from his junior year, simultaneously working for the *New York Times* on an assignment basis. In this last capacity he found covering Sunday sermons in Manhattan's different churches a source of steady income, three dollars for the story, ten cents for subway fare, and fifteen cents for the collection box. It was also a major learning exercise in the study of comparative religion and religious attitudes. Before he was through, the young reporter had visited scores of churches and synagogues in all parts of the city and discussed their differences with as many priests, ministers, and rabbis. Other assignments also came his way, the most prized being the opportunity to report Norman Thomas' campaign for mayor of New York in 1929. Riding with Thomas in the subway (the other candidates used limousines) Isaacs was impressed with Thomas' ideas, lack of affectation, frugality, and idealism. He was drawn as a result to the concept of socialism. And, like so many of his generation, despite occasional or frequent ideological differences, he never lost his personal admiration for Thomas. A friendship eventually developed which lasted until Thomas' death.

The summer vacations of his college years contributed new experiences and maturity. Curious to see what lay beyond the skyscrapers, the bustle, and the squalor of New York and to glimpse places about which he had long read, in 1927 Isaacs hitchhiked across America, worked as a seaman on the Great Lakes and a harvester of wheat in the Midwest. He mingled with many different types of people, taking the rough with the kind. One summer night followed a day during which the rides had been few and he had raised blisters after walking miles and miles. Arriving on sore feet in a small Minnesota town where the only light shone from the police station, a fatherly officer on duty helped in the only way he could: he booked Isaacs for vagrancy, locked him in a cell for the night, and, the next morning, supplied bandages, breakfast, and fifty cents for the road. (Isaacs, never forgetting this kindness, thirty years later tried to locate the policeman. But real life does not always contrive neat endings: the trail had long before gone cold.) He met with memorable kindness again when he suffered a bad ankle sprain jumping off a freight car in the railway yard of a small Colorado town. The operators of a small railway hotel abutting the yard took him in and he became a fixture there until he could walk again without crutches. (He looked for them, too, years later, but they had long since disappeared.) In Los Angeles he returned these favors by giving his last few dollars to a friend he had met in a gospel hall (where he had gone for curiosity's sake and a free bowl of soup) and went to San Pedro where he stowed away on a ship bound for New York via the Panama Canal. He worked his way home as an ordinary seaman. (Three years later he received $5 back in the mail. He has found it hard, ever since, to assume the worst at first about anybody.)

The next year, 1928, he and a friend from that same ship's crew, a Californian named Charles Renwick, went to Europe. They saw London, Paris, and the Swiss Alps. They shipped deck passage from Marseille to Egypt and saw the sun rise from the top of the Great Pyramid. They travelled the ancient road from Egypt to Jericho, Jerusalem, Bethlehem, the Dead Sea, the Jordan, and Galilee. They made a rapt discovery of the land of the Bible. They made their way back across the Mediterranean to Spain (as workaways who spent their days cleaning out the dregs of oil in the hold of a small tanker) and young Isaacs returned to New York just in time to begin his junior year.

These were exciting journeys but not nearly as fateful as the one he had already made, across the street from Columbia to Barnard where, from his freshman year on he had begun to share life's expectations with Viola Robinson.

At school, Isaacs concentrated on philosophy, especially the philosophy of religion, political thought, history, and politics. He had come to Columbia with religion much on his mind. As a small boy he had eagerly pursued a traditional Jewish education, giving it many of his after-school hours. But here too his questing mind had caught early at dilemmas and unanswered riddles. At age nine he gave a Talmud Torah teacher a bad moment by asking to know why God, in commanding the Israelites to slay the Amalekites, had specified not only the men, but also the women, the children, and their beasts. His questions multiplied as he grew up. At Columbia Isaacs wrote papers on the Old Testament, the origins of Christianity, and Jewish mysticism. He explored the history and ideas of religion in a long arc of time stretching from Plato to William James. He came out of this exploration with what he described to a student interviewer as "life-shaping conclusions."[2] These brought him to the materialistic-humanistic outlook which has governed his life and work ever since.

He had entered Columbia thinking that he would eventually study law, but abandoned that idea after his freshman year. He wanted other values, other goals, other ways of spending his energy. By the time that he finished college he knew he would spend his life, and make his living, as a writer. His bents were strongly reportorial and he saw his apprenticeships on the Columbia *Spectator* and the *New York Times* as launching him on a newspaper career. He had also decided during his last two years at Columbia that he would make his way as soon as he could to

China. He fixed on China, he has told questioners many times, because it was the farthest away he could get from where he was, and it was true that young Isaacs wanted to break away from the culture and the environment in which he had been raised and to discover what other parts of the world, other cultures, other people, and other environments were like. But it is also true that he had begun to develop a serious interest in China—in Chinese history and the modern Chinese predicament. This came partly out of his studies of nineteenth century imperialism under Moon, and partly from reading the books of Thomas Millard, founder of *Millard's Review* (later the *China Weekly Review*) whose work in the World War I decade and immediately thereafter gave Isaacs a beckoning view of what a combination of journalism, history, and contemporary politics could offer in the useful expenditure of energies and the making of the good life.[3] When he completed requirements for a bachelor's degree in February 1930, after three and a half years at Columbia, he was still half a year short of his twentieth birthday. In March, he left home and family and—temporarily—even Viola behind, and set out to expose himself, in his own key phrase of the time, "to the buffeting of circumstance."

He departed from New York as a bellhop on an intercoastal liner, and some weeks later left San Francisco as an ordinary seaman on a Matson liner. Reaching Honolulu he went to work as a police reporter on the *Honolulu Advertiser*. His experiences there were seasoning—including being temporarily "arrested" at the order of an angry local city and county attorney who accused him of "interfering" with the work of his office and staff. During his six months in Hawaii, Isaacs was fascinated by its multi-hued population. He took a summer course at the local university in the history and sociology of the islands and did the paper "Races—Hawaii" which is published for the first time in the present volume. It foreshadows in a remarkable way the interests to which he was to come in such fullness in later years. He stayed on in Honolulu long enough to turn 20. One day an *Advertiser* assignment took him aboard a Dollar vessel to interview the captain, who turned out to be the same man who had been the skipper of the freighter on which he had stowed away out of San Pedro three years before. The next time that ship came through the port, Isaacs was signed on as a wiper to spend his days in the 120 degree heat of the ship's bowels. He was rescued for some hours each day, however, when the chief engineer discovered he was literate and put him to work keeping the engine room log.

On shore again in Manila, Isaacs did some temporary stints for the United Press and wandered the islands to the farthest south, to Zamboanga and Jolo, writing freelance pieces for the Philippines *Free Press* and the Honolulu *Advertiser*. One of them was an interview in prison with a Moro datu, or chieftain, who had led a dissident band against the American constabulary, even as Moro chieftains are leading such bands in 1976 against their Filipino rulers. He was offered a newspaper job that would have kept him in Manila, but China beckoned. He left Manila—a ship's passenger at last for this final leg of his transpacific journey—and walked ashore in Shanghai in December 1930, ten months after leaving New York.

Isaacs landed a job almost immediately as a reporter on the American-owned daily, the *Shanghai Evening Post & Mercury,* and launched forthwith on his new career. A few months later a Chinese syndicate closely allied to the Kuomintang established the *China Press,* the first English-language daily owned by Chinese. Hollington K.Tong, a graduate of the Columbia School of Journalism and a former teacher of Chiang Kai-shek, became its editor and immediately hired as city editors two young Americans, Tillman Durdin, later of the *New York Times* and then 24, and Isaacs, not yet 21. Isaacs approached this new task with great enthusiasm. To write for a Chinese-owned publication challenged the long-established British and American owned newspapers and supported the aspirations of Chinese nationalists. But he was soon disillusioned. Truth, he discovered, was also capable of being distorted by Chinese for political purposes. It was not long before Isaacs' stubborn refusals to tamper with facts brought him into conflict with Tong. He was fired in the summer of 1931.

He had begun to learn about radical politics, meanwhile, from a variety of Chinese friends, including Mrs. Sun Yat-sen, from Agnes Smedley, an American writer who espoused the Communist cause, and from a wandering South African Trotskyist, Frank Glass, who introduced him to the factional complexities of the international Communist movement. That summer he and Glass went up the Yangtze River to Chungking and from there Isaacs went on alone, on foot, pony, and by bus, deep into western Szechwan almost to the border of Tibet. He returned by river junk, coming back down the Yangtze in the wake of one of the great river floods of the century. There was devastation everywhere and, for the first time in his life, he saw dead and dying and mass suffering. He also saw how callous Chiang's officials were, how little they did to alleviate the plight of the flood's victims, and how greedily they diverted American and other foreign aid into their own pockets. It was a life-changing experience for him. When he reached Nanking, he took an assignment from the United Press to cover Charles Lindbergh, arriving to make an aerial survey of the flood area. But in that week, on September 18, 1931, Japan invaded Manchuria and he found himself instead covering the Nanking Government's first responses—or non-responses—to the Japanese assault.

Back in Shanghai, the young reporter obtained a job translating the incoming news service supplied to newspapers there by Agence Havas, the French news agency. But he was looking for ways in which to serve his strong new impulse to *do* something that would be useful socially and politically.

As he has written: "The effects of all these exposures, the shocks, the encounters, the learning of that year came together for me not long thereafter when Communist friends and friends of Communists I met in Shanghai suggested the possibility of my starting up a paper of my own."[4] The first issue of the *China Forum* appeared on January 13,

1932. On its front page, it described the arrest and execution one year earlier of five young Communist writers. The second issue began publishing translations of stories by these and other Chinese writers. The *Forum's* columns were given over to reports of the harassment of intellectuals by the Kuomintang government at Nanking, the arrests, executions, and other acts of terror and perfidies of the Chiang regime, the pressures of the Japanese and Western imperialists, and news of worker unrest in the cities and the Communist-led peasant rebellion in the hinterland.

But publication of the *Forum* and much else was interrupted when the Japanese attacked Shanghai by air, land, and sea in January 1932. Isaacs saw at firsthand for the first time mass death and destruction wreaked not by nature but by men. From the protected sanctuary of the International Settlement—which literally shook with the concussions—it was possible to watch the world's first terror bombing from the air. It was like a spectacle put on for a select audience, the systematic destruction by wave after wave of bombers of the neighboring working class district of Chapei, a vast, sprawling, thickly-populated area in which thousands were killed. Along with scores of other foreign newsmen, he looked on at close range as the battle for control of Shanghai's North Station went on only yards away from the Settlement boundary. Ranging out through the city's war zones, he and others witnessed the wanton killing of civilians by shooting and bayonetting. The Japanese were resisted—in defiance of Chiang Kai-shek's orders from Nanking—by the independent 19th Route Army then garrisoning Shanghai. It fought alone and was all but decimated by the time token help came near the end of a 34-day battle. Chiang's troops arrived only to police the surrender that followed.

Reappearing after an interruption of several months, the *Forum* described these events in a way that angered both his Kuomintang enemies and his Communist friends, the former by the *Forum's* blunt characterization of what had happened, the latter by its refusal to accept their exaggerated version of the Communist role in these events.

Wu Teh-chen, the Kuomintang mayor of Shanghai, was particularly troubled by the issue of the *Forum* which appeared on 2 July. Below a large headline, "Drinking the Blood of China," was a photograph of Mayor Wu and the local Japanese consul-general. The caption beneath the photograph said that the two sipped "from their cocktail glasses in amiable sociability the blood of tens of thousands of Chinese whom both helped to slaughter here only a few months ago.... Their unity is expressive on the converse side of the union between the worker-peasant masses of China-Japan against the venal oppressors who rule them."[5]

The Kuomintang authorities formally protested about Isaacs to the U.S. Consulate-General in Shanghai. They filed seven charges against him, five of which, under their law, carried the death penalty. He was summoned by the consul-general who advised him to cease publication and threatened him with the withdrawal of the extraterritorial rights which alone protected him from the mercies of the Kuomintang. In an official cable to Shanghai, the State Department declared that the *Forum's* campaign against the Kuomintang government was "a gross abuse of his privilege as an American citizen" and was prejudicial to the interest of the United States. He had therefore forfeited rights of protection. The government of the United States would refuse to intervene if the Chinese authorities tried to prevent further publications of the *Forum* .[6]

Isaacs immediately published the news of this attempt to gag him. The issue suddenly became a broader one, involving the jealously-guarded principle of extraterritoriality. The *New York Times* carried a long story on July 28 and another on July 30 with the headline, "Our Consul tells Harold R. Isaacs, Editor, Attacks on Nanking May Bring End to Immunity. Death Penalty Possible." As a result, the State Department slightly softened its position, but consular officials in Shanghai did not intervene when Isaacs' Chinese printer was forced to stop printing the *Forum* in August. Isaacs was not touched personally. The indicated threat to foreign privilege had been sharply criticized in the local British press and nothing more was said about depriving this difficult young American of his treaty status. When the American consular attorney invited him to surrender his "rights" voluntarily since he opposed such rights so vehemently, Isaacs replied that he thought it more useful—and practicable—to use his privileges against the privileged.

It was in the midst of all these events, in August, 1932, that Viola Robinson left her teaching job in New York to join Isaacs in Shanghai. The reports of his predicament had appeared in the *Times* while she was still in New York and the *Forum* had temporarily ceased publication by the time that she reached Shanghai. But to her considerable relief, there he was on the jetty to greet her when she stepped ashore. To the bemused astonishment of younger officials at the American consulate, they were married there two weeks later. The judge of the United States Consular Court refused to preside over the nuptials of this notorious young Bolshevik but the U.S. Commissioner, who ranked under him as a kind of magistrate, thought it only right that the demure and proper and pretty young Viola Robinson should be made an honest woman. On the appointed day, the day after Isaacs' 22nd birthday—during the lunch hour—Viola came from the teaching job that she had already obtained in a local settlement Chinese school, and Isaacs arrived from his embattled office. They were duly joined together by the same legal authorities who were quite ready to allow the Kuomintang to put them rudely asunder. A young vice-consul who did the paper work for the occasion—George Allen, who eventually rose to high ambassadorial rank in the Foreign Service—later marvelled to friends: "And do you know, she is very nice!" (Twenty-five years later, when Isaacs sought Allen out to interview him for *Scratches,* Allen, then an Assistant Secretary of State, greeted him at his office door, saying: "I know you, I *married* you!")

Having lost access to commercial printers, Isaacs proceeded to set up a small printshop of his own, using handset type and a small Platen press—all supplied by friends of the Communists—and from this tiny shop the *Forum* re-emerged in January, 1933. In all there were 34 issues, the last 16 appearing in Chinese as well as English. As a whole the *Forum* trod a careful philosophical line between the approaches of Stalin and Trotsky, and, toward the end, represented a tussle between the supporters of nontruth and partial truth upon whom the *Forum* was dependent for information and distribution, and those, like the editor, for whom integrity was a concern more important even than revolution. The last issue of the *Forum* appeared in January, 1934. "Mounting disagreements between me and my Communist friends came to a head," Isaacs later wrote, "and the paper could not survive our break. It became my own small version of the experience of being caught, or nearly caught, between those same two gates of darkness."[7]

Harold and Viola Isaacs moved that spring from Shanghai to Peking. Viola went to work as a teacher in a Chinese middle school there, the first foreigner and the first woman that the school had ever hired. Harold worked for awhile as a part-time stringer for the *London Daily Express.* Together they sought to complete the translated collection of stories by radical Chinese authors, many of which had appeared in the *Forum.* Partly because of his break from his Communist friends—Isaacs was now being denounced in the overseas Communist press as an "imperialist agent" and a "counter-revolutionary"—this book was not immediately published. It gathered dust in the Isaacs' files for 40 years before finally appearing in print. In his introduction to *Straw Sandals: Chinese Stories 1918-1933* (Cambridge, 1974), he tells the poignant story of the five writers executed in 1931 and how their fates became entwined, in a deeply personal as well as political way, with his own.

In Peking in 1934 Isaacs also began *The Tragedy of the Chinese Revolution.* He had intended to write mainly of the years of the Kuomintang regime, beginning in 1928, but found himself drawn to the events which had brought Chiang Kai-shek to power in the first place. The book became a history, often since described as a "classic" in its field. It is a detailed examination of the events of the first Kuomintang-Communist alliance (1924-1927) in China. This alliance brought on a vast popular uprising in the country against foreign domination and militarist rule. It ended when Chiang Kai-shek, its military commander, seized power through a bloody coup at Shanghai in 1927 and established his own Kuomintang government at Nanking. The book examines the differences between Stalin and Trotsky in Moscow over the strategy of the revolution in China. It vividly describes and documents the events in China which gave such somber reality to Trotsky's warning that Stalin's course could lead only to disaster.

The Tragedy of the Chinese Revolution was first published in London in 1938 and has remained in print ever since in numerous editions in English and other languages. In introductions to revised editions of it in 1951 and 1961, Isaacs described his own abandonment of his early faith in radical Marxism. This shift in view changed his estimate of what might have resulted in China had Trotsky's views prevailed instead of Stalin's, but did not require him to do much more than excise as much as he could of the hortatory passages and polemical style from the original text. Indeed, the passage of time brought the issues of these events to a characteristically paradoxical outcome, as Isaacs noted in an introduction written in 1971 for a French re-issue of the original Chinese translation (which had appeared in Shanghai in 1947):

> Eventually—22 years after the 1927 defeat—Mao Tse-tung led the Chinese Communists to power without benefit either of Stalin's mechanical "stage" theory of revolution or Trotsky's puristic proletarianism: he did it by the distinctly non-Leninist strategy of sweeping in on the cities from the hinterland with Communist-led peasant armies, preserving the necessary doctrinal purity by identifying the Communist Party with the "proletariat." In power, Mao—propelled by drives with origins in China's remoter as well as more recent past—became in his turn the greatest national-Communist of them all. He broke with post-Stalin Russia to follow his own course, calling upon the world Communist movement to recognize Peking, not Moscow, as the center of true revolutionism. But the banner under which he summoned the world to follow him—from a Peking still adorned with Stalin's portraits years after Stalin's posthumous downfall—was inscribed with Trotsky's device of the permanent revolution, the ongoing, never-ending, uncompromising, ceaselessly aggressive advance of the "working class" toward the "victory of socialism" in each country, country after country, until it encompassed the entire globe. Here was a dialectic with a marvelous vengeance: Leninism producing Stalinism vs. Trotskyism out of which Stalinism and Trotskyism fuse into a "new" super-revolutionary Maoism.[8]

After nearly a year and a half in Peking, the young couple decided to return to the United States. They felt too far from any stream of events in which they could participate. They wanted to get away from being conspicuous foreigners in China and to become "two among many digits" in their own country. They also wanted to check out sources and material in Europe for the *Tragedy*. So when a job opened for Viola in the New York City school system, she accepted it, and they sailed from Shanghai in June 1935. They went home by stages, interviewing observers or participants in the Chinese events of the 1920s. They saw Albert Treint in France, H. Sneevliet in the Netherlands, and Leon Trotsky in Norway, and combed libraries for increasingly rare Communist materials dealing with that period.

In New York in the fall of 1935, Viola went back to teaching and into new activity as a member of the Teachers Union, and Harold went back to work for Agence Havas, filling the rest of his hours with work on *The Tragedy*, as a volunteer editorial hand on weeklies published by the Trotskyist and Socialist movements, and, after the Moscow Trials began in 1936, as a helper at the Trotsky Defense Committee in New York headed by John Dewey, the philospher. *The Tragedy of the Chinese Revolution* was finally finished in 1937 and appeared in London—no American publisher would take it—in 1938 with an introduction by Trotsky. In correspondence with Trotsky, the youthful Isaacs—he was still only 27—had not hesitated to challenge some parts of that introduction, especially Trotsky's judgments about the further course of Japan's war in China.

But the restricted, isolated life of impotent radical politics was losing its hold on Harold and Viola Isaacs. Its rhetorical violence and factionalisms had come to seem much more a mirror of the Soviet actuality than of some felicitous future. In a world trying to come to grips with the ultimate violence of Hitlerism, they sought some more meaningful life of their own. By the time that France fell in 1940 and the job with Havas came abruptly to an end, so had their involvements with the radical milieu. In an explicit defiance of the world's outlook, they were having their first child, their son Arnold, who was born in February 1941. The new father was making a precarious living as a script writer at the Columbia Broadcasting System, but he soon moved into the writing of radio news documentaries. He joined the staff of the major prime time "Report to the Nation" in Washington, where he remained throughout the next year. But he found, especially after Pearl Harbor, that he could not remain comfortably in the "show biz" atmosphere in which he found himself. One afternoon in 1942 he walked out of a story conference and never returned. He went to work instead at *Newsweek* for a fraction of what he had been earning, being relieved however, to return to what he felt was serious work as a reporter. In 1943, when their second child Deborah was on the way, Isaacs pressed for and received an assignment as *Newsweek's* correspondent in the China-Burma-India theater of war. Not long after the baby was born near year's end, he went off once more to Asia.

For the next year and a half, he covered stories of the war in that remote and obscure theater, flew back and forth across the Himalayan "Hump," and flew a B-29 bombing mission to Manchuria and across Japanese-occupied China in a weather plane. He covered the retreat from Kweiyang in the bleak, deep of winter of 1944, the small but bloody battles fought to open the Burma Road on both sides of the border, the Salween front on the China side, and southward from Myitkina in north Burma to Bhamo. He rode the first convoy that made the triumphant run from Burma to Kunming early in 1945. He was with the British 19th Division when it took Mandalay in Burma in one of the war's last campaigns. He had flown out from under Chungking censorship to Calcutta in November 1944 to file a long story about the dismissal of General Joseph Stilwell as theater commander. For this, on his return from a brief home leave in the spring of 1945, he found himself barred by the Kuomingtang government from re-entering China. Instead he joined Lord Mountbatten's forces preparing to land on the beaches near Singapore and was in India on the day that the atom bomb was dropped on Hiroshima. He flew off to the Philippines and on to Korea in time to go in with the occupying American army. After a brief time in Korea and Japan, he returned south to report on the burgeoning new colonial wars in Indochina and Indonesia before finally returning home at the end of the year.

Isaacs became an associate editor in New York for *Newsweek*. Nights and weekends during the rest of 1946 he finished *No Peace for Asia*, which Macmillan published early in 1947. It opens with a section called "American Soldiers in Asia," a detailed series of vignette descriptions of the painful interaction between young Americans, Chinese, and Indians in the conditions of their wartime encounter. These were notes that Isaacs took the most care to preserve whenever he went off on sundry military enterprises. When book-writing time came at the war's end, it was with these matters, not battles or politics, that he opened *No Peace for Asia.* Its initial pages, about GI's, "wogs", and "slopeys," were the forerunners of the work Isaacs turned to some years later in his examination of American perceptions of China and India. The rest of *No Peace for Asia* went on to deal with the immediate postwar developments in Asia, the new patterns of power created by the Japanese collapse and the American victory in terms of the emerging new nationalisms and the new power struggle between the Soviet Union and the United States. His chapter on Korea, filled with sharp firsthand vignettes, including one of a journey on a commandeered train that continued until it was stopped just beyond the 38th parallel by the oncoming Russians taking over in the northern half of the partitioned country, ends with these words:

> For Koreans the hysterical joy that followed Japan's collapse gave way to a bitter time of hope and fear, of aspiration and gnawing disillusion. Their land was not free. It was a little test tube for Russian and American power politics in Asia, a trial zone, an outpost, a boundary where mighty opponents eyed each other. Korea was a minor preliminary proving ground for Russian and American professions and Russian and American practices. Whichever way the tests came out, the future did not look bright for Korean freedom. Koreans are not sophisticated. Neither are they naive. A Korean friend said to me: "we spent long hard years learning Japanese. Now we must learn English or Russian. When shall we be able to concentrate on learning Korean?"[9]

But the strongest among many strong pages in this early book are those that deal with the paths taken and not taken by the United States at that great crossroads reached in Asia at the point of America's victory over Japan. Isaacs saw American policy in China as a lost cause. He saw the greatest immediate danger there coming from the onset of a Russian-American collision occurring in the guise of the Kuomintang-Communist civil war. Elsewhere, however, the new American opportunity was almost boundless. Under the heading "The Myth Glorious," Isaacs wrote of what he found everywhere in Asia in the immediate aftermath of the Japanese surrender, a myth that was "in the main an insubstantial dream filled with unrealized images" that "acquired objective reality because so many people believed in it."

> The American myth in Asia was compounded of many things. It was made up of remoteness: the United States was a distant shining temple of virtue and righteousness, where men were like gods amid unending plenty. It was made up of awe: the United States was unimaginable power, a country that could suffer crushing blows and then come back to the skies and coasts of Asia, conquer the mountains, batter down the seemingly invincible conqueror of only a few years before. It was made up of half-truths: the United States was a country that believed in freedom. Its own people were free. It was granting freedom to the Philippines. It had nothing, nothing at all in common with other Western countries, or Japan, which lived by the fruits of colonial slavery.
>
> In a continent heavy with superstition and ancient beliefs, and scant in its knowledge of the outside world, the belief grew and existed that the United States would be both altruistic and wise: altruistic enough to side with the cause of freedom for its own sake, wise enough to see that continued imperialism in the British, Dutch, French, and Japanese style would bring no peace anywhere...

Such, as far as it can be reduced from scores of conversations all the way from Delhi to Seoul to Saigon to Batavia, was the hopeful picture of the American position seriously entertained by many conscious Asiatic nationalists. From it they concluded that American postwar aims would necessarily coincide with the aims of Asiatic nationalism. From it they concluded, at the very least, that while they could not trust the promises of the British, the French, or the Dutch, they could trust the Americans. But they were disappointed. They were confused. They began, in a short span of time, the passage from belief to doubt to open hostility. This process took place everywhere. It was the most spectacular fact of the first postwar months, that puncturing of the American myth, the rude destruction of hopes that never had any foundation in the first place. Watching it happen, in country after country following Japan's collapse, was like witnessing the crumbling of castles in the sky.

Writing of this "myth punctured," Isaacs identified what he saw as the central and fateful failure of outlook and policy of the time:

In the broadest and most fundamental sense, the chief American failure was the failure to stand for change. The United States had spoken for a new order of things. It acted now for the old order of things. By what it did and by what it failed to do, the American victory brought no beginning of a solution, nor the promise of a solution, to the problems of dislocation, upheaval, conflict, and nationalist aspiration. In the struggles that erupted among colonial peoples to prevent the return of their old masters, the United States stood in fact not with the rebelling subjects but with the returning rulers. In every actual political situation in which it became involved, the United States stood not with the partisans of social change but with the defenders of archaic conservatism. Peace itself remained elusive since the United States passed out of its victory over Japan headlong into a fresh competition for power with Russia.[10]

No Peace for Asia was turned aside by most reviewers as unduly "pessimistic" even though its forecast of things to come turned out to be a distinct under-statement of what actually took place in the following years, especially in Asia.

His writing made him a natural target for the China Lobby, the activities of which foreshadowed the McCarthy era, but the editors of *Newsweek* ignored the pressure brought against their forthright and prolific associate editor. Chet Shaw, the doughtily conservative Kansas Republican who was then executive editor of *Newsweek* , once received a letter from the China Lobby that accused Isaacs of sundry crimes and misdemeanors and urged *Newsweek* to fire him. Without comment, Shaw handed the letter to Isaacs and drily asked him to prepare a reply for his, Shaw's signature. Much as he respected Shaw, and much as he enjoyed plying his craft as a reporter—and a very well-paid one at that—Isaacs had begun to chafe at the limited time he could spend on writing the things that *he* wanted to write. He was turning out cover stories on a great variety of interesting subjects—his first big postwar assignment was a description of Oak Ridge when that atomic facility was first opened to public view. He made another swing through Southeast Asia when he went to cover Nehru's conference on Indonesia in New Delhi in 1949 and from there to Indonesia itself where the Dutch "police action"—the last desperate effort to keep Dutch rule intact in the islands—was underway.

But he had become by this time primarily concerned with the problems of American policy in relation to the non-Western world. He was involved with Norman Thomas and his Postwar World Council in an effort to define the new issues of current American policy. He took part, with Thomas, and Senators Wayne Morse and Hubert Humphrey, in a major conference in 1949 designed to give thrust and content to President Truman's proposed Point Four Program. A result of this involvement was his *Two-Thirds of the World* (Washington, 1950) which espoused the need for economic aid to the developing world *with* strings attached. The strings were designed to support and foster the development of open politics in the new national states of Asia and Africa.

"In the fall of 1949", he later wrote in retrospect to the Guggenheim Foundation, "I took a major career decision, resigning, effective January 1, 1950, as Associate Editor of *Newsweek* in charge of special projects and reports, to devote myself exclusively to writing on matters of primary interest to me. These were matters to which I had been able to devote myself only fitfully in spells as correspondent abroad for *Newsweek*, i.e., the problems of American policy in Asia and in the non-Western world generally, especially the problems of retrieval following upon the debacle in China. Hence all my principal writings of this period were efforts to define the new scope of these problems and our need, as a nation and as individuals, to acquire new outlooks and a new image of a changing world. As I look back over this material now, I am struck to see how gradually yet how steadily my emphasis shifted from the first of these to the second; without surrendering any of my interest in policy-problem-situation as such, I became increasingly intent upon the more elusive aspects of outlook and image as they affected the men involved in these policies, these problems, these situations."[11]

Isaacs' work between 1950 and 1953 consists almost entirely of urgently written articles about these "policies, problems, situations." He went to the Philippines early in 1950 at the invitation of the *Philippines Herald* to do a series on a conference of south and southeast Asian nations held to consider their common problems. The Korean War broke out just after he returned from Manila and Isaacs was writing frequently for the *The Reporter*, the *Christian Science Monitor*, the *New York Post*, and other publications on issues related to the Korean war, and especially the drama unfolding in Indochina, where American support for the French and recognition of their puppet Bao Dai was opening the fateful era of American intervention there. Under the title "Another Disaster in Asia," in the April 11, 1950 issue of *The Reporter*, Isaacs wrote:

> With (this act of recognition) the United States embarked upon another ill- conceived adventure doomed to end in another self-inflicted defeat. The real problem is not how to implement this policy but how to extricate ourselves from it.

Isaacs had begun to concern himself also with Africa. He saw it as the continent where a new chapter was about to open in the changing story of Western relations with the non-Western world. He saw it as related to the problems of race relations in the American society and, above all, as a continent where the United States had a chance to avoid repeating its Asian mistakes. A first product of this interest was a

Foreign Policy Association booklet called *Africa: New Crises in the Making*, published in 1952. In 1953 he jointly edited with Alan Paton, the South African author, a special issue of the *Saturday Review* which included an article of his own, "Western Man and the African Crisis." During this time he lectured extensively at many colleges and universities, spent a term as a Visiting Lecturer at the New School for Social Research in New York and in a similar capacity at Harvard, where he helped orient a group of public health specialists on their way to Southeast Asia. He also contributed to a study made for the Ford Foundation of university programs relating to non-Western countries. These interests led to an invitation first to consult and then to join the staff of the Center for International Studies at M.I.T., which he did in the summer of 1953, becoming, he wrote later, "a naturalized though not quite acclimatized member of the academic community."[12]

Isaacs always called himself "a squatter in academe." For the next twelve years, as a research associate of the Center, he followed his inquiring bents wherever they took him. He continued to do so when his colleagues and M.I.T. tinkered still further with his identity and made him a professor in the newly-formed department of political science. He devised some added duties for himself, especially the Colloquium on Dissertation Research, a sharp inquisition for students embarking on the final stages of their doctoral work. It was another extension of his essential style, which remained the asking of questions.

His first major undertaking at the Center, begun in 1954, was an examination of American ideas about American-Asian relations. It grew into a unique exploration of how Americans perceived Chinese and Indians as people. The result was one of Isaacs' best-known works, *Scratches On Our Minds: American Images of China and India*, first published in 1958 and since in various paperback editions with the title *Images of Asia*. It is a work based on interviews with nearly 200 Americans occupying key places as communicators in society, and on a freshly re-focused re-examination of the history and literature of American-Asian relations. In these interviews Isaacs probed for the sources of the images, stereotypes, and often half-held and vaguely realized notions and memories that his subjects had about China and the Chinese, and India and the Indians. He looked for the interaction between images and events, both in the past and in the present. The product was a ground-breaking study which has remained a model and a source for similar studies ever since. It also marked the shift that had taken place in Isaacs' own way of focusing on international affairs. As he described it himself in 1959:

> With this work I had both widened and narrowed the aperture of my outlook on affairs. I had widened it by finally moving over into areas of inquiry at which I had until now directed only occasional sidelong glances...(as in) my wartime writing about the nature of the American GI experience in India and China...But this meant, also, a certain narrowing of outlook, focusing down from the larger entities of nations, classes, castes, and races, to individuals as they related to each other and all of these larger identities. I found myself drawn, through the perplexities of international politics, to

begin examining the greater perplexities of individual behavior across cultural and national lines.

The loss has been in advocacy. Confronted by large and powerful entities, or even abstractions, you enter into conflict: values and ideas drive you to affirmative action. You can be for one kind of program or policy, against another. The rigorous disciplines of reporting are not only tools of knowledge and analysis; they can also be weapons. But shift your focus to the particular individual, and your object shifts too. Once engaged, you seek only to bring more and more of his complexities into view. The juices of advocacy thin out and soon stop running altogether, and [are in danger of being replaced] by the oozing milk of human kindness. The effort to understand more if not, with humility, *all*—leads straight to forgiving more—if not, indeed, *all*—and for one not given to the pursuit of knowledge for its own sake alone, or of methodology in social science without primary heed to the substance, this is not the best of all possible consummations. One's problem becomes how to trespass on the domains of priest, psychiatrist, or novelist, without sooner or later being penalized for being none of these, how not to be immobilized by "wisdom", how not to become only a question-asker in a world without answers.

These are not light problems and I do not pretend to have solved them. But while I work at it, there are, on the other hand, the great gains: the experience of fresh discovery, the greatly enriched power to explore and to describe, the summoning to the mental councils of the scholars, the journalists, and politicians, a more sophisticated awareness of aspects of behavior, including their own, with which they say they are concerned, yet so much of which they slight or ignore completely.[13]

Of *Scratches On Our Minds*, the late Gordon Allport, dean of American social psychologists, wrote:

> I suspect that *Scratches On Our Minds* will long haunt both political science and psychology—as it rightly should do. It throws a timely challenge to both. The former needs to take account of the personal equation that undoubtedly shapes foreign policy more than it should; the latter needs to explain the deep anchoring of international images in our own particular personalities. It is a smooth and readable account of the cerebral abrasions that mark and mar American minds.[14]

When Isaacs accepted an invitation to give a seminar in 1959 he was asked to provide a title for listing it in the M.I.T. course catalogue. Having always been able readily to define his field of interest as something like "Asian and international affairs," now, he explained, he had to grope for a redefinition, and from a first answer, "changing human relations arising out of changing power relations in world politics," came the title of the seminar that he gave regularly for the next fifteen years: "Changing Outlooks and Identities in World Affairs." The theme, tackled in immensely varied individual ways by successive generations of students who shared in the seminar, had to do with the great overturns, the end of colonial empires, the re-emergence of peoples and nations, and the re-casting of all roles in world affairs. Of this theme, Issacs wrote at the end of *Scratches*:

> This is history in the large, a great continental rearrangment, bringing with it a great and wrenching shift in the juxtapositions of cultures and peoples. Western men are being relieved of the comforts and disabilities of being the lords of creation; Asian and African men can no longer merely submit, nor live on the rancors of subjection, nor revitalize their own societies by the ideas or sanctions of their own more distant pasts. All must move from old ground to new, from old assumptions to new ones, and

as they move they must constantly refocus their views. They will all be engaged, for some time to come, in more or less painfully revising the images they have of themselves and of each other.

In this revision, all the images and experiences of the past have some part. They are not effaced but are absorbed and rearranged in some new design. Much is relegated to the museums and to the memory and to the contending history books, but the great part remains to bedevil the process of change itself. All the sounds, old and new, go on in our hearing at the same time, making the great din in which we live...[15]

"I must now describe myself as being devoted," Isaacs wrote later, "to the sorting out of these sights and sounds. It is in this setting that I have embarked upon my present further inquiries."[16]

These further inquiries over the next decade produced a series of studies—all based on interviews with people directly involved— illustrating this basic theme and basic experience of our time. Having pursued in *Scratches* how perceptions affected events, Isaacs moved next to examine how events affected perceptions. The regaining of political independence and the formation of new states in Africa was clearly going to force a revision of white-black relations on a world scale. It was already powerfully affecting the process of change in the United States, where the long-imbedded white supremacy system could obviously not outlive the colonial system elsewhere by very long. He began his next inquiry by asking what the effect of the African emergence was on American race relations in general. He quickly narrowed his quest as he moved into it; it became an intensive and intense exploration of the impact of the African emergence on Negro Americans, and, above all, on their image of themselves. Between 1957 and 1962, he explored this experience with 107 black American leaders, writers, educators, and public figures. As a part of this undertaking he also spent the summer of 1960 sharing the sensations of a group of black and white American college students who went to Africa on a series of work projects in various countries. His interviews with them, before, during, and after that experience, are reported in his *Emergent Americans: A Report on Crossroads Africa* (New York, 1961). A fuller version, *The New World of Negro Americans,* appeared in 1963. Included in this work were his interviews with the American Negroes he encountered in West Africa. They had gone there in search of a renewed connection to the long-lost past left behind on the ancestral continent. This report had become the subject of much heavy and angry controversy both in Africa and the United States when it first appeared, in the *New Yorker* in 1961, under the title "Back to Africa."

It was this work of learning from black Americans which more than anything else turned Isaacs toward his quest after the nature of what he came to call basic group identity. It was during these interviews that he first clearly perceived that it was composed of deceptively simple, primordially powerful elements of body and physical characteristics, name and language, history and origins, religion, and nationality. Supported by a grant from the National Institutes of Health he set out in 1963 to make briefer examinations of other cases of groups grappling with political changes that were being forced to alter their images of themselves and of others. He explored this experience with ex-Untouchables in India, to whom political independence had brought new and wrenching pressures to lift themselves out of the cesspools of human existence to which they had been confined since the dimmest times of Hindu history. His report of what he learned appeared in *India's Ex-Untouchables* (New York, 1965). Interviews with 50 American Jews trying to become Israelis were reported in *American Jews in Israel* (New York, 1967), and what he found among English-educated Chinese in Malaysia, Filipinos, and college-age Japanese on the same journey was subsequently reported in part in various shorter pieces of writing. "Beyond these case studies," he wrote for the Center's annual report in 1967, "lies a work to be done on the nature of group identity and its interaction with political change, to map some part of the still little-known territory where students of culture, history, and politics meet students of psychology and personality." That was the work he then undertook, producing *Idols of the Tribe: Group Identity and Political Change*, in 1975.

"Having spent my entire working life trying to understand something about the nature of politics and especially political change," Isaacs wrote in the preface to this new work, "I found now that I had to learn more than I knew about the nature of basic group identity, and that I could best do so by starting all over from the elementary—and elemental—beginnings from which it all comes." And he went on:

> My quest has taken me by new paths across some old and much-traveled territory, to see some old sights with new eyes, hear some old sounds in different key, to seek some clearer answers to old questions. There is not a great deal "new" to be said about our bodies, our languages, our histories and our origins, our religions, our nationalities, until one tries, as I have tried here, to see how they come together, clustering in different ways under different conditions to make us what we are in all our differing kinds. This has been a journey full of hazards and I have no doubt stumbled But it has been a journey of discovery for me and I hope it can serve the same function for others even though they may start from different places and want to arrive at different destinations. At the very least, as the words "ethnic" and "ethnic group" become more and more a part of our everyday vocabularies, the reader of this book will at least have a better idea of what they mean than he might otherwise have had. He will also perhaps understand better, as I now understand better than I did, why era after era, generation after generation, the deepest holdings of our bodies and our spirits keep getting in the way of our deepest hopes of coming to lead a more humane human existence.[17]

Idols of the Tribe concludes by somberly accepting the fact that in all their changing shapes, "our tribal separatenesses are here to stay." It ends with questions. "The only 'new' question has to do with what kind of power systems, what kind of politics, might cope with this condition in its present form in any 'new' way. The problem as always, if we wish to preseve and enjoy the enhancing pluses of our tribal uniquenesses, is what to do with their destructive minuses...The question remains and one must still doggedly ask it: How can we live with our differences without, as always heretofore, being driven by them to tear each other limb from limb? This is at bottom a question of power, of the relative power or powerlessness of groups in relation to one another...What new politics might meet these needs, what new institutions? What new pluralisms?"[18]

On these questions, supported by a new Ford grant, Harold Isaacs is currently out interviewing again. He is trying to discover and identify the "new facts" created by the process of change in American society during the last thirty years. He seeks to see the outlines of what new pluralisms, if any, might be beginning to re-shape or, indeed, finally create, the basic group identity called "American."

In all his "Who's Who" entries, Harold Isaacs has always identified himself simply as a "writer" and there is clearly no way of "retiring" from being the kind of writer he has tried to be. The best archaeologists have a nose for the old; Isaacs has a sense of the new, for what might become futureshock in human terms. And it is in the difficult human terms that he writes. An easy rhythm, flow, and imagery mask the pain and toil that go into making complex ideas read simply and clearly. It is difficult to write easily and communicate well, two hallmarks of Isaacs, the consummate craftsman.

Isaacs' study of the ways in which ethnic groups react to their own self-images and the stereotypes of others, his humanitarian focus upon the ways in which different peoples can and cannot mix, and his life-long attempt to provide reasoned policy guidance in all of these and myriad cognate areas has stimulated abundant research and writing on the part of others. His concerns have informed the concerns of others, often in manners indirect. The following chapters contain an exposition of new work which draws upon, reflects upon, or extends to the particular many of the thrusts of Isaacs' own past and continuing creativity. Myron Weiner explores the two varieties of ethnocentrism in India. Lucian Pye investigates the development of empathetic personalities. Al-li Chin writes of Chinese-Americans. Michio Nagai follows Isaacs' own pessimistic assessment for the 1970s and 1980s. Ithiel Pool analyzes Isaacs' use of images as a means of conveying intuitive social science constructs. Chai Hon-Chan compares education and identity in Guyana and Malaysia. Hiroshi Wagatsuma uses a media example to inform us about Japanese minorities, and Robert Shaplen compares the problems of today's Asia with the problems of Asia in the days of Isaacs' first involvement. The whole is no final statement on the theory of ethnicity, nor even about the major problems of our day, but the chapters taken as a whole provide the kind of new and continuing view of stubborn and troublesome topics close to Isaacs' own long-term quest.

NOTES

*This biographical account was drafted with material, especially about the early years, supplied by Viola Isaacs, with access to the Isaacs files and published works, and at a late stage, completed with some input from the subject himself.

1 Victor Serge, *The Long Dusk* (New York, 1946).

2 Ira Wilson, "Harold Isaacs, Scratches On His Mind, 1930-1934," unpub. undergraduate seminar paper (Harvard College, January, 1976), 1-2.

3 *Ibid.*, 3-ll.

4 Isaacs, (ed.) *Straw Sandals: Chinese Stories 1918-1933* (Cambridge, 1974), xxviii.

5 Quoted in Margaret Elizabeth Mais, "The Evolution of Bias: An Interpreter of China, Harold R. Isaacs," unpub. honors thesis (Radcliffe College, 1970), 38-39.

6 Mais, "Evolution," 43-44.

7 *Straw Sandals,* xxix.

8 Introduction to Chinese edition, *Tragedy of the Chinese Revolution*, (Paris, 1973). In this reproduction of the 1947 Chinese edition, the new introduction appears only in Chinese translation. The English original remains unpublished.

9 Isaacs, *No Peace for Asia* (New York, 1947), 102.

10 *Ibid.*, 232-235.

11 Memorandum to the Guggenheim Foundation, November 18, 1959.

12 *Ibid.*

13 *Ibid.*

14 Gordon Allport to Harold Isaacs, November 4, 1957.

15 Isaacs, *Scratches On Our Minds: American Images of China and India* (New York, 1958), 407-408.

16 Memorandum to the Guggenheim Foundation.

17 Isaacs, *Idols of the Tribe: Group Identity and Political Change* (New York, 1975), xi-xii.

18 *Ibid.*, 216-218.

Bibliography
of
Harold R. Isaacs*

Books

The Tragedy of the Chinese Revolution, Secker & Warburg, London, 1938; First revised edition, Stanford University Press, 1951; Second revised edition, 1961; Atheneum paperback edition, 1966; Stanford University Press paperback edition, 1971. (Also in Chinese, Italian, French, Spanish, and Japanese editions.)

No Peace for Asia, Macmillan, New York, 1947; M.I.T. Press paperback edition, 1967.

New Cycle in Asia (ed.), Macmillan, New York, 1947.

Scratches on our Minds, American Images of China and India, John Day Co., New York, 1958; First paperback edition, under title *Images of Asia,* Capricorn Books, 1962; Second paperback edition, Harper & Row, New York, 1972. (Also in Japanese edition).

Emergent Americans, A Report on Crossroads Africa, John Day Co., New York, 1961.

The New World of Negro Americans, John Day Co., New York, 1963; paperback edition, Viking, New York, 1964; winner *Saturday Review* Anisfield-Wolf Award, 1964. (Also Phoenix House, London, 1964).

India's Ex-Untouchables, John Day Co., New York, 1965; Asia Publishing House, Bombay 1965; Torchbook paperback edition, Harper & Row, New York, 1974.

American Jews in Israel, John Day Co., New York, 1967.

Poems For Certain Occasions, Limited xerox edition of 10 copies, first reproduced June 1970.

Straw Sandals: Chinese Stories 1918-1933 (ed.), preface by Lu Hsun. M.I.T. Press, Cambridge, Mass., 1974.

Idols of the Tribe: Group Identity and Political Change, Harper & Row, New York, 1975; paperback edition, Harper & Row, New York, 1977.

Pamphlets

Five Years of Kuomintang Reaction (ed.), Shanghai, China Forum Publishing Co., 1932. ("Special Edition" of *China Forum,* May 1932).

Two-Thirds of the World, Bold New Program Series, Washington, 1950.

Africa: New Crises in the Making, Foreign Policy Association Headline Series (91) (New York, 1952), with Emory Ross.

Deseg: Change Comes to A Boston School (Boston, 1977).

---

*Compiled with the assistance of Alma H. Young.

Selected Articles

"Races—Hawaii," spring-summer 1930, published for the first time in the present volume.

"Disillusioned Delights," *The China Press Magazine of Travel,* Shanghai (June, 1931), 45.

"Pinpricks and Cancer," *China Weekly Review* (September 19, 1931), 104.

"Extradition Theory and Practice: An Inquiry into Imperialist Legalities," *China Forum,* (April 13,1933).

"Radicalism and Realities: A Fukien Closeup," *China Forum* (December 21, 1933).

"I Break With the Chinese Stalinists," (A letter to the Central Committee of the Chinese Communist Party, Peiping, China, May 20, 1934), *The New International,* New York, I:3 (September-October 1934), 76-78; Also in Chinese translation in *Hsienfeng,* (Shanghai), 6 (August 27, 1934).

"Blue Shirts in China," *Nation* (October 17, 1934), 433-435.

"Perspectives of the Chinese Revolution: A Marxist View," *Pacific Affairs,* VIII (1935), 269-283.

"One Man's Fight Against Corruption: Story Behind the Stilwell Incident," *Newsweek* (November 13, 1944), 44.

"Ignorant Men and Modern Weapons: Inside Story of the Chinese Army," *Newsweek* (November 20, 1944), 44.

"China: Today's Bitter Fiasco, Tomorrow's Sure Battleground," *Newsweek* (April 23, 1945), 60-61.

"Russia Casts Its Shadow Over Asia," *Newsweek* (May 28, 1945), 50.

"Notes on a Journey Home," *Harpers* (September, 1945), 285-288.

"When Yank Meets Russian: Korea Under Two Flags," *Newsweek* (October 1, 1945), 45.

"Saigon: French Island in a Sea of Rebellion," *Newsweek* (November 26, 1945), 54.

"Mad-dog Indonesians Go Out in the Java Sun," *Newsweek* (December 17, 1945), 50-51.

"Peace Comes to Saigon," *Harpers* (March, 1946), 284-288.

"Patterns of Revolt in Asia," *Harpers* (April, 1946), 346-351.

"Indo-China: A Fight for Freedom; excerpts from *No Peace For Asia, " New Republic* (February 3, 1947), 12-18.

"Viet Nam: The Secret War," *The Star Weekly,* Toronto (April 12, 1947).

"Korea, A Country Cut in Two," *The Star Weekly* (April 26, 1947).

"British Outlook in Asia," *The Star Weekly* (July 26, 1947).

"Pacific Is a U.S. Lake," *The Star Weekly* (August 2, 1947).

"The American Majority Man: He is a Reluctant Internationalist, *Newsweek* (August 4, 1947), 32-33.

"New Leaders, New Forces," *The Star Weekly* (November 22, 1947).

"Has the U.S. Let Asia Down?" *The Star Weekly* (November 22, 1947').

"South Asia's Opportunity," *The Modern Review*, Calcutta, (December, 1947), 444-450. (Also in *Modern Review*, New York, [December, 1947]).

"Blind Alley in China," *Newsweek* (December 8, 1947), 28-29.

"Russia in Asia," in Overseas Press Club (ed.), *As We See Russia* (New York, 1948), 77-90.

"Gandhi as Politician, Evangelist and Sage," (Review of Jawaharlal Nehru, *Nehru on Gandhi), New York Herald Tribune Weekly Book Review* (May 23, 1948).

"Fighting General Against All Odds in China." (Review of T.H. White [ed.], *The Stilwell Papers), New York Herald Tribune Weekly Book Review* (May 30, 1948).

"Number One Chinese Puzzle," (Review of J.K. Fairbank, *United States and China*), *New York Herald Tribune Weekly Book Review* (July 11, 1948).

"Toward a South Asian Union," *United Asia,* Bombay (July 7, 1948).

"Perennial Problem in Present Crisis of China," (Review of G.P. Winfield, *China, The Land and the People), New York Herald Tribune Weekly Book Review* (December 26, 1948).

"Dutch War in Indonesia and Communist Victories in China May Compel U.S. to Reconsider Basic Far Eastern Policy," *Newsweek* (January 3, 1949), 22-23.

"Chennault's Own Story of Air War in China," (review of C.L. Chennault, *Way of a Fighter), New York Herald Tribune Weekly Book Review* (January 3, 1949).

ʰ"A Thing is Good or Bad" (Interview with Ho Chi-Minh), *Newsweek* (April 25, 1949), 44.

"Will South Asia Go Red? A Roving Correspondent Reports on How Communist Gains in China Stir Up Eight Countries," *Newsweek* (May 9, 1949), 42-43.

"South Asia: Where and How America Loses Friends," *Newsweek* (May 30, 1949), 36-38.

"The Problems of South Asia, An NBC Radio Discussion by Harold Isaacs, Soedjatmoko and Phillips Talbot," University of Chicago Round Table, 585 (June 5, 1949).

"South Asia: Grinding Change Amidst Bullets," *Newsweek* (July 18, 1949), 32-33.

"A New Disaster in Asia?" *The Reporter* (April 11, 1950), 24-27.

"U.S. Recognition of Bao Stirs Political Disputes in South Asia,", *Christian Science Monitor* (April 5, 1950).

"The Men Who Make American Far Eastern Policy," a series of four articles, *Christian Science Monitor* (May 5, 8, 9, 11, 1950).

"Issues in Baguio," a series of reports, *Philippines Herald,* Manila (May 27-31, 1950).

"Conference of South Asia Nationals Fails to Solve Problems," *Christian Science Monitor* (June 12-13, 1950).

"Point IV: Inter-Racial Problems Tied to Technical Aid Problems," *Christian Science Monitor* (June 12, 1950).

"The Political and Psychological Context of Point Four," *The Annals of the American Academy of Political and Social Science*, CCLXX (1950), 51-58.

"Situation in the Philippines," a series of articles, *Washington Post* (June 13-17, 1950), (also *St. Louis Post-Dispatch*, June 18-22, 1950).

"What Korea's 'Small War' Is About," *New York Post* (June 27, 1950).

"Events in Asia Shaping U.S. Foreign Policy, *New York Post* (June 28, 1950).

"Delay Reflects India's Desire to Ride Fence," *New York Post* (June 29, 1950).

"Weak S. Korean Regime Hampers GI's At Front," *New York Post* (June 29, 1950).

"U.S. Fighting in Korea Reminds Asiatics We Don't Look at Facts," *New York Post* (July 9, 1950).

"Korea Lesson: Win or Lose, U.S. Policy in Asia Needs a Big Overhauling," *New York Post* (July 14, 1950).

"Problems of Nationalism" and "A Policy for the United States," in Phillips Talbot (ed.), *South Asia in the World Today* (Chicago, 1950), 161-173.

"Korea and America's World Policy," *New Republic* (August 7, 1950), 14-16.

"Asian Reaction to War in Korea," a series of four articles, *Christian Science Monitor* (September 1, 2, 5, 6, 1950).

"Motes and Beams at Lucknow," *The Reporter* (November 7, 1950).

"What Should Be Our Policy in Asia Now?" Harold Isaacs and Claire Chennault, Town Meeting of the Air, 639th Broadcast, November 21, 1950, in *Town Meeting,*, Town Hall, New York, 16:30.

"Yalu River or Rubicon," *The Reporter* (December 12, 1950).

"Prospect in Asia," *Nation* (December 16, 1950), 552-555.

"The Blind Alley of Totalitarianism," *The Annals of the American Academy of Political and Social Science,* CCLXXVI (1951), 81-90.

"McCarthyism Blasts Careers of Two Men," *New York Post* (July 22, 1951).

"Asia's Multiple Revolution: The Dimensions of the Crisis," *Saturday Review of Literature* (August 4, 1951), 13-16ff.

"Korean Front in Chicago," *Saturday Review* (July 19, 1952), 11ff.

"Dismal Annals of South Africa's Intolerance," *The Reporter* (January 6, 1953), 37-40.

"South African Apartheid and the United Nations," *United Asia* (Bombay) (February, 1953), 9-14.

"Western Man and the African Crisis," *Saturday Review* (May 2, 1953), 10-12ff (special issue, Alan Paton and H.R. Isaacs, eds.).

"The Rediscovery of Africa, Notes on Some Recent Books," *International Journal,* IX, Toronto (1954), 48-53.

"Communist Power and Indian Policy," *The Reporter* (May 25, 1954), 38-40.

"Mr. Gunther Assimilates Another Continent," *The Reporter* (October 20, 1955), 44-46.

"Two Americans in Saigon," *The Reporter* (February 23, 1956), 46-47.

"Scratches on Our Minds," *Public Opinion Quarterly,* XX (1956), 197-211.

"India's Racism in Reverse," *The Reporter* (May 31, 1956), 48.

"How We 'See' the Chinese Communists," *New Republic* (February 25, 1957), 7-13.

"In Little Rock He's a Controversial Figure," *The Reporter* (January 23, 1958), 46-47.

"World Affairs and U.S. Race Relations: A Note On Little Rock," *Public Opinion Quarterly,* XXII (1958), 364-370.

"Civil Disobedience in Montgomery," (Review of Martin Luther King Jr., *Stride Toward Freedom)., New Republic* (October 6, 1958), 19.

"The American Negro and Africa: Some Notes," *Phylon,* XX (1959), 219-233.

"Five Writers and their African Ancestors," Parts I and II, *Phylon,* XXI (1960), 243-265.

"DuBois and Africa," *Race,* II (1960), 2-23.

"Back to Africa," *The New Yorker* (May 13, 1961), 105-106ff.

"Identity and World Politics: A Case Study Approach," Center for International Studies, Massachusetts Institute of Technology (September 7, 1961), unpub.

"American Race Relations and the U.S. Image in World Affairs," *Journal of Human Relations,* X (1962), 266-280.

"Integration and the Negro Mood," *Commentary* (December, 1962), 487-497.

"The Changing Identity of the Negro American," in Leonard Duhl (ed.), *Urban Condition* (New York, 1963), 275-295.

"Blackness and Whiteness," *Encounter* (August, 1963), 8-21.

"Group Identity and Political Change," adapted from a lecture given at International House of Japan, December 6, 1963, *Bulletin* of the International House (April, 1964).

"The Ex-Untouchables," *The New Yorker* (December 12, 1964), 60-64ff.

"The Ex-Untouchables," *The New Yorker* (December 19, 1974), 75-76ff.

"Group Identity and Political Change: The Role of History and Origins," a paper presented at the Association of Asian Studies, San Francisco, April, 1965, unpub.

"Portrait of a Revolutionary (Frantz Fanon)," *Commentary* (July, 1965), 67-71.

"Americans in Israel," *The New Yorker* (August 27, 1966), 37-40ff.

"Americans in Israel," *The New Yorker* (September 3, 1966), 73-74ff.

"Old Myths and New Realities," *Diplomat*, XVII (1966), Special issue on China, 41-47.

"Group Identity and Political Change: The Role of Color and Physical Characteristics," *Daedalus*, XCVI (1967), 353-375.

Working paper for the National Advisory Commission on Civil Disorders (October, 1967), unpub.

"Introduction to the Italian edition," *La Tragedia della Rivoluzione Cinese, 1925-27* (Milano, 1967).

"Group Identity and Political Change: The Role of Color and Physical Characteristics," in John Hope Franklin (ed.), *Color and Race* (Boston, 1968), 75-97.

"Group Identity and Political Change: The Role of the Nation," *Survey*, 69 (Fall, 1968), 76-98.

"Color in World Affairs," *Foreign Affairs*, XLVII (1969), 235-250.

"Race and Color in World Affairs," in George W. Shepherd, Jr. (ed.), *Racial Influences on American Foreign Policy* (New York, 1970), 19-38.

"Preface to the Japanese Edition," *Scratches on Our Minds*, (Tokyo, 1970).

Review of *Gandhi's Truth* by Erik Erikson (April, 1970), unpub.

"Sources for Images of Foreign Countries," in Melvin Small (ed.), *Public Opinion and Historians* (Detroit, 1970), 91-105.

Introduction to "Documents on the Comintern and the Chinese Revolution," *The China Quarterly*, XLV (1971), 110-115.

"Group Identity and Political Change: The Houses of Muumbi," presented at the American Political Science Association Meeting, Chicago, September 7, 1971, and Psycho-History Group, American Academy of Arts and Science, October 16, 1971, unpub.

"The Houses of Muumbi," *Washington Monthly* (December, 1971), 38-46.

"The 'Tilt': American Views of South Asia," (statement on Bangladesh), Hearing before Subcommittee on Refugees and Escapees of the Committee on the Judiciary, U.S. Senate, 92nd Congress, 2nd session (February 2, 1972), 182-188.

"Nixon and China—The Mirror Turns," *Boston Evening Globe* (February 16, 1972). (Also as "Old Images of China in New Light," *Mainichi Daily News,* [Tokyo], February 17, 1972).

"Nixon's Asian Game Plan," *New Republic* (February 19, 1972), 19-23.

"The New Pluralists," *Commentary* (March, 1972), 75-79.

"Introduction to the 1972 Edition," *Images of Asia*, (New York, Harper & Row paperback edition, 1972).

"The Ex-Untouchables," in J. Michael Mahar (ed.), *The Untouchables in Contemporary India* (Tucson, 1972), 375-410.

"A Jewish View of 'Isaiah Ben Dasan'" (Review of the *The Japanese and the Jews), Japan Times,* Tokyo (March 7, 1973).

"The Politics of Retribalization," adapted from a lecture given at the International House, Tokyo, January 23, 1973; in *Bulletin* of the International House (April, 1973).

"Basic Group Identity: The Idols of the Tribe," *Ethnicity*, I (1972), 15-41.(Paper presented at the American Academy of Arts and Sciences Conference on Ethnic Problems in the Contemporary World, October 26-28, 1972.)

"Introduction to the re-issued Chinese Edition," of *Tragedy of the Chinese Revolution,* (Paris, 1974).

"Nationality: 'End of the Road'?" *Foreign Affairs*, LIII (1975), 434-449.

"Our SOBs" *The New Republic* (May 3, 1975) 4-5 (Special issue on Vietnam).

"Basic Group Identity: The Idols of the Tribe," in Daniel Moynihan and Nathan Glazer (eds.), *Ethnicity: Theory and Experience* (Cambridge, Mass., 1975), 29-52.

"Some Concluding Remarks: The Turning Mirrors," in Akira Iriye (ed.), *Mutual Images: Essays in American-Japanese Relations* (Cambridge, Mass., 1975), 258-265.

"Fathers and Sons and Daughters and National Development," A Note on which to open the 1975 Joint Seminar on Political Development, October 1, 1975, in *Political Generations and Politcal Development* (Cambridge, Mass., 1977).

"The Closing Societies," paper presented at Board of Foreign Scholarships Convocation on "International Education: Link for Human Understanding," Smithsonian Institution, Washington, D.C., May 18-20, 1976, in *A Process of Global Enlightenment* (Washington, D.C., 1976.)

"Changing Arenas and Identies in World Affairs," (based on Chap. 1, *Idols of the Tribe)* in Harold Lasswell, Daniel Lerner, Hans Spier (eds.), *Communication and Propaganda in World History* (Honolulu, 1977), II., forthcoming.

"The Road Ahead: 'Open' or 'Closed'," *Survey*, 22 (Fall, 1976), 82-85.

082155

II.

Scratches on Social Science: Images, Symbols, and Stereotypes

By Ithiel de Sola Pool

Occasionally in science different disciplines using different jargons develop equivalent theories unbeknownst to each other. Long periods may pass before their equivalence is recognized.[1] Sigmund Freud on symbols, Walter Lippmann on stereotypes, Robert Abelson on balance theory, and Harold Isaacs on images have each in their way, covered common ground. Though stemming from different disciplines and documented by different evidence, their findings nonetheless converge. All four writers examine those simplified representations that people use to order their perceptions of the buzzing confusion of empirical reality around them.

Each of the four treatments recognizes that the representations in any individual's head are related by an associative logic which does not meet the test of veridical proof. These representations in an individual's head are acquired by him early and are held tenaciously against empirical challenge.

The representations are essentially visual and descriptive; the words to refer to them are nouns, not verbs; their referents can be seen in the mind's eye with portrayable features or traits. The representations are also emotionally charged and heavily value-laden; there are among them, representations of "the good guys" and "the bad guys." The representations often come in pairs of terms both of which, by any semantic definition, refer to the same thing (e.g., courage and foolhardiness, patriotism and chauvinism, British subject or limey). Such representations of the same referent by a pair of alternative terms allow the pseudo-logic in the subject's head to be maintained. The benign element and the malevolent element can alternatively be elicited when required to represent different feelings about the same semantic meaning.

The representations which a person chooses to use, and also how he values and characterizes them, serve to define his own identity. Many of the most important representations are themselves names of organized groups or unorganized plurals of persons to which an individual may belong or from which he is excluded. Others are associatively linked to such groups or plurals. A person's sense of his identity is expressed by how he positions himself for or against these emotionally charged, group-linked representations.

We have in the above few paragraphs tried to describe the common domain among four writers, and to do so using a fifth jargon, neutral among them. The word "representation" in the last paragraphs, wherever it occurred, could have been replaced by "symbol" or "stereotype" or "image." The paragraphs would then, with other appropriate changes of language, describe at least a part of the theories of some one of the authors whose parallel writings we are describing. Let us take up the parallel theories of these four writers in a chronological sequence.

Freud developed his analysis of symbolism most fully in the *Interpretation of Dreams* (1900). But, as Freud said in 1925: "Many of the things that we study in dreams....have little or nothing to do with the psychological peculiarity of dreams. Thus, for instance, symbolism is not a dream-problem, but a topic connected with our archaic thinking....It dominates myths and religious ritual no less than dreams."[2]

The symbols that Freud dealt with refer mainly to the body, to sex, and to close personal relations. It is such symbols that occupy his interpretation of dreams. Only rarely does he discuss symbols that deal with ideology or national or group identity, but occasionally he does. Thus, where he talks of his own Jewish identity and his youthful reactions to anti-Semitism, he tells us how Hannibal (the Semite) and Rome "symbolized" for him "the tenacity of Jewry and the organization of the Catholic Church."[3] "I began to understand for the first time what it meant to belong to an alien race....The figure of the Semitic general rose still higher in my esteem."

In orthodox Freudian jargon one distinguishes the "symbols" in a dream from other entities in the dream to which the patient associates via his own unique experiences. Symbolism, as Freud used the term, refers to what he believed to be "a fragment of extremely ancient inherited mental equipment."[4] It was part of a common human language, and when a symbol appeared in a dream the patient could usually provide no associations to it. Nonetheless, much of what Freud says about symbolization may help us understand the broader processes of representation by an image, whether that image is a culturally shared one which Freud calls a symbol or an individualized representation that grows out of private experience.

Symbolic thinking, Freudian analysis tells us, is vague and prelogical. It is a method of distortion. The conscious symbol is used to hide an objectionable, unconscious idea. "The censoring ego uses regressive methods....In dreams, symbols appear...as a tool of the dream censorship and also as...archaic pictorial thinking, as part of visualizing abstract thoughts."[5]

Thus, symbolization is one of the methods of defense by which humans structure their perception of the world into an orderly and acceptable one. Symbolization operates in conjunction with a large family of defense mechanisms which people use to ward off impulses and perceptions that threaten their egos. One of these defense mechanisms is isolation. Aspects of the self which confound each other are separated intellectually to avoid confrontation. The soldier's professional killing or the businessman's professional seeking of gain is isolated as a professional role from the same man's perception of his personal moral character as a loving friend or altruistic philanthropist. One "type of isolation is represented by attempts to solve conflicts around ambivalence—that is, conflicts between love and hatred of the same person—by splitting the contradictory feelings so that one person is only loved, another one only hated....An example is the contrast of the good mother and the wicked stepmother in fairy tales."[6] Thus symbols tend to be pure in their affect. They live in a dream world where the "good guys" do only good and the "bad guys" do only bad. There are no symbols for the moral ambiguity of reality.

Walter Lippmann's *Public Opinion* appeared in 1922, nine years after the first English translation of *The Interpretation of Dreams.* In his closing summation of Part 3, "Stereotypes," Lippmann cites Freud's book:[7]

> Our access to information is obstructed and uncertain and...our apprehension is deeply controlled by our stereotypes;...the evidence available to our reason is subject to illusions of defense, prestige, morality, space, and sampling....In a series of events seen mostly through stereotypes, we readily accept sequence parallelism as equivalent to cause and effect.
>
> This is most likely to happen when two ideas that come together arouse the same feeling. If they come together they are likely to arouse the same feeling; and even when they do not arrive together a powerful feeling attached to one is likely to suck out of all the corners of memory any idea that feels about the same. Thus everything painful tends to collect into one system of cause and effect, likewise everything pleasant.
>
> In hating one thing violently, we readily associate with it as cause or effect most of the other things we hate or fear violently. They may have no more connection than smallpox and alehouses, or Relativity and Bolshevism, but they are bound together in the same emotion....Emotion is a stream of molten lava which catches and imbeds whatever it touches. When you excavate in it you find, as in a buried city, all sorts of objects ludicrously entangled in each other. Anything can be related to anything else, provided it feels like it.... Ancient fears, reinforced by more recent fears, coagulate into a snarl of fears where anything that is dreaded is the cause of anything else that is dreaded.
>
> Generally it all culminates in the fabrication of a system of all evil, and of another which is the system of good. Then our love of the absolute shows itself. For we do not like qualifying adverbs.

Lippmann, the literary American writer, refers to emotions as "a stream of molten lava"; Freud, the philosophical German, talks of them as "the id." The literary American uses the metaphor of digging in a buried city wherein objects are ludicrously entangled. The philosophical German designates the same process by such technical phrases as "free association" and "exploration of the unconscious." Freud coined a jargon; Lippman talks about symbols in symbols.

In some important respects, what Lippmann describes as "stereotypes" are a generalization from, rather than a synonym for, Freudian symbols. They refer to public affairs rather than to intimate ones. Their meaning is only occasionally and marginally hermeneutic. The "Hun" may have been a stereotype of Germans in the era when Lippmann wrote, but there was little mystery to be unveiled in that symbolism. What was meant required no free-association to bring it out; it was mostly on the surface. True, there is an element of inexplicitness. There are connotations of the metaphor that are not spelled out. Huns, we understand, are barbarian, ruthless, and cruel. But then, perhaps they may also be thought of as heathen, strong, ugly, illiterate, or successful. Many of these other traits carried over into some 1920's images of Germans, but which ones did so may differ from speaker to speaker. There is a layer of hidden meaning that only probing can bring out. Nonetheless the hidden meaning in stereotypes is shallow compared with that in the symbols in the Freudian language of dreams. Lippmann applies the shared theory of representations to a language of public discourse in civic affairs not to a hidden language of the unconscious.

Lippmann stresses that stereotypes are crude and inaccurate, short on detail, and dominated by conventional cliches. Sunsets are portrayed as red, which few sunsets are. An Italian dish is noted for garlic, only one of its ingredients. Lippmann is normative about all this. Stereotyping is not only a feature of cognitive processes empirically noted by him, but rather an abuse of thinking that makes the achievement of civic rationality difficult. Stereotypes are not only a necessary element in thought, but also a fault of uninformed, unsophisticated, irrational men. They are found among the ignorant masses more than among the thoughtful intelligentsia.

We have overstated the case. Lippmann understood that in the economy of human thinking the use of simplified images is inevitable. Stereotyping, he recognized, is not confined to prejudiced or thoughtless men. "The attempt to see all things freshly and in detail, rather than as types and generalities, is exhausting, and among busy affairs practically out of the question" (59). Yet in emphasis, Lippmann clearly perceived stereotypes as abuses. The main thesis of *Public Opinion* presumes that. The thesis is that for democracy to work, mass opinion must be raised from its defective ordinary functioning by the rational educative efforts of an intelligent, organized elite of political scientists.

Lippmann belongs to a class of writers, including Alexis de Tocqueville, M. Ostrogorski, Roberto Michels, Vilfredo Pareto, Gaetano Mosca, Max Weber, and Bernard Berelson, who may be called realistic critics of democratic theory. All of them held up Rousseauean democratic ideals against the empirical facts of democratic practice and found the theory wanting. The theory postulated that publicly-minded citizens would inform themselves about issues and then vote for what they perceived to be the common good. The empiricists easily showed that most citizens were more self-interested than publicly minded; that most knew what they wanted first, and then sought rationalizations for it; and that only the few participated on most issues. One conclusion, Mosca's, for example, was to dismiss democracy as a pious fraud. Another conclusion, Lippmann's, was to seek a means to bring the reality closer to the ideal. Lippmann's purpose was to find ways to improve the quality of public life, to reduce the stereotypic element in public affairs thinking and to make it more objective, more publicly minded, and more rational.

Stereotypes are thus, for Lippmann, unfortunate simplifications even if to some degree inevitable. They are linked to each other by obscure associations. They provide a handy but inaccurate map of the social world. Furthermore, one of their defects is their fixity. A stereotype, once held, is not readily abandoned. Instead of re-evaluating at each moment the changing facts of the real world, people selectively perceive an event (e.g., the redness of the sunset), shaping the observation to the salient features of a pre-established stereotype.

There is another reason, too, Lippmann argues, "besides economy of effort, why we so often hold to our stereotypes when we might pursue a more disinterested vision. The systems of stereotypes may be the core of our personal tradition, the defenses of our position in society" (63). Stereotypes are what Lasswell called "symbols of identification."[8] Most stereotypes can be positioned in society's ethnic and status structure. The British butler, the hard hat construction worker, the hippie student, the Kolkhoznik tractor-driving girl, are all stereotypes that belong somewhere in a population of the mind's world. And the self belongs somewhere in that world, too. Where one fits in it is symbolized by hairstyle, the clothes that one wears, the car that one chooses, the accent of one's voice.

In the decades of the 1920s and 1930s, it was in the literature on ethnicity that Lippmann's coinage, "stereotype" took hold as part of the common language. It is now a word that most well-educated high school students know. If you ask one of them to define it, more often than not, he will tell you that stereotyping is a way of talking about ethnic groups; that it refers to the fallacy of assuming that all members of an ethnic group have a common trait—usually a trait that excites derision. Lippmann used the concept more broadly, but that ethnic use of the word as a special case is true to his analysis.

It would be natural, in the context of a discussion of ethnic stereotypes, to turn directly to Harold Isaacs' work, for in recent decades that is what he has written about. However, as we are proceeding chronologically, there is another major treatment of representations which we cannot omit: that found in balance theory.

The formulation of balance theory came from Fritz Heider in 1946.[9] Its outstanding current exponent and elaborator is Robert Abelson. The most basic idea in balance theory is represented by a triangle.

Ego perceives alter as having an attribute.

Each link in the triangle can be given a sign + or − . Thus ego may like or dislike alter. The attitude object may have favorable or unfavorable attributes. Alter may have or reject, may favor or disfavor them. Thus "the great doctor saved my father's life" is plus all around.

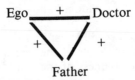

That is a thoroughly balanced statement. But "the great doctor saved the brutal dictator's life" is a different kind of statement. It arouses a certain measure of ambivalence. One is not sure how one feels about it. Such an event certainly could happen; nonetheless it creates a psychological tension in one who thinks it.

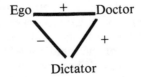

The existence of such tension is, according to balance theory, a condition conducive to attitude change. In that unbalanced situation there may be some inclination to come to think less well of the doctor or to come to think that the bond between the doctor and the dictator was not wholly positive. The doctor as professional may have done his duty, but may also have done it with distaste or been forced to do it. It is easier to accept the picture that way.

Balance theory does not assert a specific predicted outcome. It identifies, rather, a condition under which the relation among cognitive elements will be stable and a condition in which the relation among them will be unstable. (It is unstable if the product sign is negative.) If it is unstable, the individual may handle the situation by any one of many defense mechanisms including avoidance (i.e., thinking about other things), attitude change regarding the elements, or differentiation. The last is the split that we have met before in the analysis of dreams. The great doctor becomes two symbols: the skillful physician who does his job and the coerced citizen who hates the dictator.

The highly simplified formal model represented by the balance triangle is an analytical step forward in that it provides the basic element for a formal calculus whereby one can model the complex processes of symbolization or stereotyping. The triangle is but the atom with which larger models can be built. It itself is a trivially simple concept, and occasionally people whose reading in balance theory goes no further than learning about this basic atom dismiss the whole thing as trivial. As Abelson's later work illustrates, one can go far, using balance notions, to create sophisticated analyses out of such relatively elementary building blocks.[10]

The first step toward complexity, taken in an article by Abelson and Rosenberg, is to generalize from a set of three to a set of "n" elements.[11] Suppose there is a set of elements in an individual's psyche, each linked to each other by a plus, a minus, or a zero (i.e., unlinked). How can one determine whether the structure as a whole is balanced? If it is not balanced, how much change in the structure would be required in order to eliminate the tension and restore balance? Abelson and Rosenberg work out the mathematics of such n-element matrices. There are rather powerful theorems that can be used in analyzing the psychologic of associated symbols when they are presented in this way.

Abelson's most recent formalization of cognitive processes has pushed further toward Freud, Lippmann, and Isaacs, in seeking to incorporate still more of the complexity of human thinking. We noted above that balance theory incorporates the various defense mechanisms such as forgetting, selective perception, etc. as ways of responding to imbalance. When the mental world does not neatly fit into good guys doing good things and bad guys—bad things, there are various psychic gambits available to avoid the pains of ambivalence. In his most recent work, Abelson has attempted to formalize them into a finite and well defined set of strategies.[12] The particular psyche he has used as a case study is a hypothetical Goldwater Republican thinking about Communism and the United States, war and peace, good and evil.

A description of the symbols, associations, stereotypes, topoi, scratches on the mind of this prototypic right wing ideologist is formalized in Abelson's treatment. The goal of the exercise is to produce a computer-manipulable model of the man's cognitive strategies. Indeed, Abelson's point is that stereotypic psycho-logic is simple-minded enough to be successfully simulated by a computer program. The ideologist uses a limited bag of strategies. In content, the strategies which Abelson describes are perhaps most similar to the topoi, or standard arguments, in Aristotle's *Rhetoric,* but they also cover the same ground that we have covered before in discussing symbolization, association, psycho-logic, polarization, and splitting of images accordingly. The Goldwaterite true-believer is chosen by Abelson as an extreme illustration of such stereotypy, of a man with images formed early in his primary environment and carried rigidly by association into the world of politics, where he holds onto them with strong resistance to change, by means of a series of simple strategies.

Harold Isaacs' treatment of the "scratches on our minds" starts in one respect at the opposite pole from Abelson's. While Abelson stresses the universality and simplicity of the cognitive strategies used in stereotyped thinking, Isaacs delights in savoring the infinite variety of ways in which humans play that game. Abelson is a social psychologist in the mathematical tradition. Isaacs is a former journalist and observer of life. But there is no contradiction. A game—the game of cognition or any other—has formal rules, and one writer may make his mark by the codification and analysis of their logic. Another writer watches the game being played and conveys its excitement, its suspense, its uniqueness as a single event. His is an art form. But he is watching the same game and is also aware of the rules; he, too, by his description of the single case helps us to understand the general rules. Isaacs is that sort of artist.

The psychoanalytic literature, Lippmann, and the literature on ethnic stereotypes (but not balance theory) must certainly have entered quite consciously into Isaacs' thinking as he started in the early 1950s to write on American images of India and China. For a quarter of a century, Isaacs had been writing about Asian politics as a journalist and scholar.[13] In 1953 he joined a new program on international communication that the Ford Foundation had established at M.I.T. This author, Daniel Lerner, Raymond Bauer, Howard Perlmutter, Eric Lenneberg, and Harold Isaacs were its initial staff. We set out to study how foreign information affected political behavior. We were interested in the penetration of modern information into the developing world,[14] and also the penetration of information about the outside world into American public affairs.[15] Isaacs chose for his study the formation of American images of India and China.

His was a study of stereotype formation. That was also the area in which Howard Perlmutter worked at M.I.T. Their work was in a long tradition going back to Theodore Bagardus' social distance scale in 1925. That instrument asked whom one would be willing to work with, accept as a neighbor, or marry. Such work on ethnic stereotyping peaked in the 1930s and 1940s in response to both Nazi and American racism.

The classic work was by Adorno, Frenkel-Brunswick, et al.[16] Perlmutter used the F-scale from that study and found that it correlated positively not only with anti-foreign prejudice, but also with xenophilia, i.e., favorable identification with things foreign.[17] He also worked on the process of impression formation regarding foreigners.[18] Ethnicity, he showed, was the strongest dimension governing the formation of an image of a person who belonged to any other nationality than one's own. Ethnicity dominated profession, for example, as a source of images.

It was against this background of extensive social research on ethnic stereotyping that Isaacs undertook his program of interviews with Americans who had played some key role in Far Eastern policy. His interviews were rich in detail and he reported them with all their idiosyncratic drama. His interview technique was open-ended and encouraged free association on the Freudian model, a style of interviewing more congenial to an ex-reporter than the psychometric instruments that Perlmutter, for example, used. Isaacs encouraged his respondents to work back gradually to their earliest associations with the symbols of India and Indians, China and Chinese. What emerged was often a relatively fixed image formed as early, for instance, as when the child put money in his Sunday school mite box for the heathens whom the missionaries went out to save.

What came through the interviews was the same logic of stereotypes that we have been discussing in reviewing Freud, and Lippmann, and Abelson. There were good guys and bad guys. There were respondents who described "lo, the wonderful Chinese" and who held the image of Chinese as a supremely intelligent people, heroic in war and idealistic in peace. Typically such sinophilic Americans found India and Indians dark, dirty, and unpleasant. On the other hand, there was the smaller group of indophilic Americans who saw Indians as spiritual. Those typically saw the Chinese as sly and inscrutable. Reactions to the dirt of Asian cities evoked in sinophiles horror at the filth of Calcutta while indophiles were appalled by the dirt in Shanghai.

Although the India-China polarization provided for most of the respondents a neat hero-villain casting (one way or the other), the scene in their minds could rarely be quite that simple. History has thrown Americans back and forth in shifting alliances in Asia. The Chinese were our heroes against Japanese aggression until 1949. But then the mainland became Communist China beset by madnesses such as the cultural revolution. Japan became a land of delicate art, political democracy, and the postwar economic miracle. More recently, China, since the Nixon visit, once more has become a wonderland in the tales of returning travelers—as one told me, it is a land that had changed his life, for he had seen that a society based on altruism can work. Japan at the same time has become increasingly in American eyes an economic competitor, a land of environmental pollution and of ruthless economic men. Thus the splits in national stereotypes are there, with each half-image available to be used when needed to sustain consistency. There are, Isaacs tells us, the images of the benign and wise Charley Chan and the image of the cruel and mysterious Fu Man Chu. There are the images of the tea ceremony and the kamikaze pilot. These cohabit in our minds. As alliances shift the appropriate image comes forth to explain reality and keep it consistent with a viscous cognitive mass. At each moment there is one country in Asia to represent the good, the extraordinary, and the heroic, and another country to represent the devious, the inscrutable, and the cruel. The plot and symbols remain the same even if the characters trade places from time to time.

In "Scratches" the main interest is in the cognitive processes by which people acquire the images that they hold and in the strategies that they use to defend them. The debt to Freudian notions of symbolism and to Lippmann on stereotypes is clear, and was presumably conscious. The parallelism to social psychological theories of attitude structure such as Abelson's is equally clear, though there is no reason to believe that Isaacs was aware of those theories or subject to any direct influence from them. Those ideas were in the social science environment, however, and could undoubtedly have been communicated, unattributed, by informal conversation in a university environment.

In Issacs' works since "Scratches" one particular element of the theory of symbols or images, as we have described it above, is particularly stressed, namely the notion of identity. Symbols, as we have seen, often help define the self and the other. The stereotypes that one holds of people and groups position the self as *for* some people and *against* others. All of Isaacs' books since "Scratches" deal with the changing identities of groups in the post war world. Like most people who have used, analyzed, or developed the concept of stereotype, Isaacs has been particularly interested in ethnic identities—American blacks in Africa, American Jews in Israel, Filipinos caught between Spanish, indigenous, and American identities, and ex-untouchables in India released from the age-long fixity of their assigned status have been among the cases that he has dealt with.

There are various ways of talking about people's images of self and other. Harold Lasswell uses the phrase symbols of identification. Erik Erikson, who spent the academic year 1958-59 in a seminar with the social science faculty at M.I.T., talks of identity. However the notion may be expressed, it involves, first, the assignment of group names; second, the classification of people under those symbols; and, third, the attribution of traits to those groups.

The four writers whom we have discussed, Freud, Lippmann, Abelson, and Isaacs, would see themselves as very different from each other. And in some respects very different they are. But they are all feeling over different parts of the same elephant. The common theory shared by all four writers may be summarized in nine points.

(1) Humans organize the buzzing confusion of reality into simplified representations. These universal simplifications, rooted according to his theories in human sexuality, Freud called symbols. Those that had their roots in ideology or adult experience, he discussed little. The other writers were more eclectic and wrote of whatever images or stereotypes they found to occur in the realm of discourse that they were observing. Abelson described what he found in Goldwater Republican ideology. Isaacs is most concerned with the contents of the symbolism as it appeared in the psyches of important actors on the current world scene. He describes them vividly. His motivation is substantive and political rather than psychological or theoretical. The new nationalisms emerging on the world scene fascinate him, particularly where the resulting images reflect strain among conflicting traditions.

(2) The simplified representations are not an inchoate list, but relate to each other in a quasi-logic. It is not the logic of veridical truth, but an emotional or psycho-logic. Freud describes it in terms of associations. Abelson examines it most sophisticatedly, and gives it the label psycho-logic. The most basic rule is that good people do good things, and bad

people bad. Moral ambivalence is the equivalent of illogic.

(3) These simplified representations are acquired early. Freud traced those that he deals with farthest back into the childhood experience. Isaacs, too, traces those that he deals with back to the first recalled experience of them. Abelson and Lippmann are not primarily concerned with the date of acquisition.

(4) All four writers agree that once acquired, those simplified representations are defended strongly against change. They are clung to tenaciously, often in the face of evidence. Freud and Abelson classify the defense mechanisms used.

(5) Simplification and the defense of existing cognitions against new evidence are both deplored and also accepted as inevitable by all of these writers. Lippmann is most moralistic. Stereotypes, he believes, are bad things, to be overcome by educated men. Yet he, too, realizes that they are inevitable characteristics of thinking. The economy of mental effort does not permit each issue to be examined *de novo* every time, nor can every presumption be challenged if the duration of deliberation is to be less than eternity. Thinking is an allocation of scarce mental resources. Freud and Isaacs both seem deeply if not explicitly aware of the inherent agony of the resulting human condition; the impossibility of full rationality is the central object of Freud's analysis. We all think neurotically or irrationally, for to be human is to do so. Yet Freud, a liberal steeped in the tradition of progress and perfectionism, seeks to help men achieve a higher level of consciousness, to become less victimized by the mechanism of their own psyches.

(6) The representations that we are discussing are visual, referred to by nouns. They are, in short, "things." Isaacs uses the word "images." Freud is explicit about the visual quality of dreams. Heider deals with attitude objects.

(7) The things represented have rather unequivocal values on a good-bad scale. The world of the mind is a low grade Western. There are good guys and bad guys. There is no moral ambiguity there. All four writers are at one about that. The resistance of humans to living with moral tension provides the dynamic in balance theory. Change occurs to restore balance whenever it is departed from.

(8) One mechanism to maintain univocal moral balance is the splitting of representations into pairs that are given different names but stand for the same thing. Freud and Abelson describe this process. Isaacs illustrates it in absorbing detail.

(9) The representations that people hold serve to affirm their identities. Many of the representations are of groups. Others are held to with fervor because to contradict those hallowed beliefs would be a denial of one's identity. It may not be orthodox Fruedian psychology to place emphasis on symbols of group affiliation as against individual gratification, but the notion of identity is certainly present in Freud. It was there strongly enough for Erikson to bring it forth as a central notion and for Lasswell to have used it in his application of psychoanalysis to politics. It was natural for Isaacs to move in his writings from dealing with images

to dealing with identity as his central focus. They cannot be discussed in isolation from each other.

It is sometimes argued that the social sciences are not cumulative. Unlike the practitioners of modern physics, we can still read Aristotle with profit. But to some degree the social sciences are cumulative; there is progress. There is, for example, a theory of symbols, stereotypes, and images that has progressed visibly in the past half century, elucidated by a variety of authors in a variety of ways. From the cumulation of their different treatments, there has arisen a distinctly higher level of understanding. Abelson's formal models, Freud's insights, Lippmann's applications to politics, and Isaacs' phenomenological perceptiveness have all contributed, each in its way.

NOTES

[1] For example, Everett Rogers, in *Diffusion of Innovations* (New York, 1962), brought together the work done in the 1940s by rural sociologists on the diffusion of agricultural innovation with the work of sociologists of mass communication led by Paul Lazarsfeld dealing with the two step flow of communication in politics and marketing. Another instance concerns voting studies and balance theory. In *Candidates, Issues and Strategies* (Cambridge, Mass., 1964) a psychologist, recognized the equivalence of the cross-pressure voting theory of Bernard Berelson, Paul Lazarsfeld, and William McPhee as presented in *Voting* (Chicago, 1954) with the balance theories of attitude change developed in psychology by Fritz Heider and Abelson.

[2] "The Occult Significance of Dreams" in Sigmund Freud (ed. Ernest Jones), *Collected Papers* (London, 1950), V, 158.

[3] "Interpretation of Dreams," in *The Basic Writings of Sigmund Freud*, (tr. and ed. by A.A. Brill) (New York, 1938), 196.

[4] "Psycho-analysis," 1922 in *Collected Papers*, V, 116; also *Interpretation of Dreams*, 251-252.

[5] Otto Fenichal, *The Psychoanalytical Theory of Neuroses* (New York, 1945), 48.

[6] Ibid., 157.

[7] Walter Lippmann, *Public Opinion* (New York, 1965), 99-100. Cf. Freud's discussion of absolutism in dreams. *Interpretation of Dreams,* 288.

[8] Harold D. Lasswell, *World Politics and Personal Insecurity* (New York, 1935), 29-51; Lasswell and Abraham Kaplan, *Power and Society* (New Haven, 1950), 104.

[9] "Attitudes and Cognitive Organization," *Journal of Psychology,* XXI (1946), 107-112.

[10] Cf. "The Structure of Belief Systems," in Roger C. Schank and Kenneth M. Colby, *Computer Models of Thought and Language* (San Francisco, 1973).

[11] Robert P. Abelson and M.J. Rosenberg, "Symbolic Psychologic," *Behavioral Science,* III (1958), 1-13.

[12] Abelson, "The Structure of Belief Systems."

[13] *The Tragedy of the Chinese Revolution* (London, 1938; 2nd rev. ed., New York, 1966).

[14] Daniel Lerner, *The Passing of Traditional Society* (Glencoe, Ill., 1958).

[15] Raymond A. Bauer, Ithiel De Sola Pool, and Lewis Dexter, *American Business and Public Policy* (New York, 1963).

[16] Theodor Adorno, Else Frenkel-Brunswick, et.al., *The Authoritarian Personality* (New York, 1950).

[17] Perlmutter, "Correlates of Two Types of Xenophilic Orientation," *Journal of Abnormal and Social Psychology,* LII (1956), 130-135; "Some Relationships between Xenophilic Attitudes and Authoritarianism among Americans Abroad," *Psychological Reports,* III (1957), 131-137.

[18] Howard Perlmutter and Jerome S. Bruner, "Compatriot and Foreigner," *Journal of Abnormal and Social Psychology,* LV (1957), 253-260.

III.

Races — Hawaii

By Harold R. Isaacs

(This paper is presented here with neither the knowledge nor the permission of the author. Written when *HRI* was 20 years old, it was his first piece of serious independent research. As far as I know, it was never published but remained tucked away in a long forgotten file until 1973 when quite by chance in the course of searching for something else we came across its yellowing pages. Seen in the light of the many articles and books he has written since, culminating in his work on group identity, this early piece assumes a special significance, revealing as it does from its very first word one of the important threads that has consistently been woven into the fabric of all his varied works.

Having completed the requirements for his B.A. at Columbia College in January, 1930, he did not wait for the the formality of graduation but took off in March of that year to experience what he then called "the buffeting of circumstances." His first stop in the journey which would in future years take him many times around the world was in Honolulu where as a reporter on a local newspaper he became fascinated by the infinite variety of the people around him and the ways in which they lived together. Characteristically he set out to learn more about it. And that is what he has been doing ever since. --V.R.I.)

Introduction

Races! The word evokes color and a heavily blotted map of the world. Africa—ebony black. Asia—yellow and brown. The Americas and Europe in grades of white from the swarthy olive of Italy and Brazil to the fair skinned blond of Scandinavia and the blue-eyed Anglo-Saxon. Take groups of these—all excepting the African—root them from their homes and transplant them into a geographically restricted area smaller than the State of New Jersey. Force them through the exigencies of space to live closely together. Pack them one next another in stores, offices, banks, plantations, theaters and schools. Put them into streets where every day they must pass each other a thousand times; into churches where in varying degrees, together they will seek religious satisfactions on common ground.

In countries, towns and cities where the populations have remained fairly homogeneous, or where the process of change and absorption has been made easy by lines of demarcation which were merely national— and superficially, cultural, the problems of Race, of white and yellow and brown and black, remain largely academic playthings. But everywhere today these problems are engaging the attention of statesmen and sociologists. And perhaps nowhere in the world is the opportunity to study them so rare as in the Hawaiian Islands today. The streets of Honolulu are research laboratories for the student. Marriages, birth rates, rising and falling population trends all give some idea of what is happening where the races of the world have found themselves thrown together within a small, restricted area and have been forced by the necessities of living to seek some satisfactory adjustment of palpable differences. Hawaii is today the garden spot of the world for the study of inter-racial phenomena.

In Hawaii lives a population of nearly 400,000, white, yellow and brown. Of this number roughly ten percent is American-North European. More than a third, 140,000, are Japanese. Down the list in varying proportions range the Filipinos, the Portuguese, the Chinese, Hawaiians, Puerto Ricans, Spaniards, Koreans, Russians—and inextricable combinations of all these. The pure Hawaiians, the native stock upon which has been grafted this sudden and polyglot growth, were never very numerous—and they now number less than 20,000. Their fate stares out

Islands' population. They are a people with less than a century to live.

Deposited suddenly into this whirl of human color, an observer asks himself a thousand questions—and the wealth of material is such that the search for answers is a bewildering matter of choice and selection. How great the inter-mingling of cultures and bloods and traditions meeting here like strangers in a lonely place? What has been the fate of isolated prejudices? To what extent have common interests been discovered—or devised? And of the issue of this mingling, one makes enquiry. And in the confusion of initial reactions, the term Americanization becomes the one word in the language most difficult of definition. Where is there harmony and where discord? How is the first promoted and the latter eliminated? The people of Hawaii have had only the merest beginnings of a chance to answer these queries and inevitably the solution of old problems has been accompanied by the creation of new ones which further complicate the scene. I do not claim to possess the answers to the questions raised in any final or near-final sense. Anybody who does is exaggerating. But there are ways of ascertaining trends and there are already available records and figures which cast interesting but largely conjectural speculations on the future. The extent to which these races and highly diversified types have joined together and through the medium of intermarriage sought adjustment is one important index. Some striking results and frequently startling conclusions can be derived from a survey of inter-marriage in the Hawaiian Islands which the writer made over stated periods since 1913 (the first year for which such records are available).¹ Join with these the fruits of actual observation of phenomena here in the Islands and it is possible to make a study which, if not final, will at least be partially definitive.

Americans and Intermarriage

Aside from what it reveals about the fate of the Hawaiians, perhaps the outstanding result of such a survey as has been made is the genesis of a new and profound respect for the versatility of Americans. No other national group has been more prolific or has made more widely diversified choices in the field of intermarriage among Hawaii's polyglot thousands than they have. In the years 1913, 1917, 1921 and 1929 (which were selected first because they were representative within their respective decades and second, because for those years there were available the most complete records) the only groups out of twenty classifications into which American men failed to marry were the Korean-Hawaiian and Filipino-Hawaiian. This oversight was, however, negligible. Americans in those periods have variously selected brides from among groups, which aside from the British and German, have included Japanese, Chinese, Hawaiian, Filipino, Portuguese, Spanish, Puerto Rican, Russian, Korean, Chinese-Portuguese, Chinese-Spanish and from a last group gathered under the heading of "all others" by statistic-gatherers who despaired of giving those included in it any more specific a name.

While these marriages have been taking place in comparatively small numbers within each group, they have been occurring consistently and in gradually increasing numbers rather than otherwise. For example, in 1913 there were in all 151 American grooms, 75 of whom selected American brides. The remaining 76 distributed themselves in varying proportions to every group listed with the exceptions of the Filipino and Korean. Last year (1929) of 340 American grooms only 128 married American girls and the balance of 212 entered every group excepting the Filipino-Hawaiian and Korean-Hawaiian. One American here last year married a girl whose father was Chinese and whose mother was Spanish. Eleven married Chinese-Hawaiian girls. More than three times that number married Caucasian-Hawaiians. Twenty married pureblood Hawaiians and no less than fifty-nine married Portuguese girls. Twelve unions took place with Japanese, nine with Puerto Ricans and four with Chinese. Some idea of the consistency of these figures can be obtained when it is pointed out that each one of the figures represents a substantial increase over every previous year listed—with a single exception. Only 39 Americans married Caucasian-Hawaiian girls as compared to 44 in 1921.

It is in a way unfortunate that records are kept only of marriages which have been in one way or another legalized. Were it otherwise, the democratic ways of the Americans in Hawaii might be shown to be even more widespread and our respect for their versatility of course would increase proportionately. Indeed, I think this can be taken as a generalization applicable to every group in varying degrees and should be kept in mind constantly when actual marriage figures are being cited.

Britishers run the Americans a close second, the survey shows. It is impossible, however, to draw the proportions to their respective numbers because unfortunately in the population listings the Americans and North Europeans have always been counted together. But it can be taken for granted, I think that the number of Britishers is comparatively quite small. In any case, the British have only been slightly less prolific than the Americans. They are listed as having married into fifteen different groups, but of course, in considerably fewer numbers. I mention this angle because I think it gives ample basis for the contention that the Anglo-Saxons (if it is still possible to group Americans and British under that rather deceiving name) have been the chief aggressors in the matter of intermarriage, not only into alien national groups, but cutting deeply as well into other races.

American and British girls, although in very small numbers, are also shown by the survey to have developed an instinct for variety. In 1913 while 75 of them married American husbands, 22 married Englishmen, one a German, one a Hawaiian, two joined with Portuguese and four entered the inter-racial column by marrying Caucasian-Hawaiians. This last figure increased to five in 1917 and remained unchanged last year. In those years American girls were also recorded as having married Japanese, Chinese, and Filipinos, one in each case. Marriages between British girls and Caucasian-Hawaiians numbered three in 1929.

The Filipinos and Portuguese

Continuing to use the American standard of discrimination as an index, it was found that Filipino males achieved a similar record in terms of extent, if not in numbers. This has remained consistently true despite the fact that since 1922 and 1923 the Filipinos have outnumbered by a considerable margin all the Americans and Europeans in the Islands combined. But in their lesser way, the brown-skinned immigrants from America's other great island possession have shown a distinct tendency to emulate the Americans in Hawaii by diversifying their marriage records as much as possible. Throughout they have shown a marked preference for Hawaiian, Portuguese and Puerto Rican girls. Only three of them married Hawaiians in 1913 but by last year that number had increased to twenty-seven. That was one of the few cases in which they exceeded the American representation in the same column. They again topped the Americans in marrying Chinese-Hawaiians and show approximately the same number in the Caucasian-Hawaiian column. It might be apropos to inject here, for purposes of checking, the observation that in 1929 the American-North European group numbered about 38,000 while the Filipino figure had swelled to 68,769. So comparatively speaking, our Filipino residents in Hawaii have shown a fair degree of restraint. Unlike the Americans, the number of Filipino males marrying outside their own fold has never even approached the number marrying their own kind.

For example, last year 227 Filipinos married Filipino girls while only 85 stepped out of their own column seeking marital felicity elsewhere.

The Portuguese record resembles that of the Filipinos, although there are today only about half as many Portuguese in the Islands as there are Filipinos. A marked difference is noticeable, however, between the female halves of the two groups. The record of the Filipino females shows only rare marriages outside of their own race. The Portuguese women, on the other hand, show a variety of international and interracial unions equalled only by the Hawaiians themselves. This discrepancy may be due to the fact that there may be proportionately fewer Filipino women here than Portuguese.

For those unfamiliar with the history of American occupation in Hawaii it may be important to volunteer the information that the larger proportion of the Filipinos, Japanese, Portuguese, Puerto Ricans and Chinese here are not voluntary immigrants in the same sense as the Europeans who pour into America every year. American interests, coming into Hawaii during the latter part of the last century and since to develop the vast sugar and pineapple plantations found the problem of labor shortage a serious one. Accordingly they entered the labor market everywhere in the world and brought shipload after shipload in to work the plantations and this process is still going on. Only recently a load of half a thousand Filipinos was brought in by one of the big companies.

The Chinese and Japanese

The Chinese were a fairly well established unit of the population when the Japanese came to Hawaii but while the Chinese since 1913 have increased gradually from 21,500 to a present estimated figure of 25,211, the Japanese have spectacularly leaped in the same period from slightly less than 84,000 to nearly 140,000 and they now dominate the territory in more ways than one, comprising, as already indicated, more than one third the territory total.

It is noticeable at once from the survey that while the Chinese, like the Americans, have married into nearly every grouping listed, the Japanese have been less diverse in their choices. The Chinese have also intermarried in larger numbers than the Japanese. It is also noticeable that only in the case of Hawaiian and Chinese-Hawaiian girls has the number of Chinese intermarriages exceeded that of the Americans. (The two groups are probably very close with respect to population.) The Japanese, however, with a present population more than seven times greater than that of the Americans, show not only a lesser variety but a smaller number of intermarriages in every case.

The lack of sympathy between Japanese and Chinese is frequently mentioned in general discussions of the two peoples. It is usually said to take the form of a Japanese disdain for Chinese "backwardness." In pointing with pride to their material achievements during the last forty years, a record which has raised Japan to the position of primary "Power" in the Far East, the Japanese are said to find it convenient to forget that the Chinese are in many respects their cultural and spiritual mentors. However that may be, there has been intermarriage between the two groups from time to time. Their number, however, has been too negligible to permit of any generalization and I only mention it because it indicates that any barrier that does exist between Chinese and Japanese is not utterly free from attack in Hawaii.

The records show that more Japanese girls have married Chinese than Chinese girls have married Japanese. Three marriages occurred between Japanese grooms and Chinese brides in the years listed, one each in 1913, 1917 and 1929. Two Chinese married Japanese girls in 1913, however, two more in 1917, one in 1921 and the number jumped to seven last year. Both the Chinese and Japanese girls have intermarried with other groups to about the same extent, which is not very great and the Japanese girls outnumber the Chinese in most cases. The margin is insignificant, however, when their populational differences are considered.

On the whole, the tendency of both Chinese and Japanese has been to remain within their own race. With the exception of their choice of Hawaiian brides, which has been quite frequent and numerous, their other intermarriages have been scattered enough to give them the appearance of exceptions to the rule. There are no signs of the determined invasion of other peoples and races that is so marked in the American record of intermarriages in Hawaii.

The Hawaiians

An investigation of comparative population figures over a period of years would show that the pureblood Hawaiians have been decreasing steadily in number, a few hundred each year, from about 24,000 in 1913 to less than 19,000 at present. This has been accompanied by a steady rise in the death rate over the birth rate, although the rate of decrease is not so marked at present as it was ten years ago. A study of the intermarriage records reveals quite forcibly that the Hawaiians are losing ground chiefly by being swallowed up, bit by bit, into every other group, racial or national, that is listed among the territory's highly varied population. The evidences of this absorption are plain.

In the years selected for the survey, 1913, 1917, 1921 and 1929 there wasn't a single group of males who did not have at least one representative in the Hawaiian bride column. Only one other group of brides—the Portuguese—can show a column as solidly and widely filled with figures. But that fact in the present discussion is immaterial.

While for many years the number of Hawaiian girls who married Hawaiian men remained in the majority (i.e., of the Hawaiian brides for any given year), this preponderance was gradually sliced down and last year, 1929, 108 girls were recorded as having married within their own race, while 141 married outside of it. The largest single group of these latter married into mixed strains of Caucasian-Hawaiians. There were 40 such unions. Twenty-seven married Filipinos and 20 united with Americans. The others distributed themselves freely into every other group but the Russian. Only one Russian-Hawaiian marriage was noted in the study and that took place in 1928 between a Russian groom and an Hawaiian bride. These marriages, which have been increasing steadily, are causing, with the passage of time, the constant addition to the list of such inter-racial subdivisions as Caucasian-Hawaiian, Japanese-Hawaiian, Chinese-Hawaiian, Filipino-Hawaiian and Korean-Hawaiian. The last two named are the latest additions, six brides of those categories having been listed for 1929. They have not as yet produced any grooms. The utter confusion of races that will result after several generations is apparent and the emergence of a new race from the welter of crisscross is a possibility filled with interesting prospects. It is an intermingling of bloods in which the weaker strain of pure Hawaiian is fast giving way. It is commonly said that the Hawaiian strain, unlike that of the American Negro, for example, will disappear entirely after a generation or two and never recur.

It is easy to visualize the picture of varied races and nationalities, drawn from practically every source in the world (with the notable exceptions of the American Indian and the Negro), swarming into the Islands in large numbers, always increasing, and taking for wives the attractive, softly-tinted brown-skinned Hawaiian girls. It is easier still to grow sentimental over it, because it is a picture upon which is predicated the disappearance of a race whose kindliness, beauty, grace and hospitality have been bywords ever since the whites first came. That flash of anger which marked the end of Captain Cook has recurred only seldom in the history of white penetration into these islands. Predictions as to the nature of the race in the process of formation, and of the time when it will emerge as a visible entity, I leave to hardier observers than myself. It is a question that will find its answer only in the passage of more generations than we can reasonably concern ourselves with for the purpose of our present discussion.

In the case of Hawaiian men, what is happening makes itself readily apparent from the survey. The number of them marrying pureblood Hawaiian girls has been decreasing steadily since 1913. They have been turning instead, in regularly increasing numbers, to the part-Hawaiian groups, predominately the Caucasian-Hawaiian. The extent to which this is hastening the eventual disappearance of their race is obvious. Their marriages with girls of ancestries variously American, Chinese, Japanese and others have been taking place in small and isolated numbers. But it is perhaps worth noting that these numbers, however, few, have been on the increase rather than on the wane. Only one Hawaiian married a Japanese in 1913 but four similar unions took place in 1929. Only one married a Chinese in 1913 but seven followed suit last year. The same has happened with regard to their unions with Portuguese but in the other groups the numbers have varied between one and four and have shown little tendency to change.

Aside from the Caucasian- and Chinese-Hawaiian groups, Hawaiian girls have in recent years been marrying more Filipinos than they have Americans, although the figures for both have been steadily increasing (from 3 to 27 from 1913 to 1929 for the Filipinos and from 17 to 20 for the Americans in the same period). It is perhaps notable that while this increase has been taking place, the number of Hawaiian girls marrying Chinese and Japanese has dropped, from 8 to 6 for the Japanese in the stated period and—more notably—from 34 to 8 for the Chinese.

If these figures are indicative of anything at all, it would seem that the trend of absorption of Hawaiians is away from yellow to brown (Filipino) and white. The Hawaiians themselves, of course, are brown. But it is hardly reasonable to suppose that Asiatic-Hawaiian marriages will cease altogether. Furthermore, the volume of such marriages which has already taken place during the last two decades, even if it has been decreasing, has been sufficient to add an Asiatic-Hawaiian element to the population which will defy elimination for many generations.

But the pure strain Hawaiian will be an historical figure before the passing of another century.

While a bit less spectacular than the intermarriage figures, the birth and death rates and population records lead just as inexorably to the same conclusion. In the sixteen-year period since 1913 the pure Hawaiians have averaged a yearly decrease of 277 in actual numbers. Since 1917 they have averaged an annual decrease of 8.66 per 1000 population. The high and the low for the entire period fall in the consecutive years of 1920 and 1921 with a decrease of 650 in the first and only 83 in the second.

The figure of 650 in 1920 represented a decrease of 15.18. In 1921 this dropped sharply to 4.25. But the rate's wavering progress makes one think of a dying man wobbling along an uncertain path before finally giving up the ghost. We can start, for example, in 1917 with a decrease of 10.33. This dropped slightly the following two years but in 1920 jumped, as I have shown, to 15.18. Then came the reaction in 1921, but for the next four years the rate increased steadily and in 1924 it stood at 9.21. It declined again thereafter and dropped as low as 4.31 in 1926, a rate which represented a loss of only 91 in actual numbers. In the three years that followed, however, it rose again and the last available figures (1929) report a decrease of 11.70.

But a race is doomed when you begin to count it a gain if the rate of loss declines. That thin wavering line is not fluctuating; it is trembling. The movement back and forth does not represent a struggle for existence—but only the death throes.

On the surface, the effects of this racial disintegration are obvious. They are implicit in the disappointment of every tourist who comes to Hawaii expecting to see the natives in grass huts and the hula girls in grass skirts. The authentic originals of both are gone. Grass huts are preserved by the roadsides and in museums as curiosities and many of the hula girls who perform for tourists at the big hotels are dancers from the mainland. Only in the remote corners of some of the other islands are there still remnants of the old life and these are rapidly disappearing and their equipment is going into the museums.

But some of the old Hawaiian customs have been preserved and among them are several quite picturesque. Not the least of these is the wearing of leis. These garlanded neckpieces of interwoven flowers are commonly seen. It is the usual custom—and a pretty one—both to greet and bid farewell—Aloha—with leis. The arrival and departure of steamers are always made colorful affairs by the omnipresence of flowers. Friends greet friends by framing them in lovely leis and they say goodbye in the same fashion. It is an old Hawaiian custom, as the saying goes, and it is now formally preserved in an annual day—May Day—set aside for the purpose—although the wearing of leis is still a daily affair. It is perhaps the one unique feature that saves Honolulu from bearing too close a resemblance to Los Angeles.

There is the music, much of which remains and is often played, although many people feel that it has been sadly diluted by mainland syncopation. Likewise the dance. The hula in principle is retained. In method it conforms to the more rapid rhythms of characteristic American music. But somehow even the Great God Jazz has failed to deprive Hawaiian music and dancing of all their charm. In each case, a certain quality all its own is retained. It is a quality I can describe only by calling—distracting. They jazz up the music, perhaps, but still it is Hawaii. It isn't Broadway. And infrequently one comes across a dancer who has grace and technique as well as daring—and the art to reconstruct the glory of the days when Kamehameha I reigned upon the Hawaiian throne. These things have been enthusiastically adopted and will probably continue to live long after the Hawaiians have gone. It would be nice, in any case, to think that the music and the dance have a charm and a grace inherently genuine enough to survive the passing of the race that created them—and to stay on as that race's monuments. Sentimentally, it is nice to think that they go with the land and the lava hills and the blue-green sea on all sides, and that like the flowers, they'll continue growing.

There are the lithe beach-boys who ride the surf on their boards, erect and graceful alongside the athletic tourists who grotesquely try to imitate them and usually gain nothing more than a ducking for their pains. There are the outrigger canoes that still dot the water. Finally there is the language. The names of places and streets and many expressions that find daily use on the tongues of nearly all still remain. The musical and rolling syllables of the old native tongue too are showing more vitality than the people who first spoke them. For the pure strain Hawaiian himself will be an historical figure before the passing of another century.

Others

Naturally the youngest portion of the survey is that which deals with the inter-racial subdivisions. Here we begin to see the first signs of activity among the issue of the earlier unions among the members of the solid racial or national groups. As yet these are not sufficiently numerous to indicate any general trends or apparent preferences. Under the circumstances we can only give space to them here as interesting sidelights in a many-sided situation, although wrapped up in them is the answer to all the queries which are today necessarily unanswerable. Given perhaps another fifty years or a century, they will doubtless dominate the intermarriage records. People who enjoy guessing will probably find considerable enjoyment in the figures as they stand today. But guessing around a dinner table and in print are two different things.

Of the several interesting unions, I have already noted one. That took place last year between an American and a Chinese-Spanish girl. Two Americans, two Portuguese, two Filipinos and one Puerto Rican have married Japanese-Hawaiian girls. No less than 11 Americans last year married Chinese-Hawaiians. Britishers, Germans, Japanese, Portuguese and Koreans have married similarly. In the majority of these crisscross marriages, however, we find Hawaiian blood acting as a common denominator. Thus there have been comparatively large numbers of unions among individuals variously Japanese-Hawaiian, Chinese-Hawaiian and Caucasian-Hawaiian. These have been especially frequent between the last two named.

Perhaps most intriguing of all are two marriages that have taken place (1921 and 1929) between Caucasian-Hawaiian grooms and Chinese-Portuguese brides.

Except to say that these give some evidence of the inextricable intermingling of bloods, cultures and traditions that is going on in Hawaii and that they suggest vaguely the coming confusion of the next century, I leave these citations without comment. From mere speculation about them with no facts at all as bases, only confusion issues.

Color Line

The widespread intermingling of races in Hawaii that has been described doubtless raises any number of questions in the mind of the reader. What has been its issue? Have these intermarriages turned out "happily"? What now are the relationships among these peoples? What is the position of the still-pure whites? Even the most casual student of race relationships would be interested in the results of a marriage between a Caucasian-Hawaiian groom and a Chinese-Portuguese bride. So is the writer. Unfortunately there are serious obstacles in the way of entering people's homes and asking them if they're "happy." There are many who do it, but they're known as reformers. Happiness has always been so difficult to define anyway.

The task of ascertaining the results of this wide and diverse intermarriage is far more difficult and laborious than merely discovering its extent. One prominent sociologist, connected with the University of Hawaii, has been collecting family and individual case histories for nearly ten years. He is unwilling even to approximate a date when any generalizations will appear from a sufficiently large number of them to make them convincing.

If one were to return from a walk through the streets of Honlulu and attempt to generalize his impressions of the people he's seen, he would probably hit upon the absence of "that harrassed look." Everyone, at his job or passing by, seems contented enough. As a criterion for serious study, however, such a conclusion is negligible. Some of the most contented-looking cows among New York's millions are frequently in their own private opinions the unhappiest people in the world. There is available considerable data on the careers of the children of Hawaii's mingled races in the schools and I shall take the opportunity elsewhere to describe the changes being wrought through educational channels. I will concern myself here with an attempt to describe the apparent effects of this intermingling on the everyday relationships between and among the races as they can be noted under various conditions and in different groups. But here again, it is impossible to get into the minds of these people and describe the workings there. Nor is it possible to make any definite statements about their "true" feelings. But questions put to the right people in the right places often elicit illuminating bits of information. Nor are expeditions into the streets and public places utterly fruitless.

It doesn't take a visitor long to discover that any "color line" that does exist in Hawaii is frequently invisible and at all times extremely flexible. People here, like everywhere, divide themselves into strata determined by the common interests and similarity of backgrounds, although that last is less noticeable in Hawaii. People will ordinarily seek and enjoy the company of friends with whom they can exchange ideas on the same plane and whose idea of "a good time" is similar enough to their own to make that exchange a pleasant one. This normal tendency holds true, of course, within the different racial groups, and carries over without important changes, I think, into places where those lines cross and crisscross. Where the lines cross a tendency for "traditional prejudices" to disappear, so far as race or nationality is concerned, is an obvious result, else the lines would not perhaps have crossed in the first place. They would certainly not be continuing to do so over a long period of years. This is one important factor in explaining why the color line in Hawaii is so nebulous a quantity.

Hawaii, like most other communities in the world, has its "aristocracy," either by self-appointment through birth or through the sanctions of wealth—or as is more usual—a combination of the two. This type of the "better families" with their tiny snobberies, whose activities are listed in the "Society" columns of the town papers, is so well known, that for the purposes of our study here they can be in the main ignored. Suffice it to say that Hawaii is not exempt from the presence of such a group and among them are numbered some of the wealthiest and most influential families in the Islands.

It is possible to list for our purposes here a type which we may safely term the "better" class judged by standards usually strange to the "aristocrats." Include among these the more intelligent and educated within every racial group. Include also those members of the aristocracy whose experience and education has been sufficient to lift them from their accustomed category. Include many of those engaged in educational work of different kinds—from teachers in the kindergartens to professors at the university. Among these, with all their varied backgrounds, convictions, ideas and tastes, the color line seems to have become quite flexible.

It is inconceivable for example, that a professor in a southern university should invite as a dinner guest to a hotel a negro friend, even if he be Booker T. Washington himself. (Indeed, it is doubtful if a southern university professor would have a negro friend.) That professor would be run out of town on a rail and Booker T. Washington probably lynched by the self-respecting citizens of any Alabama town, for example, should such an incident occur. The color line in the Alabama sense is practically unknown in Hawaii. Whites and orientals of the university or Booker T. Washington type mingle freely, dine together, and moreover, marry each other if they choose. The remarkable and perhaps unique feature of this situation, as one professor pointed out to me, is the absence of any social law which makes those who intermingle the objects of general disapproval. No important stigma seems to attach to intermarriage. Such people as disapprove seldom do more than shrug their shoulders. "Each to his own taste" is a dictum quite generally respected.

Intermarried couples among intelligent groups have been known to make a successful go of it on the basis of a give and take adjustment which their intelligence would naturally suggest. Their positions are made infinitely easier by the fact that they are not subjected to the ostracism and contempt which they would probably meet on the mainland. Their children face the same circumstances. And at this point generalizations must cease. Each case solves its own problems, or fails, depending on the individual and always differing circumstances.

Among whites of lesser consequence (that is, whites with little wealth who are desirous, through the acquisition of wealth, of "crashing the gate" into the aristocracy), the color line in so far as Orientals are concerned is usually as stringent as in California. People who someday hope to have it recorded that they dined twenty at dinner prior to closing their town house at the end of the winter season will usually steer clear, if possible, of any social contacts with Orientals. It is difficult to say how many such people there are. Bank clerks, lesser clerks, cashiers, express agents, store managers, lesser merchants, shipping company department heads—are all as a rule included. It is illuminating to note, however, that in a growing number of these positions whites are being gradually replaced by the incoming generations of educated and comparatively intelligent Orientals or different varieties of white or Oriental Hawaiians.

Among that varied group that so many Americans like to call "the backbone of the people"—the laborers, white-collar underlings, waiters, truck-drivers, store-clerks—the color line frequently seems to have disappeared altogether. Although among those of this category who want to ascend through the ranks of the "lesser whites" and into the aristocracy it again recurs and usually sharply because the struggle to maintain it is fiercer. But the great majority of this class in Hawaii is yellow, brown or part-white. Among them the line is to all intents and purposes non-existent—or at least, invisible. People who still think racial prejudices are "fundamental" and "inherent" have a lesson to learn in Hawaii where intensive contact over a relatively short period of time seems to have erased discords of allegedly "ancient" standing.

This seems to be remarkably true of the second and third generation in Hawaii, many of whom are approaching manhood and womanhood. Arm in arm and happily down the streets they go, couples frequently as far removed from each other by tradition as the two ends of the world. Americans, Europeans, Japanese, Chinese, Filipinos, Portuguese, Hawaiians, of every shade and color, boys and girls together and apparently oblivious to the breach which tradition ordinarily assumes between or among them. The children of Hawaii's many races, Hawaiian born, seem to be erasing the lines they find between their respective parents—they are playing and studying together. Later they are working and marrying and living together. The thousand tiny difficulties, the disagreements, the doubtless unhappy attempt to solve "in-law" problems, must all certainly play their big part in the lives of these young people. Such intermingling in so short a space of time would be inconceivable without these accomplishments. But the ultimate achievement of a satisfactory adjustment is not hard to imagine although it is far more difficult to predict what form that adjustment will take.

The daily difficulties of adjustment and especially the "in-law" problem must be quite serious in their magnitude but it is next to impossible to get at the facts. One would have to become an intimate part of the lives of hundreds of people. One would have to be there to watch their tiny struggles and one would no doubt discover that no two are alike. The case histories would be as variable as there are varied degrees of intelligence and circumstances. The compilation would in itself be a lifetime's work for one generation of students and the results even then would perhaps defy generalization. So it is only possible to point out that the intermingling is taking place and that in the process many prejudices commonly thought of as "in the blood" seem to be disappearing rapidly.

Reasons for the apparently widespread readjustment of many whites to "inborn prejudices" against Orientals (even among some of the aristocrats) are not wholly based, however, upon a sudden change for the better in the intelligence quotients of these people. There are additional and important reasons for expediency, chiefly economic. Together the Japanese and Chinese comprise nearly half the territory's population. It is no exaggeration to say they dominate it. Many of them are wealthy and consequently influential. Alongside the palatial homes of the established whites, they are building mansions of their own. They are bankers, merchants and landowners of premier importance. It is often extremely unwise for many whites, even aristocrats, to insist upon adherence to the dictates of traditional prejudices which are usually based upon some vague notions of "white supremacy." The Orientals show too many positive signs at least of equality, if not outright superiority. They are not forcing their way in or "demanding" recognition. They are earning it by playing the whites' game at least as well as the whites play it. Just to what degree in this process they are sacrificing their own traditions, or some features of it, is a question left to further examinations. But a big part of the Orientals' success is undoubtedly their Occidentalization.

Privately and often publicly some whites find these conditions a matter of serious concern. Students of race problems see in it evidences of eventual harmony. Many of them realize that harmony can perhaps only be attained at the expense of the fiction of "white supremacy." But the point is moot. While the conditions, political and geographical in the Hawaiian Islands, may peculiarly favor inter-racial intercourse, they provide none the less a rare and revealing object-study for a world whose history for the next several hundred years will probably be determined by the solution of world-wide race problems.

NOTES

[1] In subsequent years vital statistics were no longer kept in terms of racial categories and, much to the regret of some social scientists, this kind of study no longer could be carried out....vri

IV.

Empathy and Idealization: The Dynamics of Goodwill

By Lucian W. Pye

The fashion today is to acknowledge the "reality" of ethnicity, boldly to proclaim one's recognition that a fact of life is the power of biological and national bonds. Two decades of extolling the vital importance of everyone's search for identity has had its unmistakable consequences: The primordial has been legitimized and any champion of universalism is suspected of hypocrisy. Those who have sought to put aside or generally discount their tribal ties are viewed as artificial men, afraid to tell it like it is.

The current enthusiasm for the durability, indeed, the integrity of ethnicity has obscured the significant social fact that some people have deep antipathies for their own kind, and even more have powerful affinities for others. The range can go from those who are merely bored by the parochial and fascinated with the unaccustomed all the way to those who will unhesitatingly sacrifice the interests of their community and their private interests in order to favor those who are manifestly different.

We seem in danger of losing sight of the fact that the xenophobe is balanced by the xenophile and that it is no more "natural" to defend one's clan unquestioningly than to scorn one's parents' habits in favor of one's neighbors' contrasting customs. Although ethnic spokesmen may trumpet the psychic importance of unabashedly praising one's ethnic identity as the proper route to self-esteem, the fact is that many people seem only able to find themselves by standing apart from their crowd. For some people this capacity to empathize with the interests of other communities is clearly an important ingredient in their achievement of maturity.

Indeed, in the era just prior to the current rediscovery of the authenticity of ethnicity it was commonly believed that the public good was best served by a citizenry who, for whatever private motivations and idiosyncrasies, readily and easily associated with others of different backgrounds. There was a time, as Harold Isaacs has frequently reminded us, when it was honorable and certainly not neurotic to strive to join the brotherhood of the "detribalized." It was then widely assumed that such people would provide the basis for a better and more enlightened community.

Other chapters in this volume deal with the dynamic of rising ethnic feelings and the legitimacy of the new concepts of community without integration. Our concern in this essay will be with some individuals who have been steadfast in empathizing with other ethnic causes than their own. What are the psychology, character, and the motive drives of such people? What led them to empathize with others? And how have they reacted to rebuffs from those who now are too filled with the importance of their ethnic identity searches to appreciate the universalistic people who once offered them help?

In the spirit of Harold Isaacs' style in searching for human understanding we limited our investigations to in depth interviews with three civil rights activists who have made considerable personal sacrifices for the cause of social integration and three overseas development workers who altered their careers to help developing countries. Statistically they are not significant as a sample for we know nothing about the universe from which they have been drawn. Rather we have selected them because they serve our purpose, which is to document the human and psychological dimensions of people who best approximate an "ideal type": the American liberal who has upheld the faith in dark times. We do not have the space here to present the full stories of each of these six people. Instead we shall identify several themes which seem to run through all of their accounts and which may help to explain their steadfastness in seeking to understand and defend others.

First, however, we shall briefly identify the six. Of the civil rights workers, one is a suburban matron, the wife of a successful businessman, who answered the call to work in Mississippi, maintains friendships with several black women leaders, and, although not religious, is a leader of programs in the "Y" devoted to better racial understanding. She thinks of herself as being "...born into the liberal tradition—my family is related to the Adamses—and in college it was natural for me to identify with the liberal issues. I remember how surprised I was when I learned that my father thought I was going too far in my open support of the New Deal and the labor movements." The second is the wife of a professor at a small, isolated college in the mountains of the South. She grew up in a border state and, completely on her own, traveled to Selma, Alabama to give witness to her support of the civil rights confrontation. Our third civil rights worker also participated in the Selma events, but he grew up in a mid-Western farm community, and after working his way through college sought a career in the ministry and has written on liberal theological matters.

The three overseas development workers all spent their childhoods in small towns: one in the South, one in western New York state, and the third on the Pacific coast. They all graduated from professional or technically oriented colleges: the Southerner earned a degree in agricultural economics, the Easterner planned to be a public accountant, and the Westerner trained in mechanical engineering. For all three, World War II gave them their first experience with foreign societies. All three were committed to domestic careers, were married, and were raising families when they made the decision to become involved in helping nations to develop. The Southerner went to India for an agricultural extension program of a state university under contract to A.I.D.; the Easterner became involved in foreign assistance through an Eisenhower administration program of recruiting businessmen and in time was assigned to posts in various Muslim countries, administering various technical training programs; the Westerner came to foreign assistance in the wave of excitement of the early New Frontier days and became deeply involved in several aspects of aid to India. We have allowed ourselves to become slightly confused and vague about aspects of their careers in order to maintain their anonymity, but we are absolutely certain of one fact: all three developed deep attachments to the idea of helping specific foreign countries, and even to specific programs of their foreign governments, and all three are aware that their labors have been denounced by those whom they sought to help.

These two women and four men are extremely intelligent, reflective, and complex individuals. They all appreciate the complicated changes taking place in America and the world, which have affected the relations of nations, communities, and races. To do justice to the views of any one of them would require more space than we have for all six in this book. Fortunately, all six vividly share certain characteristics which appear to account, no doubt in differing degrees, for why they developed strong sentiments of empathy for another ethnic community and why their feelings have not been appreciably affected by the rise of ethnic and racial separatism or nationalism. Let us now turn to these themes and see how different strands of belief and conviction were in all cases woven together in much the same manner to produce the strong qualities of character which have resisted the pulls of more current fashions.

The Absolute Inadmissibility of Injustice

All six of our respondents at one point or another in their interviews gave vent to impassioned statements about the injustices experienced by others. And they all noted that they had once been quite unaware of the extent, viciousness, and damage done by racial injustice. The three civil rights workers spoke with emotion about prejudice in a way which was reminiscent of the literature on that subject of the 1930s and 1940s. For the overseas development workers, prejudice was replaced by colonialism, which they spoke about in terms used by nationalists of nearly a generation ago, but so vividly that European domination seemed a matter of only yesterday.

For the civil rights workers the concept of prejudice was in itself enough to explain the plight of blacks and the motivation of whites. One of the interviews began with the respondent holding forth so intensely

about the effects of prejudice that it seemed for a while impossible to
move on to other subjects.

> I feel very strongly that there is only one problem and that is white prejudice. We
> blame the blacks for everything that is wrong when it is really white society that is at
> fault. I honestly believe we are trying to carry out genocide—that is what the Nixon ad-
> ministration is doing. If it wasn't for our prejudiced, racist society the government
> wouldn't be able to get away with this unjust treatment of blacks. I can't blame the
> blacks for a single thing because everything follows from white prejudice.

Another commented that "The more I learned about the suffering of the
Negroes, the more I realized how deep and vicious prejudice is in our
society."

The overseas development workers spoke about the evils of colonialism in almost the same words and style as the civil rights champions
spoke of prejudice:

> In Egypt I first realized that just about every reason why the country was poor and
> backward could be traced to their colonial sufferings. This became even more obvious
> in India. The curse of colonialism was everywhere, holding back the country. Every
> day in my work I seemed to be fighting the heritages of colonialism. The inefficient
> way things were set up all came out of British practices. ...Sure the Indians seems to
> have a lot of hang ups, but all of them can be explained by what they had to go through
> because of colonialism.

Another observed that "I am sure that colonialism must have been the
most evil thing that ever existed. Its scars run so deep; I don't know if
they will ever disappear."

The themes of prejudice and colonialism were emotionally
presented, but, at the same time, they were largely abstract concepts for
all of the respondents. This was the case because they freely used the
terms as presumably self-evident, explanatory concepts. In their own
thinking, no right-thinking person could possibly argue about the obvious evils of prejudice and colonialism. The ease with which they accepted the explanatory powers of these concepts led us to inquire more
about where they first learned of the nature of prejudice and colonialism;
and possibly not surprisingly all spoke quite vividly of courses which they
had taken in college in the late 1930s and early 1940s which dwelled extensively on these evils. For one, all of the psychology she could
remember from three courses were the readings and lectures about
stereotypes and prejudice. One respondent did admit to the feeling that
the ultimate proof of education was to be free of all prejudices and that it
was essentially the uneducated who were infested with prejudices. The
theme of colonialism had appeared in courses which dealt with the causes
of wars and the requirements for enduring peace after World War II.
Thus, almost in a nostalgic mood the interviews carried us back to the
spirit of the Atlantic Charter and the denunciation of "gentlemen's
agreements." Needless to say, "colonialism" was a complete abstraction
in the college context, but, surprisingly, prejudice was almost equally an
abstraction. Those who talked of being influenced by what they had
learned in college about prejudice admitted that the subject was really

directed against anti-Semitism. Yet, only one of the civil rights workers could remember any first-hand examples of anti-Semitism. The one who did tells of the horror and of the tears that were shed by the girls on her dorm floor when the Jewish parents of a roommate were denied a hotel reservation in Florida.

Thus, all of the respondents, when of college age, were deeply impressed with the imperative need to oppose certain evils of behavior and thought—evils which in their daily lives they never had the chance to confront. In a sense they were armed to fight a major foe, they were intellectually and emotionally prepared for the conflict, but they were not given a chance to do battle. It was only years later in the civil rights movement and in their work in developing countries that they felt that at last they were meeting the evils which they had been so ready for so long to fight.

Personal Discovery: "They Can't Take That Away From Me"

In all six cases the critical confirmation of what they had learned in the abstract took the form of a personal discovery through a particular friendship with someone whom they saw as a victim of prejudice or colonialism. These experiences all had the characteristics of being extremely positive, and of a highly private, or at least of an individual nature. In each case friendship with a black or an Asian provided "solid" evidence which thereafter could repeatedly be called upon to support generalizations about the characteristics of different peoples.

The minister had as a roommate in seminary a black whom he quickly came to admire for his steadfastness of faith, his capacity for human understanding and sympathy, and his determination to have a useful career.

> My friendship with John taught me what blacks really are like. After having known him and the richness of his spirit I could never thereafter remain silent in the face of any demeaning remarks about blacks.

The wife of the businessman established her decisive friendship at the time her first child was born. At that time she brought into her household a live-in-maid who was educated, had been trained for office work, but who had never been able to find an appropriate job. This maid became a complete part of the family—her own son was brought up with the family children and sent to college just as the other children.

> She was without question one of the most wonderful persons I have ever known. Maybe she is the woman I have been the closest to in all my life. She was always tremendously wise, full of understanding as to everybody's needs, feelings and sufferings. She was absolute proof to me of how prejudice denies opportunities for there isn't anything she couldn't have done or been if she had been given the chance.

The wife of the college teacher worked in the university library while her husband was doing his graduate work, and one of her co-workers was an older black woman who was dedicated to the institution she worked for and who contributed to a strong sense of group identity among all the employees: "She was just a natural leader. It was she who took interest in me first, and I soon found that I cared very much about all the things which were important in her life."

Of the three development workers, each recounted a friendship which became for him proof that he was personally more acceptable than Americans or Westerners in general, and that, because of his personal capacity for sympathy, he had broken an almost mystical barrier which separates Westerners from the victims of colonialism.

> Most of the people in the Mission were only interested in their diplomatic invitations, but I and my wife developed a couple of real friendships.... We were accepted into his home and we learned about his life.... Although we haven't corresponded in years, I know that we could pick up right where we left off.

> I developed tremendous respect for the dean of the college. He was trying to break out of the old British structure of education and to interest young people in agriculture. We became very close friends and he would tell me all of his problems and I was the only American he ever invited to his home.

> Most Americans never got to know anyone, but I became very close to several Indians I had to deal with. It wasn't easy because they had always distrusted our mission, but I showed them that I was on their side. I really couldn't fault them because after what they had experienced from the British it was understandable that they never wanted to invite a Westerner into their house.... No I was never invited to an Indian home, but I did have some real friends."

Both the civil rights and the overseas development workers were not only greatly influenced by the experiences of their special friendships and the human aspects of coming to know persons of different backgrounds, but also tended to assume that such friendships made them unique— pioneers in an area of human contacts. They spoke as if they were the very first white people to have had close friendships with blacks or Asians. Even when they were challenged on the uniqueness of their friendships, they tended to defend the special character of their experiences by suggesting that theirs must have been far more frank and intimate than the usual cross-ethnic contacts.

Friendships thus worked as both learning experiences and ego boosters. Personal contacts were without question eye-opening events for all of the respondents. Those who came to know blacks spoke more concretely and convincingly of the richness of their experiences, while those who spoke of their friendships with Asians seemed to be making much over far less. Possibly those who grew to know well particular blacks began by expecting little and were greatly impressed by the deeply human and personally genuine dimensions of their friends, while those who dealt with foreigners began with a certain awe of Asians and were thankful for whatever experiences they were allowed.

Whatever the differences in the character and intimacy of the relationships, it is clear that these personal experiences became, in slightly different ways, a constant reference point which each used thereafter to disprove the generalizations that others might make and to prove their own generalizations. It was the quality of friendship which convinced each that he truly "knew" something, and that no other authority, however important or prestigious, could cast any doubts on the truth revealed by those friendships. Thereafter, no one could ever take away what they had gained. Any contrary opinion of others could only be manifestations of prejudice or exceptional events of little importance.

Intellectualization and Idealization

The correctness of these experiences of friendship were in all cases balanced by strong commitments to abstract concepts which served as the bases for various forms of idealization. Two of our informants became deeply attached to political liberalism, the cause of labor, the principles of welfare, and the ideals of the New Deal; one was close to them except that his vision was that of liberal theology and the doctrine of opposition to all forms of orthodoxy; and three came to sense great potency and virtue in Keynesian economic doctrines and believed that they possessed the knowledge which could make possible unlimited economic growth, if only they could command the resources of the American government.

The objection may be raised that nothing could be more trite and self-evident than for civil rights enthusiasts to be committed liberals and for champions of development to believe in economic theories. Yet, at the risk of being banal, we must insist that commitment to these abstract systems of thought, when linked to personal experiences, provided all of our respondents with impenetrable shields against critical opinions. The contents of these belief systems or theories were of course important, but they also seem to have had a functional role in facilitating the dismissal of all awkward ideas by making it possible to classify all such challenges as being either uninformed and ignorant or informed but heretical.

Liberal views and economic theory thus served as a filter for discriminating between good and bad, proper and improper, and the right-minded and the wrong-minded. At the same time that liberal views and economic theory provided these discriminating or evaluating functions, they also had the merit for their users of being nonmoralistic, anti-orthodox, non-ideological, and mere secular good sense, which all intelligent people will in time come to accept. Since liberalism was opposed to prejudice, it had to be free of all distortion and prejudice; since Keynesian economics was opposed to classical economics, it had to be liberating and free of cant.

All of our respondents in some degree idealized what they intellectualized. Theories about the economy became not just explanations of reality but the bases for describing utopias. Those who had strong views about the various dimensions of the New Deal saw such policies as social security, minimum wage, the rights of labor, and the like as not just necessary or appropriate policies, but as key ingredients of the good society. It would be tempting to suggest the easy paradox that in professing opposition to orthodoxy and doctrinal views, our civil rights and overseas development workers were adhering to ideologies of their own. This, however, would be going too far for they were committed to both ideas and ideals; about the former they were prepared to be flexible, imaginative, and even subtle, but it was in their need for ideals that they seemed to become rigid and uncompromising. Had they been pragmatic liberals without strong ideals, they probably could have shifted easily with the times. This, however, was not possible because there were certain things which for them were completely unthinkable because of their need to idealize. Thus, instead of suggesting that their liberalism hardened into a rigid ideology, it seems more accurate to think in terms of a personality style in which certain matters have to be treated in idealized terms. None of our respondents subscribed to the full doctrines of liberalism or held strongly to elaborate theories of economic development and progress; but rather all had certain subjects that they refused to see as other than pure and glorified.

> I know of no example in America in which there has been a truly well integrated school in which everyone isn't better off than when the races are separate.

This use, by all six respondents, of the defense mechanism of idealization appears to have two important consequences for their general behavior. First, it helped to blur the distinction between self and virtuous cause which therefore made it possible to identify the self with the cause without overtly suggesting that the self was excessively virtuous. Secondly, idealization made it possible to hold steadfast to certain beliefs and principles while accepting that much was going wrong in areas where reality could be more critically accepted. We must examine each of these approaches for they seem to have been critical in helping all six people to maintain their beliefs while coping with a changing world.

The Self Pinned Down in the Activist Role

There was a variety in the ways in which the six were brought to activist roles—some had to be enticed, even tricked, while others took the initiative and sought out ways to become involved. The differences disappeared, however, once they had become activists: In every case activism meant assuming a position or role the performance of which reflected on their sense of self-esteem:

> I was on the "Y" board and so I had no choice, I just had to go on.

> I was afraid about going to Selma, because those were violent times. But I guess I was even more afraid not to go because of my position at the time it was unthinkable for me not to go.

> All my life I had heard criticism about how bad government bureaucrats are, but once I got into A.I.D. I realized how wrong all that talk had been. We really worked hard and well, and I was never personally involved in any foolish policies.

Self-esteem was generally reinforced by vivid feelings of self-sacrifice. The good cause was also a hard one:

> I wasn't at all sure about going to Mississippi but my husband and children all said that I had to go. It was one of the most difficult things I had ever done. We worked long hours. Just listening to the experiences of others was tiring but it also reminded me of the dangers of just wanting to be a human being in our society.

> People like to picture American aid officials as living like diplomats in big houses with servants. Let me tell you that it was a hard strain; tough on the kids who had to give up their friends; tough on my wife to be away from her family and friends; and tough on me to have to take all the guff from two governments—ours and theirs.

Personal sacrifice and pride in one's abilities combined to elevate the honor and the importance of the cause. In all cases activism sealed the commitment which made interracial and inter-ethnic relations an ultimate value for each of the six. All had previously been active people, involved in many endeavors, but what made their identification with interracial, inter-ethnic causes special were the higher stakes, the greater sense of individual commitment, and the awareness that there could be no reversals or retreats.

> After Selma I had to give talks to many different groups, and from then on I was known by everyone as the most active local person in the cause of integration.

> When I first came back from India I was something of a hometown celebrity. I was interviewed by the press and on radio. Lots of questions were raised as to why we gave so much foreign aid and what we expected to get from it all. I really enjoyed defending what we were doing in India.

The Dialectic of Good and Evil

Although all six spoke of their own sense of rightness in their personal activism, they were more comfortable and eloquent in defending the virtue of their cause and talking of the dark, ignorant, and, indeed, evil qualities of those who opposed them. The instinctive reactions of the two women and four men were the same: Any criticism of blacks or the developing countries was dismissed by sharp attacks on those whom they saw as the enemies of those with whom they empathized. Initially, they could dismiss critics as being merely prejudiced and ignorant.

Interestingly, whereas many people in recent years have tended to rethink questions of rights and wrongs with respect to integration and "black power" and with respect to involvement in the development of foreign countries, these six civil rights and overseas development workers warded off increased criticism by elevating the status and power of those who were the evil foe. Whereas originally the "enemy" consisted of the illiterate, prejudiced, and uninformed, they now spoke of the source of trouble as President Nixon, the Senate, and essential elite institutions. They could continue to idealize their peoples by demonstrating that "things were harder" for them because of the increasingly hostile attitudes of those in power.

> I just cannot accept any of the criticism about "black power" because I know that many blacks have been driven to extremes by the hardhearted policies of the current Administration. The fact that the cities aren't burning, the blacks aren't revolting,and crime may be down a bit in the cities really means that the blacks have lost all hope because of the lack of sympathy of Washington.

> Some people say that the blacks pushed too hard, that their language was too violent, and that they tried to hold up everyone else, but that isn't true because all they were doing was reacting to the awful practices of our racist society. They had to fight back because the government became their enemy....Yes, it is true that the violence was the worst with Johnson who did more than any president for the blacks, but the reason why was explained by the Kerner Commission Report. Now there is just no hope at all because of Nixon's policies.

The three civil rights activists refused to admit that conditions had in any way improved for blacks or that there were any grounds for criticizing the behavior of black extremists. They uniformly dismissed the "affirmative action program" as a trivial matter of only symbolic importance because it was inconceivable that anything the Nixon Administration might do could be of any help to blacks. Similarly, the overseas development activists continued to find it impossible to criticize the developing countries because whatever faults they might seem to have were as nothing compared with the great failing of Washington to maintain and even raise aid levels in the face of ever rising needs in the poor countries. The trend toward military rule in Africa was explained by one as an understandable response to declining American concern and help for Africa. All three insisted that a more forthcoming spirit in Washington would have prevented India from being driven to its anti-American stands.

No one would admit to disappointment over the behavior of the spokesmen for either blacks or the developing areas because, although not necessarily approving of specific actions, they found legitimacy in all—including even violence and intemperate posturing. Above all, no one would entertain for a moment the idea that their actions, backed by the very best of intentions, could have encouraged in any way unintended and undesirable results. There were too many other ways of explaining and justifying all that might be and has been criticized in the behavior of both minority leaders and liberal activists. As the world became worse they could further idealize both those whom they empathized with and their own commitments.

Their firm need for the defense of idealization also meant that none of the respondents admitted to any sense of betrayal as a result of black attacks on liberals or Indian denunciations of American aid. All of the civil rights workers had been personally insulted in confrontations with black radicals, and their work in seeking integration denounced as merely symbolic by young blacks; yet, the three were able to brush aside these attacks as understandable acts of frustrated youth.

> One very tense evening was when we sat through a play put on by young blacks in which an endless stream of obscenities were directed against whites. I felt very embarrassed for some of the mothers who were my friends who must have been ashamed of their children, just as I have often been embarrassed by the actions of my children. When you think of how rude young white radicals have been, then the behavior of the blacks doesn't seem so extreme.

> It has not been pleasant to have to listen to and to read the rantings of Indian intellectuals who criticize everything the U.S. has done to help the Indians get on their feet. But I think I understand their frustrations and their need to seem to be politically in favor of change. Sure, they keep saying that American aid was unnecessary, that it has held back Indian development and the GOI should never accept anything in the future. The fact, however, is that India is approaching a crisis, she is in desperate need of further aid and she just cannot get along without it. She is going to be facing famine and awful hardships. This is why I think it is a real disgrace that Washington is drifting towards less and less aid. Whatever harm Indian intellectuals may do to U.S.-Indian relations is nothing compared with the failure in responsibilities of the Administration and Congress in providing what is clearly going to be needed.

Speculations, Interpretations, and Projections

There is probably little that is surprising or novel in the words of our six respondents. Their views are essentially those of committed liberals who believe strongly in the ideals of an integrated society in America and of advancement in the developing world. Much of what they have to say may seem banal, as are the views of most people, and often they seem slightly naive and certainly somewhat old fashioned. They represent their generation and do not seem to feel any urgency to identify with more current fashions. When directly confronted with questions about the rise in ethnic consciousness and the decline of interracial and internationalist sentiments, they indicate awareness of these presumed trends but hold that such developments should have no effect on their cherished goals. The growth of prejudice and parochialism suggested only the need for greater commitment.

The perseverence of our six in their liberal beliefs seems to stem in almost equal measure from social norms and personality characteristics, with the former, a cause for pessimism for future generations and the latter, a source of possible optimism. All six were very strongly influenced by the normative doctrines which denounced ethnocentrism and extolled the ideals of accepting all people regardless of race or ethnic background. As one stated: "I guess we believed much too uncritically that the 'melting pot' worked in America. My conclusion now is that we will have to work much harder to make it succeed." Given the public mood, the standards of sophisticated discourse, and what is taught in civics courses and college social science subjects, it is hard to picture the next generation having such deep commitments to interracial cooperation and harmony. These six respondents demonstrated that the assault that American education made on prejudice and anti-Semitism did have lasting consequences which were relevant for the cause of racial integration and international assistance. To the extent that it is no longer fashionable to teach about the evils of prejudice but rather to display tolerance for ethnic identities and inward-looking nationalisms, people will not be leaving college with the feeling that parochial sentiments are unbecoming of educated men and women.

Certainly the recent tone of higher education with its legitimizing of the inward search for identity will produce quite a different pattern of commitment among conformists than did the earlier stress on forgetting the self in favor of tolerance for all peoples. If bright and energetic members of the current college generation are going to display the same enduring commitments to the normative tone of their college cultures as our six respondents did, then we must be pessimistic about the prospects of future activists for racial tolerance and international understanding.

On the other hand, we also found that our six displayed some striking psychological qualities, and there is no reason to believe that future generations will not contain within them people with these same qualities. In particular, there are two qualities which all had in great abundance—a capacity for empathy and a need for idealization. In our interviewing there was no way in which we could explore deep enough into the personalities of our respondents to learn about the sources of these two striking qualities. We can only report their existence and the powerful effects that they had on the behavior of the six.

The capacity of each of them to identify with others was remarkable; indeed, they all essentially defined themselves by their statements about their feelings for others. None of them seemed interested in their own inner, isolated sentiments, and certainly none was concerned or intrigued with questions about his or her identities. Although these were outwardly directed people, they were not the shallow, "other-directed" people described by David Riesman because they were concerned with the inner feelings and sufferings of others, and were not hypersensitive to the views of others.[1]

The basic concept of empathy, which is the denial of traditional man and the essence of modernity as defined by Daniel Lerner,[2] is the opposite of the concern for identity, the holy grail of Erik H. Erikson's complete personality. Presumably fashions can shift back and forth from outward concerns for others and inward concerns for the self, but it seems likely that at a more basic level of personality the distribution of people in the American population who are capable of, and indeed compelled to manifest, empathy is likely to be fairly constant. In short, the dominant styles may change but the inherent potential for identifying with others probably endures at about the same proportion of the population.

Much the same can probably be said about the other personality characteristics which the six all manifested—the heavy utilization of the defense mechanisms of idealization. Again, we must acknowledge that there was nothing in the interviews which would help us to understand how they came as individuals to the use of idealization; rather, we learned only that their capacity to hold to their positive views of other ethnic peoples and to ward off all criticism depended upon such a psychological mechanism.

No doubt the times in which these people began to apply their basic defense mechanism to blacks and developing peoples was a period in which idealization was highly popular and acceptable. What one wanted to see as good and worthy of support one readily idealized and thereafter defended against all negative characterizations. In American society today, just as identity searching is more "in" than manifesting empathy, so probably the utilization of cynicism as a defense mechanism is more in tune with the dominant tone of life than is idealization; but this probably has nothing to do with the actual distributions of peoples who rely upon the one or the other basic defense mechanisms. A given proportion of people are still learning how to use idealization to protect and defend their egos. The change is only a decline in the readiness of such people to set the tone for public life.

Cynicism and idealization are readily paired defense mechanisms since they both operate to protect against the reality of objective criticism and evaluation. With cynicism what is truly valued is spared any sustained scrutiny, any exposure to reality, by the device of pretending that it is self-evident, without any investigation being necessary, that what is valued is flawed. With idealization what is valued is protected from reality testing by asserting that it is self-evident that what is valued is perfect. With idealization there is always the underlying anxiety that what the psychic energies are seeking to protect will be exposed as being flawed; with cynicism the anxiety is exactly the same and what is protected may be exposed as worse than what is pretended. The one uses pretty wrappings and the other uses shabby wrappings to prevent full exposure and penetrating observation.

Our six informants have shown us how it is possible to combine empathy and idealization so as to provide a solid, indeed impenetrable, basis for constructive public roles. Presumably among future generations there will be countless people with the same psychological potentials and the same cravings to act out with respect to constructive public issues. This thought should be a source of optimism for the future except for the fact, which we have just noted, that the fashions of today, as shaped in schools and expressed in the mass media, are ones that do not encourage the harnessing of these psychic qualities to the cause of opposing ethnic parochialism. On the contrary, empathy and idealization now seem to be legitimized mainly in defense of parochial identities.

With the swings of fashions and moods there will always be some element of the counterfashion and the countermood. We have certainly learned that during the period when our six informants were acquiring their hostility toward prejudice there were others who were keeping alive the fires of parochialism and ethnic separation. Therefore, it may be reasonable to expect that during a period when the dominant style is to accentuate ethnic differences there will be some who will maintain the faith in what Harold Issacs has called "de-tribalized" man and society.

Notes

[1] David Riesman, *The Lonely Crowd,* New Haven, 1950.

[2] Daniel Lerner, *The Passing of Traditional Society,* Glencoe, Illinois, 1958.

V.

Political Change, Education, and Group Identity

By Chai Hon-Chan

The two decades following the end of World War II were a period of optimistic faith in the instrumental value of education in socializing the young into the new civic cultures and creating generations that would be allegiant to the post-colonial governments. Foremost among the aims of the rapidly expanding mass education was nation-building, at the heart of which was the process of changing individual and group identities so that an overarching national identity could take precedence over, if not actually replace, the primordial group loyalties of the disparate ethnic or racial components of the polity. As the key to modernization, education, therefore, had to be made a direct arm of government in most of the new nations. This entailed, in many instances, structural changes in the educational system to harmonize conflicting sub-systems, bridge discontinuities between one level of education and another, ensure that certain cognitive and affective outcomes of education were consonant with national ideals, and generally extend or consolidate the scope of government control.

The integrative role of education in political development and nation-building, says Coleman, is "more or less self-evident," but in the transitional period education may be dysfunctional to political integration and malintegrative in two respects: it may "perpetuate the *elite-mass* gap and it may "perpetuate and even intensify divisions among different ethnic, regional, and parochial groups out of which nationbuilders, partly through education, must forge a larger sense of national identity."[1] Different ethnic groups, by virtue of their cultural orientation and value system, may exhibit differing capacities for utilizing and absorbing modern secular education; and these initial differences, coupled with differential levels of access to schools, may widen the inherent social and economic inequalities between them. As aspirations and expectations rise with expanding education, group frustrations and hostility are also likely to rise. The relative strength of one group may give rise to a policy of "equalizing opportunities" by preferential educational sponsorship of the disadvantaged group and "positive discrimination" in its favor in employment. Since education is inherently achievement-oriented, the injection of ascriptive criteria in education may generate a feeling of distrust toward the system which, in time, may even be disesteemed. In this way education is likely to heighten any underlying tensions between groups and may be the focal point of political conflict.

Interethnic or interracial violence in some of the new states, notably Nigeria, Mauritius, Sri Lanka, Guyana, and Malaysia, suggests that education has not been as effective as expected or hoped in creating a national identity; at least not effective enough to break down or substantially modify the primordial group identities which are recognizably the primary source of interethnic or interracial suspicion, prejudice, and hostility. In some instances, the politicization of education has tended to exacerbate existing tensions between ethnic groups whose different perceptions of the role of education in satisfying their social, cultural, and economic aspirations reflect deep-seated anxieties over their respective cultural identities and their place in the new polity. In extreme cases, education has come to be seen by groups alienated by the political process not as an instrument of national development and integration but as a device to maintain the power of the privileged or to undermine, if not destroy, the corporate identities of those perceived as a threat to the larger national identity.

The dilemma of nation-building in such societies may be characterized as the tension between the primordial urge or compulsion, on the part of all ethnic or racial groups, to maintain and assert their ethnic or racial identities, and the desire for political order, economic progress, and social justice. The latter can be realized only within the larger framework of a modern polity whose capacity to function effectively and to satisfy the competing demands of various sectional interests requires, at the minimum, the compliance, if not the allegiance, of all groups. These centrifugal forces, which ironically may be stimulated by education, threaten the nascent political institutions and the stability of the new states. The breakdown in nation-building in many of these new states in recent years is symptomatic of what Geertz describes as the "conflict between primordial and civil sentiments," the deeply felt "longing not to belong to any other group" which is fundamentally more dangerous to the viability of the state than any other kind of conflict.[2] The traumatic severance of Bangladesh from Pakistan, preceded nearly a generation earlier by the partition of the Indian subcontinent into Pakistan and India, the abortive attempt to establish Biafra, the violence between Turks and Greeks in Cyprus, and the separatist movements in Ethiopia and the Philippines, are some of the more dramatic instances of the "longing not to belong to any other group." In all these conflicts, a common factor appears to be the fear of one ethnic or racial group being dominated by another or, if it is already dominated, the desire of that group for equality. The source of conflict is the identification of political power with one particular ethnic or racial group.

In the on-going reshaping of old societies into new states and the re-ordering of peoples in the new hierarchies of race and ethnicity, communalism is likely to persist as a dominant feature of the political process. Instead of diminishing the importance of race or ethnicity, both economic development and political modernization have increased the prominence of primordial group identities in nation-building. The moving force in the new power arrangements is what Isaacs calls *basic group identity*, by which he means

> ...the set of identifications which every individual shares with others from the moment of his birth: his ethnic being, his family and group name, his color and physical characteristics, the history and origins of the group into which he is born, its whole culture-past providing him with, among other things, his language, religion, arts, modes and styles of life, and inherited value system. It lays upon him his nationality or whatever other condition of national self-awareness in his group. He is endowed, finally, with the total structure of his family's culture, with all its intersecting, concentric, and multiple enlargements, the social-economic threshold of the family through which he enters upon life, the geography, politics, and economics of the country of his birth, and all the impinging circumstances of his time.[3]

The primary function of this basic group identity, says Isaacs, is to sustain a person with "self-esteem" which springs in part from acceptance and respect by others; but when it fails to provide this support or subjects him to "a pattern of self-rejection," it becomes a problem and, "sooner or later, a matter of crisis." Failure or success is influenced by different conditions and occurs at different times and varying levels, but cardinal, and probably decisive, are the *political* conditions in which a group functions in relation to other groups. "How dominant or how dominated is the group to which the individual belongs and how, therefore, is he able to bear himself in relation to others? This is the cardinal question, and it is essentially a question of politics or power."[4]

The salient feature of political change in multiethnic societies is the political polarization of communal groups, with a concomitant tendency toward the ethnicization of all centers or sources of political power. There may be varying forms of group coalitions and arrangements of power sharing, depending on the relative strength of each communal group, the way political elites view the problems of national integration, the kind of political ideology, if any, they espouse, and the policies they adopt for economic development; but the trend seems to be toward the concentration of political power in the hands of one ethnic or racial group. The symbols of power and dominance are often such that they leave no doubt as to which group is superordinate and which subordinate. To be sure, in most of the new states political power does not always coincide with economic dominance, but this relative balance of power precisely engenders a pervasive feeling of "relative deprivation" in which each of the contending groups believes it is "deprived," leading to the common "zero-sum" syndrome where one group's gain is perceived by another to be its own loss. Under such conditions the economic and political insecurity of one group or the other and non-rational economic or political behavior tend to be maximized and exploited to the best advantage of the group concerned. Conversely, the group perception of threat to its corporate identity may elicit group reaction and behavior that may be perfectly rational in the context where ethnic solidarity has been politically rationalized. In this setting education, as one of the most decisive sources of political power and group-identity maintenance as well as change, is apt to become the focal point of ethnic and racial rivalries. Just as the political process tends to polarize primordial loyalties, so education is prone to divide rather than integrate these contending groups.

These trends and issues manifest themselves in various forms and different circumstances in most of the developing multiracial or multiethnic nations, but in few have they been as starkly dramatic as in Guyana and Malaysia. In both these countries the change from colonial dependency to national independence activated the dormant centrifugal forces which, in Guyana, split the East Indians and the Africans into two opposing camps and, in Malaysia, aligned the Malays against the non-Malays. The struggle for power and succession in Guyana precipitated racial riots and violence which hardened the primordial group loyalties of the East Indians and the Africans and crystalized the pattern of ethnic politics for at least the next generation. In Malaysia, the facile separation of powers—with the Malays predominant in the political realm and the Chinese and the Indians in the economic sphere—temporarily maintained communal peace, which was the precondition for independence from Britain, but the veneer of national unity did not conceal for long nor could it contain the competing and clashing political and economic aspirations of the non-Malay and the Malay masses. Twelve years after independence, race riots shattered the illusion of national harmony and set the course for drastic changes in government and in economic and social policies for the "restructuring" of Malaysia's plural society.

Clearly there are fundamental differences between Guyana and Malaysia in the structure of society and the economy, in the educational system and the style of government, and in the history and culture of the contending groups. And all these in their different combinations have produced contrasting patterns of race relations. Nevertheless, the salience of race in political and social change provides a framework for the comparison of the interactions of politics, education, and group identity in these two countries.

Guyana

Political Change and Racial Polarization

Guyanese nationalism has its roots in the early history of the country, but the modern organized movement dates from 1947 with the formation of the Political Affairs Committee, led by Cheddi Jagan, an East Indian dental surgeon, his American wife Janet, and a handful of radical labor leaders. It was essentially a coterie of intellectuals whose action-oriented Marxist philosophy required an organization which would enable them to translate their views of Guyana's colonial condition and "capitalist exploitation" into a political program. Accordingly in 1950 the PAC was replaced by the People's Progressive Party which was established under the dual leadership of Jagan and Forbes Burnham, an African barrister recently returned from England. This was the symbolic union of the two major racial groups in the country in their common fight against colonialism, a union representing a mass movement which apparently transcended communal interests. The PPP was committed to a program of radical reform of a society riddled with class and color prejudice and to a drastic reorganization of the economic system dominated by expatriate sugar interests.

The espousal of a socialist ideology which stressed, above all, the community of economic interests between the Africans and the East Indians, proved to be only a veneer which temporarily glossed over but was unable to control the underlying mutual suspicion and distrust, as well as the divergent economic and political interests, of the two major racial groups. Ironically the success of the PPP in the 1953 elections under a new Constitution, considered one of the most advanced at the time in British colonies, was also the beginning of the split between East Indian and African loyalties to the emerging national leaders. Having won eighteen of the twenty-four elected seats in the Assembly, which gave them control over internal affairs, the PPP leaders set about implementing their social and economic policies, but not before the ideological differences between the Marxists and non-Marxists, as well as personality clashes within the party, were exposed. The major thrust of the PPP policy was to establish control over the labor movement to widen and consolidate their base for popular support. But the new government's program for socioeconomic change so threatened the status quo that the British Government suspended the Constitution in October, 1953, and deposed the PPP leaders after 133 days in office. The PPP was charged with, among other misdeeds, an attempt to turn the country into a communist state.

This setback to Guyanese nationalism aggravated the widening ideological cleavage between the Marxists and the non-Marxists, and eventually led to a party split, with Burnham leading one faction and Jagan the other. That it was not a racial split was attested by the fact that two of the most prominent East Indian personalities, aside from Jagan himself, followed Burnham, while several influential Africans remained with Jagan.

Given the charismatic appeal of Jagan and Burnham, and the underlying racial and cultural divisions between the vast majority of rural East Indians and urbanized Africans, the prospect of a national contest for power between these two leaders was the catalyst for mobilizing the masses along racial lines. To be sure, both factions were sincere in their non-racial strategies to mobilize support, but Burnham and Jagan, primordial symbols of African and East Indian aspirations respectively, ineluctably attracted and drew together those whose history and blood-ties would identify them with one or the other. The differences between Burnham and Jagan might revolve around political ideology and tactics, but for the masses racial solidarity seemed to be the overriding concern.

The 1957 elections under a revised Constitution proved to be the turning point in racial politics. Of the total East Indian votes cast, it was estimated that 98 percent went to Jagan's faction and 91 percent of the African votes to the Burnham faction of the PPP.[5] Jagan formed the new government with a multiracial cabinet, and Burnham, conceding the PPP mantle to Jagan, went on to form the People's National Congress. From then on the country was effectively, possible irretrievably, split between East Indians and Africans. The political process became a vortex of increasingly abrasive conflicts between the PPP and the PNC. The political arming of East Indian cultural and religious organizations, such as the *Arya Samaj*, the *Sanatan Dharm Maha Sabha* (both Hindu), and *Anjuman* (Muslim, but practically East Indian) and the use of the Hindi phrase " Apan Jaat" (literally "own race") as an election slogan among PPP party hacks underlined the strength of primordial sentiments among the East Indians. Faced with this threat, PNC supporters found it difficult not to resort to similar tactics. Indeed, most of the African population was so alarmed by what it perceived as "East Indian racialism" that it hardly needed any persuasion not to support the PPP. In an attempt to counteract the East Indian cultural organizations, Sidney King, one of the original supporters of Jagan who subsequently broke away from the PPP, established ASCRIA (African Society for Cultural Relations with Independent Africa) as a focal point of African identity.

The 1961 elections, which returned the PPP to office, showed that racial solidarity had hardened. It was estimated that 95 percent each of East Indian and African votes went to the PPP and the PNC respectively.[6] At this juncture it may be relevant to point out that the population of Guyana in 1960 was roughly 560,000, of which the East Indians comprised 48 percent, the Africans 33 percent, the "Mixed" 12 per cent, the Amerindians 4.5 percent, and the Chinese, Europeans, and "Others" less than 3 percent. The demographic change for the first three groups, by far the most important politically, may be seen from the corresponding figures from 1946, when East Indians made up 44 percent, Africans 38 percent, and "Mixed" 10 percent of a total population of roughly 376,000. In 1960 close to 85 percent of East Indians were rural compared with 57 percent of Africans.[7]

Between 1962 and 1964 race riots and general violence wracked the country which, in 1964, was virtually in a state of civil war between the East Indians and the Africans. Some 2,700 families, involving more than 15,000 persons, became refugees in their own country; 176 persons were reported killed and hundreds injured; property damage and losses, including more than 1,400 homes destroyed by arson and home-made bombs, were estimated at over 4 million Guyanese dollars, and the resultant unemployment affected more than 1,300 families.[8] When the size of the total population and the scale of the society are taken into consideration, the human casualties and the material losses represented an enormous waste of resources. More importantly, the violence left the vast majority of East Indians and Africans psychologically scarred and deeply embittered. Prior to the civil disturbances residential patterns were fairly integrated in the rural areas, but the spate of riots physically separated East Indians and Africans, who sought safety among their own kind. Schools which had been racially integrated became uniracial not only in enrollment but also in the teaching staff.

Under a new system of proportional representation imposed by the British Government, the 1964 elections resulted in the PPP capturing 45.8 percent of the votes cast and 24 seats in the Assembly. The PNC obtained 40.5 percent of the votes and 22 seats; and the United Force, formed in 1960 as an alternative for those who supported neither the PPP nor the PNC, secured 12.4 percent of the votes and 7 seats. An analysis of the voting pattern showed that 93 percent of East Indian votes went to the PPP and 95 percent of African votes to the PNC.[9] Since no party had a clear majority of over 50 percent of the votes, only a coalition between two parties could form a new government. The PNC and the UF agreed to join forces against the PPP, which was then ejected from office after seven turbulent and bitter years of government. For the next three years the PNC-UF coalition, which won independence from Britain in May, 1966, ruled uneasily. In 1968 a few PPP and UF members defected to join the PNC which then was strong enough to discard the UF as a partner in the government. As the sole ruling party the PNC succeeded in introducing a law which enabled expatriate Guyanese (mainly in Britain, Canada, and the United States) to vote in the 1968 elections, which gave the PNC 94 percent of the overseas vote (amounting to about 5 percent of the total votes) and 51 percent of the domestic vote, thus giving it a clear majority to rule. For the East Indians, the defeat of the PPP was seen as the frustration of their aspirations and the triumph of African power.

Institutional Discrimination and Group Identity

As the last group of immigrants to arrive in Guyana, the East Indians were resented and despised for taking the jobs on the sugar plantations from which the vast majority of Africans, on emancipation, had escaped and which the Portuguese and the Chinese had also rejected after serving their indenture. Unlike the African slaves who were systematically detribalized by the slave-owners, the East Indians were able to preserve their basic group identity through Hinduism and Islam, which were kept alive by their respective religious teachers. A generation after emancipation (1834), a significant proportion of Africans had become literate in English through education instituted by various Christian missionary groups. Without any organized religion of their own, the Africans took easily to Christianity, undergoing that basic change in identity symbolized by their adoption of Christian names. Through the various churches and the English language they soon internalized the values and mores of the white man who, despite his social distance from the Africans and his obvious dominance in a colonial society, became effectively the only role model for the Christianized and increasingly Anglicized Africans.

As the colonial government took no direct responsibility for education, schools were established and operated exclusively by the various Christian denominations whose primary objective was the conversion of "the heathens." Right from the start, therefore, the East Indians, as Hindus and Muslims, found themselves in conflict with the educational institutions which alone could provide them with the skills to move out of their lowly social status as "coolies." They were constantly under pressure to convert to Christianity, and many East Indians were reluctant to send their children to denominational schools. An additional psychological block was the fact that the first generation of school teachers was African. In the eyes of most of the caste-conscious East Indians, the color and physical characteristics of these teachers branded them as *Chamar*, the lowliest in the Hindu hierarchy of social groups. But as the local heirs and exponents of English culture, the Africans were the very individuals who could, and did, provide the education for the East Indians' social mobility. However, in the rigid colonial Guyanese social structure, in which, all other things being equal, color was the final determinant of social status, high educational achievement did not confer the social status and high social rewards that might have been expected in an open society. Consequently many East Indians sought and achieved high status, at least within their own community, through business activities which gave them economic power if not social prestige within the larger Guyanese universe.

Nevertheless, increasing numbers of East Indians went to the denominational schools, but, when the first generation of East Indian school teachers emerged, they found that employment in the church schools and professional mobility in the school system depended, in most cases, on affiliation with the particular denomination concerned. This applied also to the Africans, of course. Given the jealous sectarian interests of the churches, professional mobility for school teachers was rigidly circumscribed. Consequently, as Despres points out, "the structure of educational activities within the villages not only threatens to denationalize them by providing the role models unrelated to the kinds of activities by which East Indians have achieved the economic status they now enjoy."[10] In a survey of six Guyanese villages, Despres found that, on the question of "dual control" of schools by the church and the government, 86 percent of East Indian respondents opposed the system, while 68 percent of African respondents favored its continuation. The East Indians complained bitterly of discrimination against their children if they did not conform to Christian values.[11] The denominational schools were therefore perceived as a threat to their cultural identity. Furthermore, as the majority of African teachers were Christian, the East Indians tended to see them as the churches' agents in undermining their identity.

It was partly to secularize the schools and partly to respond to the pressure of the East Indians that the PPP government in 1961 took over fifty-one denominational schools (out of a total of 298 such primary schools) which had been built with government funds but handed over to the church authorities for administration. This move was resisted by the churches and, because of the racial undercurrents, the majority of Africans saw it as an East Indian challenge. Although education had the manifest purpose of socializing Guyanese children into Guyanese culture, Hindu and Muslim East Indians did not, as a whole, consider the schools with a Christian bias as suitable for the transmission of the East Indian cultural values which they considered central to their identity. This accounts, in part, for the spread of East Indian cultural organizations which were established to counteract the early prejudice against East Indians and their rejection from a Christianized creole society. Their exclusion was also partly because they were not Christian and partly because they were not educated enough to be receptive to Western mores. The falling back on East Indian culture was to reinforce their self-esteem and group identity and to counteract African prejudice against them as "coolies." According to Smith, the East Indian's defensive insistence on "the glories of Indian culture" was really "a mode of expression of his desire to be treated on terms of equality within a Guianese universe" and was not "an expression of separatist tendencies."[12]

African fears of East Indian domination were stimulated by the rapid increase of the East Indian population, their relative prosperity (which tended to be highly visible in the form of better homes and other material possessions), their increasing access to, and success in, education, and their competition for better-paid jobs in the civil service and the teaching profession. All of these were perceived as a threat to the position of the Africans who, although they did not claim Guyana as "their country," certainly felt that they would soon become a minority under East Indian rule. These fears were expressed as early as 1954 during an inquiry by the Constitutional Commission, which reported that the success of the East Indians in agriculture and commerce had begun "to awaken the fears of the African section of the population." Furthermore,

> Guianese of African extraction were not afraid to tell us that many Indians in British Guiana looked forward to the day when British Guiana would be a part not of the British Commonwealth but of an East Indian Empire. The result has been a tendency for racial tension to increase...the relationships are strained; they represent an outward appearance which masks feelings of suspicion and distrust.[13]

Official views at the time tended to feed the amorphous fears of the Africans and to reinforce the idea that the East Indians were "a sort of disruptive element, a truculent minority which is getting out of hand," while the East Indian viewpoint was that their self-assertiveness was "a demand for recognition as equals after years of being discriminated as 'coolies' ."[14]

The Africans' contempt for "coolies" can be traced back to the post-emancipation period when the East Indians were brought in to replace the manumitted slaves who scorned the menial tasks on the plantations. The same contempt was extended to the indentured Portuguese and the Chinese. According to Skinner,

> The Negroes fought the entry of these laborers [from the Madeira Islands, India, and China] with all the weapons at their disposal. They terrorized the East Indians, ridiculed the Portuguese with the appellation of "white nigger," and appealed to the abolitionists and missionaries to save them from the "introduction of masses of sensual and idolatrous Asiatics...[who] will render nugatory the effort of the emancipated labourers...who are endeavoring to inculcate upon their rising families a practical respect for the claims of chastity and other Christian virtues."[15]

Middle-class Guyanese looked down on and rebuffed East Indians who lacked formal education, spoke "pidgin" English, did not wear Western clothes, ate with their fingers, wore no shoes, and were dirty and smelly. But as they became better educated, spoke "proper English," dressed modishly, and furnished their homes "Western style," they were resented as social upstarts who had no right to such pretensions. Skinner's study of Guyana concluded that there was a general "unwillingness of the Negroes to reward East Indians for acquiring 'English' ways, while at the same time basing status on the acquisition of these cultural traits."[16] Resentment against East Indian assertiveness is best summed up by what an African school principal said to the present writer during an interview: "*We* first taught them how to read and write. Now *they* want *our* jobs!"

An Indian school principal, when asked what he thought of some of the stereotypical images of East Indians, had this to say:

> It *is* true that many Indians are ignorant, superstitious, dirty—but so are many Negroes. The simple fact is that they are ill-educated and poor.... We live in a Western-oriented culture, and there is no reversing our social history. The Negroes despise us for being "coolies," for not being as "cultured" as they think they are. The only way for Indians to succeed socially is to beat them at their own game; that is, to be better educated, more "cultured" in the Western sense, but *without* losing our Indian culture. This is what we have, and this is what Negroes envy us for.[17]

The Africans' stereotype of the East Indians (and this was also shared by the majority of local whites) was that they would do anything for money and were therefore unscrupulous, mean, untrustworthy, and clannish. They were dirty, superstitious, "ethnic," secretive, violent, too fecund, and had "long memories." (In connection with the last trait, Africans would say that they were willing to forget the racial violence of the past, but the East Indians would brood over real or imagined wrongs for which they would plot a revenge.) In the inimitably colorful creolese, the African would cry in mock despair, "Man, de black-man is goin' down, 'cause black-man is for coolie, and coolie is for coolie!" The expression succinctly summarizes the general feeling amongst Africans that although they were prepared to cooperate with the East Indians, the latter were not disposed to reciprocate, being concerned only with their own welfare.

In the face of an aggressive East Indian cultural resurgence, the more militant Africans felt that they, too, must revitalize their own group and assert their identity as *African*, turning to their ancestral land for cultural and emotional reinforcement. The formation of ASCRIA (African Society for Cultural Relations with Independent Africa) was a direct response to the East Indian cultural challenge. Its leader, Sidney King, changed his name to Eusi Kwayana and called on all Africans to discard their English names and take on African names, and to wear an "African shirt" rather than the Western shirt and tie. ASCRIA maintained a school in the village of Buxton, about twelve miles from Georgetown, where classes were held to "de-brainwash" Africans by propagating information on Africa and African philosophy and culture. Its supporters were urged to prefer things African rather than the mores and life-style of Europe and North America. ASCRIA would support any militant African organization in any part of the world, including the "Black Power" movement in the United States. "So long as black-men are considered inferior, black-men must unite—from Africa to the Caribbean to the USA— to oppose whatever...offends the dignity of man and the dignity of the black-man in particular, and the dignity of Africa."[18] Just as the East Indian cultural organizations attached themselves to the PPP, ASCRIA made itself the militant wing of the PNC. By ranging themselves behind these political parties, East Indian "culture" and African "culture" were openly and directly in conflict with each other.

Clearly both the *Maha Sabha* and ASCRIA sought to assert East Indian pride and African dignity respectively, the former as a response to the early denigration of East Indians as "coolies," the latter as a reaction to the East Indian attitude that Africans were "inferior." By being racially exclusive, they exacerbated the divisive forces in Guyanese society. However, an important difference between the two is that while the *Maha Sabha* has more or less universal East Indian support, ASCRIA tends to be frowned upon, if not ignored, by the majority of urban middle-class Africans. In a society divided politically along racial lines, there are obvious limitations to these cultural organizations, but to dismiss them as "racial lunatic fringes" is to fail to understand the group frustrations and anxieties of both the East Indians and the Africans.

At the same time, in the context of the urgent need for cultural integration and social cohesion, they tend to be obscurantist in the values each tries to stress and propagate. Each looks *outward* for cultural inspiration, for emotional and intellectual affiliation, trying to revive cultural ties which either did not exist or have long since decayed. It is, above all, symptomatic of the inability or unwillingness of both groups of adherents to these cultural organizations to look to the existing Guyanese society for a common basis for national integration. Insofar as the East Indians have a readily identifiable culture that is distinctively "Indian" on which they could fall back if they wished, the Africans cannot easily point to a culture that is cohesively "African." Although there has been no attempt to adopt one of the African languages to reinforce African identity, the vast majority of East Indians, on their part, have lost their own native tongues.

The stronger and more positive force for social integration appears to be the English language and Guyanese education. There are indications that education is succeeding in orientating the younger generations away from either East Indian or African culture as such, if their lack of interest in going to India or Africa to work and live is a valid test. To ascertain whether students were oriented toward Guyana or other countries, one of the questions in a general questionnaire administered to about 500 Form Five (eleventh grade) students in twelve high schools in various parts of Guyana was: "If you had the choice, where would you choose to work and live?" Of the 404 responses, only seven students (five African and two East Indian), representing less than 2 percent of the total, indicated any interest in "Asia" or "Africa"; 16 percent (N = 26 Africans, 25 East Indians, and 16 "Others") chose Britain, Canada, or the United States, while 49 percent (N = 103 Africans, 77 East Indians, and 17 "Others") opted for Guyana. About 30 percent gave no response to this question. Among African students about 52 percent chose Guyana and 13 percent chose Britain, Canada, and the United States. Among East Indian students the corresponding figures were 50 percent and 16 percent respectively. Significantly, among "Others" (mainly Portuguese, Chinese, and expatriate Whites, of whom there were only a few), about 33 percent (N = 16) chose Britain, Canada, or the United States; 4 percent (N = 2), Australia/New Zealand; and 35 percent (N = 17), Guyana.[19] As far as these high school students were concerned, there was an almost total lack of interest in India or Africa, suggesting that the local educational system was a more powerful acculturating agency than either the East Indian cultural organizations or ASCRIA in orientating the younger generation toward the source of Indian or African culture.

In the many permutations and convolutions of race relations, skin color plays a variety of roles, depending on the shades of skin contrast and the relationship between color and class. In colonial Guyanese society, color was closely associated with social status. Although the Africans were the first group to be Westernized, the "pure" black Africans were in the early days less favored than the "coloreds," the offspring of white slave-owners or plantation managers and African slaves. This was not because of color as such but because the coloreds were better educated, more Anglicized in speech and life-style, than the blacks. The initial advantage in education thus ensured the coloreds a relatively privileged position in a creole society that was becoming stratified according to educational attainment and a command of the dominant white culture, and this happened to coincide with color and "race." The coloreds tended to marry among themselves or others of lighter skin color, so that in time class snobbery merged with color snobbery. While the ruling whites did not quite accept the coloreds as social equals, the coloreds tended to hold the blacks at a greater social distance.

Nevertheless, the English-speaking whites, the coloreds, the blacks, and the yellows (mainly Chinese) all came to share a common conception of colonial society in which everything "white" or English was highly valued and everything "black" or African was correspondingly disesteemed. Thus straight hair was "good hair" and kinky hair was "bad hair." So apparently complete was this acculturation to "white" values that educated Africans themselves subconsciously accepted their "inferiority" vis-a-vis the whites.[20]

The obsession with color has been so morbid that the coloreds among themselves distinguish subtle shades of brown or pinko-grey. The blacks resent the superior airs of the coloreds, and those whose color and facial features resemble the whites are often derisively called "Red People." The Portuguese, although white, were originally despised by both the coloreds and blacks because of their occupation as shopkeepers and pawn-shop owners. The Chinese, by and large, remain a group apart, although they have become a highly respected subcommunity of business and professional people. The attitude of the Africans and others toward the Amerindians ranges from admiration and envy for their independence in a world of their own in the interior of Guyana, to pity and contempt for their "backwardness" and lack of a command of a Western life-style. The East Indians appear to be an anomaly in a color- and race-conscious society. Their dark skin color, ranging from light brown to deepest black, and their European-type facial features and straight or wavy hair often inspires a mixture of scorn and admiration, although in the early days they were mostly despised because they were "coolies" with the lowliest jobs.

The East Indian stereotyped views of the Africans are generally negative. The Africans are considered to be spendthrifts who love to "sport," buy expensive and fancy clothes rather than spend their time making and saving money; happy-go-lucky but uncooperative, ungrateful, and "ethnic"; and dirty and "bad smelling." A pervasive image is that African men are sexually more potent than East Indian men, who must therefore guard their women carefully. On the whole, a larger proportion of East Indians hold negative views of Africans than the proportion of Africans with unfavorable views of East Indians. There is a remarkable coincidence of East Indian, African, and Others' perceptions of how East Indians perceive Africans, that is, negatively. This is reinforced by Africans' perception of East Indian negative attitudes toward interracial marriage, specifically between East Indians and Africans, when Africans, on the whole, have no objection to it. At the same time, East Indians think that the vast majority of Africans also view them negatively, whereas a substantial proportion of Africans hold positive feelings about East Indians. The East Indian feeling of superiority, which ostensibly is based on their European-type physical characteristics and Indian cultural traits, and the African perception of this East Indian feeling of superiority, have led to what Landis describes as the East Indians' "superordinate racial attitudes" and the Africans' "defensive racial attitudes" which stem, in large part, from East Indians having a much more positive image of themselves than Africans of themselves.[21] Clearly the differences in the degree of self-esteem have been conditioned in no small way by the racial values of colonial Guyanese society.

Although less than 20 percent of East Indians, compared with 55 percent of Africans, are egalitarian in their attitudes toward other groups, better educated East Indians tend to be more egalitarian than those with less education, whereas for Africans education makes very little difference. Landis suggests that the longer East Indians remain in school, the more likely they are to make friends with African classmates, thereby modifying their superordinate racial attitudes and becoming more egalitarian, and that education may be successful in inculcating modernity, including the internalizing of democratic and egalitarian values which provide the basis for East Indians to share a common European-oriented culture with other Guyanese.[22]

In Guyana there is a public norm of non-racialism that condemns color prejudice and racial discrimination since no particular group, not even the Amerindians who are the true indigenous people, has a prior claim over others in social and political rights. In a speech in early 1966 welcoming Queen Elizabeth II, the first reigning British monarch to visit Guyana, the Guyanese Prime Minister declared, "Our country's population is as diverse as its history....The descendants of the sons and daughters of Africa, India, China, Portugal and Britain, we are today Guyana's children. Guyana for us can be our only motherland."[23]

The national norm of racial equality places a high premium on social and cultural integration, about which there is no serious fundamental disagreement between the East Indians and the Africans. But the East Indian antipathy toward interracial marriage and the relative strength of Hinduism and Islam would suggest that their racial and cultural identity as East Indians will persist and grow stronger for as long as they do not feel and believe that a government based on the PNC can ever represent East Indian interests in any significant way, however objectively fair the government may be. "If we are to continue in unity," said Burnham, "we must banish racialism. Each racial group is entitled to feel pride in its cultural traditions, and heritage, but we must not have racial differences reflected in the politics of our country."[24] But given the fact that, on the whole, Africans have polarized their political support around the PNC, and the East Indians around the PPP, racialism will remain very much a part of Guyanese politics, as the voting patterns since 1957 have shown, no matter how strenuously each party tries to maintain a multiracial image at the leadership level. Indeed, there is a strong tendency for the majority of Africans and East Indians to consider any member of their own racial group who joins the opposition party as a "traitor" to his own race. All this presupposes that whichever party forms the government, a large proportion of either East Indians or Africans is likely to feel that the government is less than legitimate.

A survey in 1967 of East Indian and African views on the economy, government discrimination, and their preference of party leaders showed that these views were diametrically opposed. On the economy, 80 percent of East Indians interviewed (N = 424) thought that it did better under the PPP, while 84 percent of Africans (N = 348) thought that it was better at the time of the survey, i.e. when the PNC was in power. On government discrimination, 75 percent of East Indians considered that the PNC-UF coalition government was discriminatory, while 84 percent of Africans felt that the PPP had been discriminatory. On the choice of party leaders, 74 percent of East Indians preferred Jagan, 1 percent favored Burnham, 2 percent D'Aguiar (leader of the United Force), while 22 percent expressed no preference. Among Africans, 58 percent favored Burnham, 2 percent Jagan, 1 percent D'Aguiar, and 39 percent had no preference. These findings suggest that the majority of East Indians tend to perceive and evaluate social and political "realities" from a standpoint favorable to the PPP, while Africans as a whole are apt to favor the PNC.[25]

Such being the political realities, the political process is likely to rigidify racial polarization, feed the negative views of one group by another, and sustain the contending group identities of East Indians and Africans. Given the larger East Indian population and, what is more important, its higher rate of growth, the PNC government's ability to maintain its power will depend, in large part, on its credibility in the eyes of the East Indians as the authority for satisfying their needs and demands. But so long as the majority of East Indians feel that they are "dominated" by Africans, they will seek to unseat the PNC through the electoral process. Politically frustrated, they are likely to channel their energies and talents to economic activities and education where they may establish and maintain a balance of power. The East Indians have shown a greater capability than the Africans in agriculture, particularly rice production, and in business and commerce. However, since declaring the country the "Co-operative Republic of Guyana" in 1970, and changing the original date of independence from May 26 to February 23 (to commemorate the first slave revolt in the eighteenth century as the first blow struck for independence), the PNC government has embarked on a socialist program of increasing state control of the economy through a cooperative movement which the government declared "will serve as the instrument in the work of bringing about qualitative change in economic and social relationships."[26] The East Indians, whether businessmen or rice farmers, have interpreted this as an attempt to curb their preference for free enterprise and therefore their economic power. If, in fact, this is so, the only channel that is still relatively open is education, which is therefore likely to become the focal point of competition between Africans and East Indians. "For us education is the corner-stone of equality," said Burnham, "and one of the chief instruments for the abolition of snobbery, the removal of discrimination, the development of creative beings and the production of a race of men who will never surrender to medocrity or dictatorship of any kind."[27]

Except for the earlier discrimination against the East Indians by the denominational schools, the Guyanese educational system is largely open and egalitarian. Although still predominantly rural, the East Indians have made remarkable gains in education achievement. Data from a 1967 survey of Form Five (eleventh grade) students in twelve secondary schools showed that, out of a total of 404 respondents, East Indians comprised 38.4 percent; Africans 30 percent; "Mixed" 19.6 percent; Chinese 4.5 percent; Portuguese 3.5 percent, and Europeans 2.2 percent. Conspicuous for their absence were the Amerindians. Among the East Indian students 81.3 percent were born in the rural areas, as against 54 percent of African and "Mixed" students with the same origin. Measured against their fathers' education, the East Indian students showed that they had achieved a higher rate of educational mobility than the African students.[28] That their predominantly rural origin had not been a barrier to the educational mobility of the East Indians was further attested by the enrollment pattern in Queen's College, the national premier boys' secondary school in Georgetown. Out of a total enrollment of 707 students in June, 1967, ranging from Form One to Form Six (grade seven to grade thirteen), East Indian students formed 34.2 percent, the single largest group in the school. The next largest group were of "Mixed" students, representing 31.5 percent, and African students, comprising 23.8 percent, formed the third largest group. At the Form Six level, the East Indian students were also the single largest group. In the University of Guyana, in the 1966-1967 session, East Indians comprised 58.5 percent, Africans 33.7 percent, "Mixed" 5.2 percent, and others 2.6 percent of the total enrollment.[29] These figures suggest that, despite the urban bias in secondary school facilities, the East Indians as a group were not as disadvantaged as they were made out to be, or as they believed themselves to be.

The rapid mobilization of both the Africans and the East Indians, but particularly of the latter, is likely to put new strains on the polity. As the number of secondary and university graduates increase, the pressure will correspondingly increase on the government to provide employment, if private enterprise is restricted. A projection of the growth of the labor force and employment for 1975 showed that about 17 percent of the labor force would be unemployed, based on trends in economic growth in the 1960s.[30] By sponsoring not only the social but also the psychic mobility of the younger generation, education is apt to swell the tide of rising frustrations if the aspirations of school leavers find no satisfaction in the world of work.[31] When this happens in the context of interracial rivalry and conflict in the economic and political spheres, it may be difficult for the government to resist the pressure to give priority to satisfying the demands of its supporters, thereby running a high risk of further alienating its non-supporters. The ethnicization of politics generates its own imperatives of racialism in all spheres of public life, and this is likely to have a predictable impact on the private sector of the economy as well. As the East Indians and the Africans compete for scarce rewards in an economy not noted for rapid growth and development, there seems to be a strong likelihood of both groups falling back on racial solidarity to reinforce their rival claims to a share of the national wealth. If economic opportunities remain restricted, the feeling of relative deprivation among both the East Indians and the Africans will become more acute. When economic competition and political rivalry coincide with racial antagonism, whatever integrative functions education may have in nation-building will be undermined. The key to breaking this vicious circle lies in the sharing of political power between the East Indians and the Africans. But as long as neither group trusts the other, the "vendetta syndrome" between the PPP and the PNC and their respective supporters will remain an insuperable obstacle to any move toward a national reconciliation. For the forseeable future, the primordial group identities of the East Indians and the Africans will remain locked in conflict.

Malaysia[32]

The Politics of Education

The central theme of Malaysian politics has been communal survival in a society of divergent and clashing group interests. The cornerstone of British rule had been the protection of Malay rights in a country which, with British encouragement, had undergone such a demographic transformation that the immigrant Chinese and Indians were seen by the indigenous Malays as a threat to their social and political survival. The post-World War II British proposal for the Malayan Union which, among other things, offered equal political rights to the Indians and the Chinese, directly stimulated the mass mobilization of the Malays to resist the scheme which they felt would effectively reduce them to a political minority in their own country.

The 1947 census showed that, out of a total population (West Malaysia) of 4.9 million, Malays and other indigenous groups comprised 49.2 percent, Chinese 38.6 percent, Indians 10.9 percent, and "Others" 1.3 percent. Apart from the numerical strength of the non-Malays, the Chinese were perceived as the dominant economic group whose financial power, if combined with full political rights, would enable them to "take over" the country. The United Malays National Organization (UMNO) was established in early 1946 specifically to articulate Malay interests and to overturn the Malayan Union, which was replaced by the Federation of Malaya in 1948. The Constitution of the Federation effectively guaranteed the "special rights" of the Malays and assured their political supremacy by restricting the number of non-Malays who could claim citizenship.[33] The Malay position was that, until there was ample "proof" of the loyalty of "aliens" to Malaya, granting them citizenship *en masse* and therefore political rights was too dangerous to be considered. An insurrection, led by the Malayan Communist Party whose leader and majority of followers were Chinese, had broken out in June,

1948, and this served to underscore the Malay fears of Chinese disloyalty.[34] Subsequently legislation on citizenship was concerned with the attempt to narrow down the multiracial population to a specific "Malayan" political community, in the hope that this definition would lead to "the emergence of a united and well-integrated Malayan sociey, in which communal sympathies would be replaced by a rising national spirit."[35]

It was against this background that the government turned to education as the instrument of political integration and nation-building. The first task was to integrate the quadralingual education system, which had evolved under colonial policy, into a national system with the aim of orientating students to Malaya and fostering a national, as opposed to a communal, identity. The Malay, Chinese, Tamil, and English schools varied in curricula, quality, and cultural orientation. Each of the first three types of communal schools socialized the child to a Malay, or a Chinese, or an Indian world-view which had great relevance to the maintenance of the cultural to the maintenance of the cultural identity of each group, but they were all increasingly incongruent with the rapidly changing political, economic, and social conditions of a country preparing for national independence. The English schools were the only institutions which were multiracial, but because they were mainly in the urban centers, those enrolled were predominantly from Chinese families, who formed the bulk of the urban population. Although the English schools were oriented toward English culture, they did provide a basis for the social and cultural integration of the three communities. The English schools effectively weakened the traditional group loyalties of those who became Westernized, especially those Chinese and Indians whose Westernized values and outlook tended to make them strangers in their own traditional communities. Thus the result of a quadralingual educational system was the social and cultural isolation of the Malays, the Chinese, and the Indians, and the emergence of a fourth group, drawn in varying proportions from the three traditional communities, with English as a common bond.

The impetus for educational change came mainly from Malay nationalism which was closely linked to the growing dissatisfaction of the Malays with their economic position vis-a-vis the non-Malays, especially the Chinese. They attributed their economic weakness to the neglect of Malay education, or more accurately, the neglect to educate Malays on the same scale as the non-Malays were being educated. The educational system was biased in favor of the non-Malays. The best schools were English schools in the urban centers and thus favored the Chinese. Whereas the English schools provided an open channel for social mobility, the Malay schools, predominantly rural, only went through five or six years of primary education of poor quality.

There were many reasons for the backwardness of Malay education. British colonial policy was to disturb as little as possible the traditional Malay way of life, the operative guideline being the British undertaking not to interfere with Malay custom and religion (Islam) at the time when the Malay States came under British rule. Consequently the school system which the British developed for the Malays had the main objective of teaching them to read and write in Malay so that they might be better farmers and fishermen. Coupled with this was low educational motivation among the majority of rural Malays, whose low valuation of education was often reinforced by the poor quality schooling they received. Thus Malay education effectively bound the Malays to their rural background and their traditional subsistence economy.

There were, however, small numbers of Malays who went to the English schools, either directly from the first grade or *via* the "Special Malay Classes" which served as a bridge for bright students selected from the Malay schools before they joined the mainstream of secondary education in English. They provided intensive coaching in English for Malay students after four or five years of primary education in Malay.

In response to complaints that the Malays were not getting a share in the administration of the country, which was conducted in English, the British at the turn of the century established the Malay College specifically to educate the sons of Malay royalty and the aristocracy. They were then recruited into the Malay Administrative Service, a subsidiary arm of the main Malayan Civil Service which was staffed exclusively by the British. The Malay College, which did not open its doors to Malay commoners until after World War II, became the premier training and recruiting ground for Malay elites who were educated in English along the lines of the great English Public Schools.

The vast majority of Malays were confined to rural Malay primary schools. There were no opportunities for post-primary education in Malay until 1922, when the Sultan Idris Training College was established to train Malay school teachers. It was from this institution that many of the radical Malay intellectuals and nationalists emerged in the 1930s and 1940s. The growing Malay disenchantment with the post-World War II educational establishment prompted the government to appoint a committee to study the problem of Malay education. On the question of neglecting Malay education, the Barnes Report (after the chairman of the committee) declared:

> ...it would be quite impossible to sustain a charge that Malay education has been in any relative sense neglected; rather has it been preferentially fostered. In underlining this we do not, of course, suggest that the political case for educational discrimination in favour of the Malays has not been a good one. We simply take note that such discrimination exists, is of long standing, and has been carried to a high degree of elaboration...this discrimination appears to have done little or nothing to predispose the Malay community in favour of the educational treatment it receives—a negative result which some observers may find paradoxical and even unnatural.[36]

Of the four types of schools, only Malay schools were free, i.e. subsidized completely by the government. The English schools, operated either by the Christian missions or the government, were subsidized but they charged fees. The Tamil schools were found mainly on the rubber plantations and, though subsidized by the government, were the responsibility of the plantation managers. The Chinese schools, established mainly by Chinese guilds and clan associations, received no government support until the 1920s when government control over them was established in return for financial support. The Chinese bias toward education, whether in English or in Chinese, gave them a major social and economic advantage over the Malays, and it was this fact which loomed large as a threat to the Malays.

Although the terms of reference for the Barnes Committee were confined to Malay education, it decided that the problem had to be seen in the context of a multiracial society.

> Our approach is governed by the belief that the primary school should be treated avowedly and with full deliberation as an instrument for building up a common Malayan nationality on the basis of those elements in the population who regard Malaya as their permanent home and as the object of their loyalty. This we regard as an essential part of the process of achieving self-government within the Commonwealth.

> ...Thus our first step is to call in question the public provision or maintenance of separate vernacular schools for any racial community, and to suggest instead a single-type primary school open to pupils of all races and staffed by teachers of any race, provided only that those teachers possess the proper qualifications and are federal citizens.[37]

It was further suggested that the ultimate aim should be bi-lingualism in English and Malay, and therefore that the Chinese and Tamil schools should be abolished, or at least discouraged by the withdrawal of government financial aid.

The publication of the Barnes Report raised a storm of protest in the local Chinese press, which regarded the proposed abolition of Chinese schools as a policy to suppress "Chinese culture." The bitterness was sharpened by the memory of official (British) hostility toward the Chinese schools in the 1920s and 1930s when they were alleged to be centers of both Communist and Kuomintang propaganda.

Coming at the height of the Chinese-led communist insurrection, the threat to the Chinese schools and "Chinese culture" seemed ill-timed. At that time it was vital that the Chinese community as a whole should give its support to the government in its effort to isolate the communists. To placate Chinese feelings, the government appointed another committee, comprising Dr. William P. Fenn, an American, and Dr. Wu Teh-yao, a Chinese official of the United Nations to look into Chinese education. The Fenn-Wu Report pointed out that the leaders of the Chinese community were hostile to the idea of "Malayanization" on the ground that, in the absence of anything that could properly be called "Malayan" the term would imply the conversion of everything into *Malay*. They perceived the intention of the government to be the elimination of Chinese schools and the relegation of the Chinese language to an inferior status "with the ultimate result, if not the present purpose, of the extinction of Chinese culture in Malaya." It added that in a multiracial society "there can be no justification for turning Malaya into a cockpit for aggressive cultures. By virtue of its composite population it should be a land where the developing culture draws its validity from the acceptance of the high value of other cultures.''[38]

The Fenn-Wu Report suggested, *inter alia,* that what might be considered was not the elimination of Chinese schools and the "suppression of Chinese culture," but a system of education whereby the Chinese schools would undertake the study of both English and Malay, making the Chinese school students tri-lingual and all others at least bi-lingual. The Chinese schools could not be eliminated until the Chinese themselves decided that they were not needed. With the aim of creating a Malayan nation, the government would naturally wish to direct educational policy to such a goal, but the Report warned that care should be taken "not to prostitute education to political purposes," though education remained the most effective, perhaps the only possible, bridge between cultures. To this end it recommended that the Chinese schools should be integrated into a national system of education without destroying them in the process.

The Indians, specifically the Tamils, were similarly concerned about the future of Tamil schools, and they made their representations to the government through their own community leaders. The major confrontation, however, was between the Chinese and the government. The Indians and the Chinese were not against the principle of a national system of education; their apprehensions were centered around the question of the medium of instruction in the schools. The non-Malays felt that a national identity did not have to hinge on the elimination of their cultural identity as Chinese or as Indians, but the government viewpoint was that the persistence of Chinese and Tamil education was inimical to national integration. It became clear that the heart of the problem was the language of instruction, and this was the recurrent motif in the politics of education for the next two decades.

As the leaders of the Alliance party—a coalition of the United Malays National Organization, the Malayan Chinese Association, and the Malayan Indian Congress—were preparing to negotiate with Britain for independence, it was imperative that the delicate racial balance should not be upset by the educational issue which could plunge the country into greater turmoil than it was in already. At the same time a national policy was needed to accommodate Malay nationalist demands for educational reform. On the eve of independence a compromise solution was proposed by the Abdul Razak Committee on Education, the main proposals of which were adopted and incorporated into the Education Ordinance of 1957. With the view to ultimately using Malay as the main medium of instruction, the national educational system stipulated that:

(a) There should be only two types of schools: independent (i.e. private) or government-assisted, and the latter should be treated alike as regards State and Federal financial aid.

(b) Existing primary schools should be converted to standard schools (Malay-medium) and standard-type schools (Chinese, Tamil or English), with all teachers receiving the same kind of training.

(c) Malay and English should be compulsory subjects in all primary and secondary schools, although instruction in other languages would be made available when needed.

(d) Only one type of national secondary school should be established, open to all races by competitive selection and with a common syllabus, a flexible curriculum permitting the study of all languages and cultures represented in the country, and with provision for diversity in the media of instruction.

(e) Common-content syllabuses and time-tables for schools with a national orientation should be introduced.

The Razak Report concluded that an education policy "acceptable to the people as a whole must provided at least two things: it must satisfy the legitimate aspirations of each of the major cultural groups who have made their home in Malaya and it must offer the prospect of a place in a school for every child born in the country."[39]

Independence was achieved on August 31,1957, under a facade of unity and amity. As the elites in the Alliance were mainly English-educated, the policy of moderation and gradualism appeared the most sensible and pragmatic. To a large extent they reflected the feelings of the English-educated segments of the Malay, Chinese, and Indian communities. The Constitution (Article 152) provided that "the national language shall be the Malay language" and that:

"(a) no person shall be prohibited or prevented from using (otherwise than for official purposes), or from teaching or learning, any other language; and
(b) nothing in this Clause shall prejudice the right of the Federal Government or of any State Government to preserve and sustain the use and study of the language of any other community in the Federation."[40]

For a period of ten years after Independence Day, and thereafter until Parliament otherwise provided, English might be used in both Houses of Parliament, in the Legislative Assembly of every State, and for all other official purposes.

Independence from Britain was achieved on the basis of compromises made among the leaders of the Alliance party, under which a racial balance of power was maintained. The non-Malays, especially the Chinese, were allowed "free play" in their economically dominant position in return for their agreement to, among other things, Malay political supremacy. The "Alliance pact" was essentially made among the Malay, Chinese, and Indian elites. Subsequent events showed that the vast majority of Malays and non-Malays neither understood nor accepted the Alliance compromise.

Soon after independence, the language issue emerged as one of the most divisive, not only between the Malays and the Chinese but also within the Malayan Chinese Association, which suffered a split in 1958 partly because of its stand on the question of the national language. When the time approached for the status of the national language to be reviewed, the government was under pressure from the National Language Action Front *(Barisan Bertindak Bahasa Kebangsaan)* to enforce the use of Malay as the sole official language after September 1,

1967. At the same time the Chinese-educated section of the Chinese community as well as the Tamil community pressed for a more liberal use of Chinese and Tamil for official purposes. Caught between these cross-pressures, the government pushed through Parliament the National Language Bill, 1967, which characteristically struck a compromise whereby English, Chinese and Tamil were permitted to be used at the discretion of the Federal and the State governments, while affirming Malay as the sole national language. While this pleased the non-Malays, it deeply angered the Malays who considered the move retrograde. They believed that it was an affront to the dignity of the Malay language and undermined the very sovereignty of Malaysia as an independent nation.

The "soft line" taken by the government seemed to embolden some of the opposition parties to make language, education, and Malay special rights, among other things, issues in the 1969 general elections. For the first time since independence the election campaign exposed the underlying discontent, frustration, and anger of all groups, and the strident racial appeals to the masses contributed in no small measure to inflaming the communal feelings that led to the riots immediately following the elections. The upshot of the 1969 general elections was the passage of the Constitution (Amendment) Act of 1971 which provided that Article 152 (national language), Article 153 (Malay special rights), Article 181 (powers and prerogatives of the Malay Rulers, subject to provisions of the Constitution), and the whole of Section III (citizenship rights of non-Malays) may no longer be questioned, "it being considered that such sensitive issues should for ever be removed from the arena of public discussion."[41]

Following the recommendations of a committee to review the implementation of education policy under the 1957 Education Ordinance, the Education Act of 1961 amended and consolidated the law relating to education, the most significant being the withdrawal of government aid to Chinese secondary schools. The result was that the majority of those schools which had been receiving government aid were converted to English-medium secondary schools, while the private schools continued to maintain their independence. In 1961 there were 84,347 students in government-aided English-medium secondary schools; in 1962 the enrollment suddenly increased to 119,217, the bulk of which, of course, came from the converted Chinese-medium secondary schools. Thus, the change in educational policy channeled a larger proportion of Chinese school students to the English-medium schools than to the private Chinese-medium secondary schools where the total enrollment increased from 17,948 in 1961 to 34,410 in 1962.[42]

Almost coinciding with this development was the opening of the first Malay-medium secondary schools in 1963. Under pressure from the Federation of Malay School Teachers, the government had established secondary classes in existing Malay primary schools from 1958, but the shortage of trained teachers and textbooks in Malay made it necessary to delay the operation of full Malay-medium secondary schools until 1963. Thereafter they increased rapidly, providing for the first time an integrated primary and secondary education in Malay. At the rate the rural Malays were being mobilized educationally, however, it was a matter of time before a new crisis would emerge at the university level where the issue of language would once again focus attention on the future of education.

As of 1963 the national educational system provided six years of free primary schooling in Malay, Chinese, Tamil, and English. Except for the English-medium schools, all the others were practically uniracial in enrollment although all schools conformed to a national syllabus. Government-aided secondary education was confined to English- and Malay-medium. The English-medium secondary schools, charging fees but with a liberal remission for poor students, were multiracial, while the Malay-medium were free and mainly uniracial. At the same time a number of new English-medium secondary schools, with boarding facilities, were established in some of the urban centers for Malays, mainly from the rural areas. These were designed to accelerate the educational and social mobility of the Malays, and they reflected, in part, the ambivalence of the government in regard to a complete integration of the educational system, at least at the secondary level, and the use of English and Malay in developing secondary education.

Although more than 90 percent of the primary age-group of all races were enrolled in the primary schools, the drop-out rate after Standard Six (grade six) was high, even though opportunities for education up to Form III (grade nine) had been widened considerably since 1961. In large part the problem stemmed from the difficulty of transferring large numbers of pupils from the Chinese- and Tamil-medium primary schools to either the English- or Malay-medium secondary schools. Apart from the switch in language from one level to another, poverty was also an important factor in the high drop-out rate.

The Lower Certificate of Education examination at Form Three (grade nine) selected about 35 percent of the students for upper secondary education through Form Five. At this point students sat for the national Malaysia Certificate of Education examination which, for the vast majority, would be the terminal point of their formal education. The cream of the Form Five students would then be selected for the Form Six (pre-university) classes. The Higher School Certificate examination (taken at grade thirteen) would determine students' eligibility for admission to university at home or abroad.

In 1970 government-assisted primary schools had about 1.42 million students, of whom the Malay-medium made up 42.8 percent, the English medium 23.8 percent, the Chinese-medium 27.7 percent, and the Tamil-medium 5.7 percent. In government-assisted secondary schools, however, with a total enrollment of over 460,000, the Malay-medium had only 27.5 percent, while the English medium had 72.5 percent. In the private secondary schools, the English- and Chinese-medium together enrolled more that 97 percent of nearly 36,000 students. Table I gives the detailed figures. It should be pointed out that a significant proportion of students in Malay-, Chinese-, and Tamil-medium primary schools transfer to the English-medium secondary schools *via* the "Remove Classes" which give them intensive English language coaching prior to their joining the regular secondary stream at Form One (grade seven).

Table I. Enrollment by Language-Medium of Government-Assisted and Private, Primary and Secondary Schools, 1970

Language Medium	Government-Assisted Primary			Secondary	Private Primary		Secondary	
	No.	%	No.	%	No.	%	No.	%
Malay	609,226	42.8	127,273	27.5	161	2.0	999	2.8
English	338,799	23.8	336,187	72.5	2,712	33.1	18,985	52.9
Chinese	394,166	27.7	---	---	5,136	62.8	15,890	44.3
Tamil	79,278	5.7	---	---	171	2.1	---	---
Total	1,421,469	100.0	463,460	100.0	8,180	100.0	35,874	100.0

Source: *Malaysia, Ministry of Education,* Educational Statistics of Malaysia, 1970 *(Kuala Lumpur, 1972), 22-23.*

The figures in Table I suggest that the preference of all groups was for secondary education in English. Considering the fact that historically the elites came from the English-medium schools, the bias toward English-medium education was hardly surprising. English-medium education has been the main channel through which all racial groups have attained, albeit at differential rates, high occupational and social mobility, and it also served to maintain high social status for the second generation of the English-educated. All this has reinforced the popular perception of English-medium education as having high exchange value not only within the country but also especially in other English-speaking countries. A significant trend in the late 1960s was the increasing number of Malay students enrolled in English-medium schools. It would appear that the system which was evolving was acceptable to all. But, as pointed out earlier, the 1969 elections exposed many community tensions and frustrations that could be traced directly and indirectly to the educational process.

It will be recalled that the National Language Act of 1967 affirmed Malay as the sole national language and English, for practical purposes, as the second language, with a liberal provision for the use of Chinese and Tamil for non-official purposes. No radical change was proposed for education, except the stepping up of the use of Malay in teaching music, art and crafts, and physical education in the English-medium primary schools. The University of Malaya (which until 1970 was the sole institution of higher education granting degrees) continued to use mainly English. The first batch of Malay-educated students entered the University in 1965 and found themselves at a disadvantage vis-a-vis the English-educated, most of whom were non-Malays. As the Malay-educated students' frustrations increased, the Malay Language Society at the University became more vocal in its demand for increasing the use of Malay in teaching.

The frustrations of the Chinese-educated, at the same time, led to a demand for a Chinese-language university. Malay counter-reaction was to pressure the government to establish a Malay-language university since the University of Malaya did not really cater to the needs of the Malay-educated who were graduating in increasing numbers from the Malay-medium secondary schools. The Chinese demand for a Chinese-language university was deemed to be illegitimate and denied, but as a consolation a junior college, the Tunku Abdul Rahman College (named after the then Prime Minister) was established in 1969, using mainly English for teaching. Although open to all, its enrollment has been heavily Chinese.

In 1970 the National University *(Universiti Kebangsaan)*, using mainly Malay for teaching, was established, with the enrollment predominately Malay. Since 1970 the University of Science, the University of Agriculture, and the National Institute of Technology have been established to meet the rapidly rising demand for higher education. Concurrently the MARA *(Majlis Amanah Ra'ayat)* Institute of Technology, first established in 1965 to provide para-professional training for Malays, expanded rapidly but maintained an exclusively Malay enrollment, although English has been used for most of the courses of instruction.

In all these crosscurrents of community demands on education, the language issue remained unresolved. As long as the national language remained in an equivocal position in the national system of education, the government would be under constant attack by its Malay supporters. Although Article 12 of the Constitution (pertaining to rights in respect of education) does not specifically guarantee Chinese and Tamil primary education at public expense, in fact it has come to be the accepted practice and policy of the government. To abolish them would be too provocative to be considered politically viable. Any change in language policy would therefore be directed at the English-medium schools. Since English could not be claimed by any group as its mother tongue and therefore central to its cultural identity, it could be attacked without any real risk of community conflict. It stood as the sole challenge to Malay as the national language, and its removal from its preeminent position in the national system of education was seen as the only way to satisfy the Malay nationalist demand for the *de facto* affirmation of Malay as the sole national language. Symbolically, too, it was an attack on the first generation English-educated, Westernized elites, at the head of which was the revered Prime Minister since independence, Tunku Abdul Rahman, whose pragmatic but equivocal stand on the national language question cost him the support and respect of Malay nationalists. The burning of his effigy by Malay students and his resignation as Prime Minister signified the end of an era in which the English-educated, whether Malay, Chinese, or Indian, had held sway for more than two generations.

The Nationalization of English-Medium Education

Soon after the race riots of 1969, which led to the suspension of Parliament, the Minister of Education, Dato Haji Abdul Rahman Ya'akub, announced that the final step toward the "full conversion" of the English-medium schools into national schools would be taken in January, 1970. With the opening of the school year, Malay would be used in teaching mathematics and science in Standard One (grade one). Since 1968 Malay had been used in teaching all other subjects except English, mathematics, and science in the English-medium primary schools. The level of all-Malay-medium teaching would rise progressively as the first 1970 cohort of students moved up the educational ladder. At the same time a progressive conversion to the use of Malay in teaching would begin from 1972 at Form One at the secondary level so that by 1980 all subjects except English and science at Form Six would be taught in Malay. By 1983 the conversion would be completed up to the university level.[43]

In step with these changes the Cambridge (Overseas) School Certificate (which, for more than two generations, had served as the passport to white-collar jobs as well as higher education) was discontinued and replaced by the Malaysian Certificate of Education. To be awarded the MCE, a candidate must have the minimum of a "Pass" in Malay and five other subjects, in the same way as the former Cambridge School Certificate required a minimum "Pass" in English plus five other subjects. As the conversion to Malay proceeds, examinations for the Lower Certificate of Education, taken at Form Three, the MCE, the Higher School Certificate, and at the university level will progressively be written in Malay.

The importance of securing a "Pass" in Malay was dramatically highlighted in 1971 when the results for the MCE examinations showed that, out of roughly 29,000 candidates, about 16,000 failed to get the certificate because they had failed the Malay paper, and without the MCE students were ineligible for admission to the pre-university classes in government-assisted schools. In response to the public outcry, the Ministry of Education instituted an inquiry and declared that it was satisfied that there were no irregularities in the conduct of the examinations. The Ministry maintained that the high failure rate, which was the first of its kind, was due to the "indifference" of the non-Malays to the Malay language, and excoriated students, teachers, and parents for their "apathy," warning them that examination standards would be strictly maintained. However, the Ministry, under protest, did allow some students to re-enroll in the Form Five classes and to re-sit the examination in the following year. Meanwhile, the two Malay language papers (one for Malays, the other for non-Malays) were amalgamated to remove any doubts about "double-standards." In 1972, 37,126 candidates (27,784 non-Malays and 9,342 Malays) sat for the MCE examination. When the results were announced in early 1973, 14,331 candidates (including 165 Malays) or 38.6 percent were deemed to have failed because they failed the Malay paper. Those who passed included 6,751 Malays and 9,314 Chinese.[44] Failure to obtain a "Pass" in Malay in the MCE examination denies the candidate employment in government and semi-government agencies as well as access to higher education in Malaysia.

Apathy, no doubt, was one of the factors for the high failure rate, but considering the cruciality of a "Pass" in Malay to obtain the MCE, it was argued that students who aspired toward better employment and higher education would not be so foolish as to neglect a paper that was essential to their success in the examination. Enmeshed in this problem is the question of the effectiveness of teaching methods and the adequacy of teacher-supply. Whatever the reasons, it was unfortunate that thousands of non-Malays were frustrated and alienated by a process that should be integrative and supportive of nation-building.

The progressive elimination of the English-medium schools appears to have had a significant impact on the enrollment in the Chinese-medium primary schools. Between 1957 and 1963, these schools showed a progressive decline in their share of the national total primary school enrollment, and between 1963 and 1969 it had more or less stabilized. But since 1970 the proportion has been rising, suggesting that a significant number of parents who had been sending their children to the English-medium schools are now enrolling them in the Chinese-medium schools. This would mean that, by 1976, the Chinese-medium secondary (private) schools are likely to register a marked increase in enrollment. In 1963 the total enrollment in the Chinese-medium secondary schools was 35,799, declining to 15,890 in 1970. In 1972 it showed a significant upswing to 18,250, a rise of 16.5 percent in two years.[45]

As there is no Chinese-language university in Malaysia, secondary education in Chinese is necessarily terminal, unless students are sufficiently proficient in Malay (which, together with English, is taught as a second language, though how effectively is not known) to be able to sit for the MCE examinations. However, given the milieu of the Chinese schools, it seems unlikely that a significant number will succeed in this way. If higher education is closed to these students, and there are no prospects of employment in government or semi-government agencies, their future will depend entirely on the private sector, family businesses, self-employment, or higher education outside Malaysia. The last alternative itself, if they are proficient only in Chinese, will be restricted to Singapore, Hong Kong, and Taiwan, unless they take a one-way ticket to China. In the past, some of the leading Chinese secondary schools, such as the Chung Ling High School in Penang, had successfully fielded bilingual (English and Chinese) students in the Cambridge School Certificate examination, but they were relatively rare. It is left to be seen whether significant numbers of bi-lingual (Chinese and Malay) students will emerge from these schools.

In the transitional period there is the prospect of a sizeable pro-portion of the younger generation Chinese withdrawing into a world of their own. Their own educational process outside the mainstream of the national system will fortify their group identity as *Chinese* Chinese. In a rapidly changing political and social environment they are apt to regard themselves and be regarded by others as "outsiders" because their participation in national life will be circumscribed by their non-Malay orientation. Their feeling of "relative deprivation," which had been strong under British colonial rule, is not likely to diminish in a Malay-oriented social order.

On another dimension, the elimination of the English-medium schools will mean that the future elites are likely to be mainly Malay-educated. Given the fact that English will be taught as a second language, there is the possibility they might be bi-lingual, but on the whole they are likely to be more literate in Malay than in English. For the Chinese in particular, it will mean a new generation whose outlook and values will be influenced, if not molded, just as their parents' values were Western-ized by the English language, by the Malay language which will effective-ly be their sole functional language. To be sure, the new Malaysian culture will be a melange of Malay, Chinese, Indian, and Western elements, but the language through which a person is socialized during the educational process into the national culture will leave a stronger im-print on the personality than the home language, if the latter is restricted to elementary cognitive learning. In this process, traditional Chinese or Indian values are likely to be blurred by the new Malay values. Where formerly the Chinese community had been split between the Chinese-educated and the English-educated, the future division will be on the Malay-educated and Chinese-educated dimension. The same will hold true for the Indians. The discontinuities in the education of one genera-tion and another for the Chinese and the Indians constitute some of the more poignant human dramas of intergenerational change in Malaysia.

For the Malays, it will be a period of new pride, new confidence, and new self-esteem in a world in which the linguistic norm will be recognizably their very own. However, the current educational transformation, though essentially an assertion and certainly a con-tinuity of Malay culture, will bring about such changes in the Malay language through the impact of science and technology that the older generation of Malays may feel as out-of-place as their Chinese or In-dian counterparts. New words and phrases, with their etymological roots in English, are being absorbed into Malay at such a rate that the current Malay language revolution may have the effect of bifurcating traditional Malay culture from the new, which will be shaped as much by the new generation of Malay-Chinese and Malay-Indians as the Malays themselves. What new group identities develop, and how these emerging groups re-order themselves in the changing Malaysian, Malay-language dominated society will be the subject of research a generation hence.

Crucial to the process of national integration, in the last analysis, is not whether education in Malay will transform the group identities of the non-Malays into something more Malay, but rather the way in which Malays will come to perceive and interact with the new Malay- educated, perhaps wholly Malay-speaking, Chinese and Indians. An increasing proportion of the Chinese and the Indians will, through the Malay language, symbolically enter the Malay world which hitherto had been closed to them mainly by virtue of their former non-Malay education. How will the Malays value them? What roles will they be assigned or per- mitted in the political process? If they are not Muslim, and as long as the dichotomous distinction between "bumiputra" ("son of the soil") and "non-bumiputra" persists in social and political categorization, not- withstanding the efficacy of the overarching political identity of *Malay- sian*, the fundamental cleavage is unlikely to disappear. In the past their lack of proficiency in Malay— indeed, their lack of interest in it—has been held as a sign that they did not really "belong" to Malaysia. When the Chinese and the Indians come to speak and think in the same language as the Malays, will they be less "alien" in Malay eyes?

Clearly a common language will achieve some degree of social if not cultural homogenization and will, no doubt, provide a concrete base for national integration. But the *basic group identity* of the Malays, the Chinese, and the Indians is likely to remain distinct even though changed, and will continued to be changed, by the complex of social, economic, and political forces. The peripheral social and cultural characteristics of each identity may be stripped away by the educational process, but the core within each group will remain as ineffably Malay, Chinese, or Indian as the East Indians and the Africans in Guyana have remained distinct and different despite their relatively long common socialization through the English language.

Conclusion

From this necessarily selective outline of political and social change in Guyana and Malaysia, two critical themes emerge: (1) the saliency and persistence of ethnicity and communalism in the process of moderniza- tion, and (2) the destabilizing effect of mass education on interethnic relations.

Recent events in a number of multiethnic societies, both "developed" and "developing," reinforce the conclusion that com- munalism is not merely a manifestation or projection of "primordial sentiments" and cultural differences: social change and modernization have led to the emergence and formation of "entirely new communal groupings which crystallize around new foci of culture and identity" because communalism is "an inherent aspect of social change in culturally heterogeneous societies."[46] However, the critical difference is that, in the new multiethnic polities, ethnicity is the *primary* political factor which affects all aspects of social change at all levels of public life, whereas in the developed societies ethnicity is relatively unimportant, or at least not crucial, at the national level of political life. At the present stage of Malaysia's political development, for example, it is unthinkable that a non-Malay should aspire to be the prime minister, or even the deputy prime minister. In Guyana the rift between the East Indians and the Africans is so wide that, whether the prime minister be an African or an East Indian, a major section of the population is likely to feel that he is less than legitimate. The same kind of polarization applies to Cyprus. In Nigeria, the symbols of power have to be carefully arranged so as to ensure some degree of identification between the government and the various ethnic groups.

If this be the pattern of political change in the new multiethnic societies, the emergence of the Africans and the Malays as the politically preeminent groups in Guyana and Malaysia respectively raises a critical question of nation-building: is this to be the emerging norm of ethnic relations in the post-colonial world?

It would appear that the distribution of power depends upon the number and strength of communal groups within the polity. On the one hand, according to Melson and Wolpe, "the greater the number of equally powerful communal groups, the greater the likelihood that institutional coherence and impartiality will be retained."[47] On the other hand, where only two groups of roughly the same numerical strength exist, political power tends to be weighted in favor of one group or the other, and ethnic competition is apt to be intense and widespread. In the case of Malaysia, the pattern since independence has been a coalition of Malay, Chinese, and Indian groups; and the transformation of the old Alliance party into the new National Front in 1973, incorporating some ten parties, followed this pattern, with the Malays as the "senior" partner in the government.

Given the strong centrifugal forces, the high level of distrust among communal groups, and the volatility of the mobilized masses in any multiethnic society, the paramount consideration of any government is the establishment of political stability and order, without which economic and social development will not be possible. The crucial problem is not who wields political power but what happens to the society as a whole and what changes are brought about in the status of other ethnic groups in the political process.

No government can remain long in power, at least in societies where democratic elections are maintained, if it does not attempt to articulate some of the interests of the other ethnic groups and to satisfy some of their demands so as to establish a minimum degree of legitimacy in the eyes of all groups. But if political institutions are subordinated to the interests of particular communal groups, communal conflict will be reinforced and politicized.[49] If the government allows its autonomy to be eroded by the demands of one particular communal group, it is likely to destroy its legitimacy and undermine political stability and order. On the other hand, its legitimacy would be enhanced if it could provide adequate, if not equal, opportunities for all groups in social and economic development and could institutionalize procedures to articulate and reconcile conflicting demands.

Clearly political order will depend in large measure on the commitment or obligation by all groups to "some principle, tradition, myth, purpose, or code of behavior" which they have in common so that the national political institutions, involving and reflecting the "moral consensus and mutual interest" of the nation, will sustain the political community.[49] However, whether any universalistic ideology is able to transcend ethnic loyalties depends on how it is translated into practice: its espousal may not guarantee ethnic harmony or consensus, but its absence certainly provides no basis for any principle for nation-building.

Malaysia's proclamation of "national ideology"[50] in 1970 and Guyana's declaration of its "Co-operative Republic" in the same year are symptomatic of the move toward a set of ideas or principles which would provide the basis for binding together peoples whose history, culture, language, value system, and basic group identities have set them apart. But an ideology, to be functional, must be set in the framework of economic and social development with the promise of raising the living standards of all groups and the reduction of social and economic disparities between and within ethnic groups. Malaysia, for example, has made it clear that national unity depends upon the Malays' receiving an equitable share of the national wealth. The "new economic policy," as embodied in the Second Malaysia Plan, aims at the "eradication of poverty, irrespective of race," and the "restructuring of Malaysian society to correct economic imbalance, so as to reduce and eventually eliminate the identification of race with economic function."[51] Similarly, Guyana's stress on cooperation instead of competition between the East Indians and the Africans through its national cooperatives may be seen as an attempt at creating greater economic and social equality between the two groups.

The quest for equity presupposes economic modernization which entails the mobilization through mass education of large number of people from the traditional to the modern sector of the economy. But education, by accelerating social mobilization—a process whereby "major clusters of old social, economic, and psychological commitments are eroded or broken and people become available for new patterns of socialization and behavior"[52]— is apt to raise the aspirations and expectations of the younger generation much higher than the capacity of the society to satisfy them. When the social and economic rewards do not match the expectations of the mobilized masses, the consequent competition tends to be politicized and defined in ethnic terms and therefore is likely to intensify ethnic conflict.

Historically the nature of Western contact, environmental opportunities, and cultural predispositions have been responsible for interethnic differentials in the development process,[53] with the result that the "late-comers" of intranational modernization find themselves handicapped in the competition for national rewards. The differential rates of education development between the Malays and the non- Malays, on the one hand, and between the East Indians and the Africans, on the other, accounted for much of the ethnic tensions in Malaysia and Guyana. For the future, at least in the short run, these differentials may take different forms as the demands of modern education, especially in science and technology, change, and therefore the educational process is likely to widen existing disparities. The urge toward economic equality is apt to lead to educational policies to "equalize" access to education and, if necessary, to aid the disadvantaged group with "positive discrimination," which, because of its ethnic overtones, may be counter-productive of national unity. But given the fact that the demand tends to outstrip the facilities for education, the competition for access to education is again likely to exacerbate ethnic tensions and could well be the flashpoint of open conflict.

Education may homogenize different ethnic groups by socializing them to the same needs and wants. But in the more fundamental aspects of cultural and identity change, its efficacy will depend not so much on the cognitive or affective outcomes of schooling or on the socialization to a national culture as on the overall political process which will determine the subjective feeling of each ethnic group about its status as citizens and its social and economic prospects in the changing political order.

NOTES

[1] James S. Coleman, "Introduction," in James S. Coleman (ed.), *Education and Political Development* (Princeton, 1965), 30.

[2] Clifford Geertz, "The Integrative Revolution," in Clifford Geertz (ed.), *Old Societies and New States* (New York, 1963), 111.

[3] Harold R. Isaacs, "Group Identity and Political Change," *Survey*, LXIX (1968), 77.

[4] Ibid., 77.

[5] Joseph B. Landis, "Race Relations and Politics in Guyana" (unpub. Ph.D. dissertation, Yale University, 1971), 160.

[6] Ibid., 175.

[7] Government of British Guiana, *British Guiana Population Census, 1960: Census Bulletin No. 1.*

[8] Government of British Guiana, *Report of the National Rehabilitation Committee* (Georgetown, 1965), 4.

⁹ Landis, "Race Relations," 284.

¹⁰ Leo A. Despres, *Cultural Pluralism and Nationalist Politics in British Guiana* (Chicago, 1967), 103.

¹¹ Ibid., 127.

¹² Raymond T. Smith, *British Guiana* (London, 1964), 111.

¹³ *Report of the British Guiana Constitutional Commission, 1954* (London, 1954), 15.

¹⁴ Smith, *British Guiana,* 140.

¹⁵ Elliott P. Skinner, "Group Dynamics and Social Stratification in British Guiana," *Annals of the New York Academy of Sciences,* LXXXIII (1960), 904.

¹⁶ Ibid., 908.

¹⁷ Hon-Chan Chai "Education and National Development in Plural Societies: A Case Study of Guyana" (unpub. Ph.D. dissertation, Harvard University, 1968), 65.

¹⁸ ASCRIA bulletin entitled "Ascrianism Defined in the Presence of Zambian Foreign Minister" (Georgetown, 1966).

¹⁹ Chai, "Education and National Development," 68.

²⁰ Smith, *British Guiana*, 41.

²¹ Landis, "Race Relations," 117-119, 104.

²² Ibid., 115, 131.

²³ Forbes Burnham, *A Destiny to Mould* (New York, 1970), XXX.

²⁴ Ibid., 8.

²⁵ Landis, "Race Relations," 316-317.

²⁶ Guyana, Ministry of External Affairs, *Guyana Journal*, I (1970), 81.

²⁷ Burnham, *A Destiny*, 10.

²⁸ Chai, "Education and National Development," 155-159.

²⁹ Ibid., 160-162.

³⁰ Ibid., 228.

³¹ Daniel Lerner, "Toward a Communication Theory of Modernization: A Set of Considerations," in Lucian W. Pye (ed.), *Communications and Political Development* (Princeton, 1963), 333.

³² "Malaysia," created in 1963, comprised the former Federation of Malaya, Singapore, and the Borneo states of Sabah and Sarawak. The Federation of Malaya itself drew together the former Federated Malay States, the so-called Unfederated Malay States, and the former Straits Settlements of Penang and Malacca. In 1965 Singapore was separated from Malaysia. In this paper the problems discussed relate mainly to peninsular or West Malaysia, sometimes referred to simply as Malaya, although the larger issues of national integration are pertinent to the whole of Malaysia.

[33] The "special rights" of the Malays grew out of the original privileges of the Malay Rulers and the aristocracy with whose consent the British ruled the country. As the number of non-Malays increased the "special rights," which were never quite defined, were extended to all "Malays" as a protection against the more aggressive Chinese and Indians. The 1957 Constitution formally defined these rights in Article 153. Since 1971 the provisions under Article 153 have been placed outside the realm of public discussion or questioning.

[34] Soon after the outbreak of the communist insurrection, the government declared an "Emergency" which was to last till 1960. Although the Chinese accounted for the greater proportion of casualties, the bulk of the armed forces fighting the insurrection was made up of Malays, together with British and other Commonwealth forces.

[35] K.J. Ratnam, *Communalism and the Political Process in Malaya* (Kuala Lumpur, 1965), 66. For a detailed discussion of the citizenship problem, see espec. ch. 3.

[36] Federation of Malaya, *Report on the Committee on Malay Education* (Kuala Lumpur, 1951), paras. 28, 29.

[37] Ibid., paras. 2, 3.

[38] Federation of Malaya, *Chinese Schools and the Education of Chinese Malayans: the Report of a Mission invited by the Federation Government to Study the Problem of the Chinese in Malaya* (Kuala Lumpur, 1951). See espec. paras. 3, 5.

[39] Federation of Malaya, *Report of the Education Committee, 1956* (Kuala Lumpur, 1958), 28.

[40] Malaysia, *Federal Constitution* (Kuala Lumpur, 1970), 155.

[41] Mohamad Suffian bin Hashim, *An Introduction to the Constitution of Malaysia* (Kuala Lumpur, 1972), 278. Under the new law any person or publication which questions these sections of the Constitution may be charged with an offence under the Sedition Act of 1948, as amended by the Emergency (Essential Powers) Ordinance No. 45, 1970, or with an offence under any law made by Parliament prohibiting such questioning. A person or publication may be guilty of a "seditious tendency" regardless of whether such questioning actually arouses hostility and enmity between two persons or groups of different races. R.K. Vasil in *The Malaysian General Election of 1969* (Kuala Lumpur, 1972) gives a detailed analysis of the results and effects of this election.

[42] Malaysia, Ministry of Education, *Educational Statistics of Malaysia, 1938 to 1967* (Kuala Lumpur, 1968), 41, 42, 46.

[43] Malaysia, Ministry of Education, *Education in Malaysia* (Kuala Lumpur, 1971), 10-11.

[44] M.G.G. Pillai, "The MCE Drama," *Far Eastern Economic Review*, LIV:17 (1973), 16.

[45] Malaysia, Ministry of Education, *Educational Statistics of Malaysia, 1972* (Kuala Lumpur, 1973), 23.

[46] Robert Melson and Howard Wolpe, "Modernization and the Politics of Communalism: A Theoretical Perspective," *American Political Science Review*, LXIV (1970), 1129.

[47] Ibid., 1121.

[48] Ibid., 1120.

[49] Samuel P. Huntington, *Political Order in Changing Societies* (New Haven, 1968), 10.

[50] Malaysia, *Rukunegara* (Kuala Lumpur, 1970). The "national ideology" embodies five "beliefs": a united nation, a democratic society, a just society, a liberal society, and a progressive society; and five "principles": belief in God, loyalty to King and Country; upholding the Constitution; rule of law, and good behavior and morality.

[51] Malaysia, *Second Malaysia Plan, 1971-1975* (Kuala Lumpur, 1971), 1.

[52] Karl Deutsch, "Social Mobilization and Political Development," *American Political Science Review*, LV (1961), 494.

[53] Melson and Wolpe, "Modernization," 1115.

VI.

Tradition and Modernization of Japan

By Michio Nagai

In the 1960s Japan was often cited as a case of successful economic development; some even spoke of the Japanese case as a miracle. To me, if Japan is miraculous, most other nations are perhaps equally so. It is important, however, to point out that Japan is unique among today's nations. She is not part of the Western world, and though one of the highly industrialized nations of the contemporary world, only a century ago she was a backward nation. Because of this combination of successful rapid industrialization and a non-Western background, she does present a unique, though by no means miraculous, case.

Before talking about the modernization of this country, it is necessary to sketch her history briefly, for present-day Japan emerged only after centuries of preparation in earlier development.

Japanese society is influenced by four major cultures. Western culture, the latest arrival, exerted only weak influence during the sixteenth century; it was not studied seriously and incorporated into the daily life of people until much later, in the latter half of the nineteenth century. Much earlier, during the period between the seventh and ninth centuries, strong cultural influences began entering Japan from the Asian continent. Among them, the two most important were Chinese Confucianism and Indian Buddhism. In addition to these three major world cultures, the indigenous Japanese culture, which existed before Japan developed close contact with the continent, established roots that survive even today.

Although the United States is said to be a melting pot of different races, the basic cultural orientation of that country is predominantly Western. The many different races who went there, as well as those who had been there previous to the founding of the country, went through the processes of acculturation called "Americanization." In contrast to the American case, the racial composition of Japan is homogeneous. It is not at all easy, however, to identify what the Japanese culture is today, for it has emerged from the mixture of four different cultures.

For these reasons some understanding of Japan's earlier contact with the continent is indispensable if we wish to gain insight into the modernization of Japan during the last hundred years, and also to anticipate what may come in future.

Between the seventh and ninth centuries the Japanese learned a great deal from the Koreans and the Chinese, with the government of Japan sending sixteen student missions to China to study various aspects of Chinese culture. This activity resulted in important technical and cultural transfer of knowledge. Indeed, the Japanese learned much from the Chinese about such basic concepts as development of a national political administration, the technology and skill necessary to build large buildings, tax system, and systematic rearrangement of agrarian land. Through the Chinese and the Koreans, the Japanese were also introduced to another important culture of the Asian continent: Indian Buddhism. Interestingly enough, Buddhism became more popular in Japan than it had been in China and Korea, and since then it has come to be regarded as the foundation of the basic world-view held by the Japanese. Some Chinese, and a number of Koreans, came to Japan to teach, then settled and actually became Japanese. Fortunately, the Chinese empire then had no intention of conquering Japan, nor were the Japanese afraid of the Chinese in a political sense. The culture transfer between the two countries was peaceful.

In the first half of the ninth century, however, the government of Japan decided that official missions would no longer be sent to China—a decision that intensified the process of Japanization. Hence, most of the great Japanese achievements in art and literature began to flourish in the tenth century. One must appreciate the fact that to absorb another great culture takes two or three centuries, and to adapt that borrowed culture to one's own tastes takes even longer.

The second important foreign influence was Western science in the seventeenth century. To the amazement of Westerners, Japan accepted it quite readily. In Europe, certain scientific concepts were considered incompatible with the religious view of the world, and the Copernican view of the world, for example, caused sharp conflict. In Japan, however, it did not take more than ten years for Japanese intellectuals to become adjusted to the scientific view of the world. Initially, the Japanese learned primarily from the Dutch and a little from the British, since other Europeans who came to Japan in the seventeenth century were more interested in missionary activities, toward which the Japanese felt suspicion and fear. There was little hesitancy on the part of Japanese to accept Westerners who had no intention of conquering Japan or making religious converts. Ambitious Japanese were excited about "Dutch learning," the nickname used to describe Western science, even though there was not even a dictionary then to aid in translating Western works. The first translation—a book on anatomy—was by Sugita Genpaku, Maeno Ryotaku, and Nakagawa Junan. Not only did they translate the book, but they also examined the body of a criminal who had been killed and compared the body with the book. This, evidently, was the beginning of the scientific world-view in Japan. If science is to be defined as a logically conceptualized body of knowledge about empirical reality, the Japanese began to entertain such a system of knowledge, when a few intellectuals became interested in Dutch learning.

Rapid diffusion of the scientific view was another important fact of history. Though Sugita, one of the translators of the book on anatomy, did not expect large sales, much to his amazement the book was widely read. The existence of a demand for scientific knowledge is indispensable for its development, and there was evidently such a demand in Japan.

A large number of Japanese were then living in urban centers; in fact, in those days the two largest cities in the world were London and Tokyo. E. Kaempfer, a German physician serving with the Dutch trading station at Deshima, wrote a detailed travel account of the Japan of that time, in which he described numerous things which sound somewhat surprising today.[1] He wrote that people in Tokyo were more publicly minded than people in most Western cities. Tokyo was much better planned than other cities that he had seen. Not only anatomy, but also astronomy, medical sciences, and mathematics had been introduced to Japanese in the eighteenth century.

The latter half of the nineteenth century was a turning point in Japanese history. Nineteenth-century Japan was the epitome of confusion and chaos. As the travel account by Kaempfer describes, Japan in the seventeenth century was not radically different from European society in terms of urbanization, diffusion of ideas, and arts and craftmanship. However, when Commodore Perry came to Japan in 1853, thus ending the long period of Japanese seclusion, Japan was at once confronted with the fact that there had been radical changes in the nineteenth-century West about which the Japanese knew very little. Although the Japanese knew what science was by this time, they did not know that an industrial revolution had taken place at the end of the eighteenth century in Europe and about half a century later in the United States. Perry's steamboats were thus a symbol of industrial revolution for the Japanese—a revolution which the Japanese soon found would be accompanied by changes in the political and economic structures also. At the same time, they observed that leading countries in Asia were now coming under heavy pressures from the Western powers. India and China, which the Japanese had looked up to for centuries, became a colony and a "half-colony," respectively under Western domination. Japanese, especially sensitive intellectual and political leaders, were afraid that Japan might be forced down the same path.

Under such circumstances efforts were made by determined leaders to abolish feudalism and establish a modern state in Japan. The social changes in the latter half of the nineteenth century are so many that detail is impossible to give here. Only three points will be made.

The first is the way in which internal social change was linked to external impact. It was evident that Japan did not reach the stage of modern-state sovereignty solely on the basis of self-innovation. At the same time, one should not disregard the fact that internal changes had been occurring since the eighteenth century. As Figure I shows, gradual changes in all sectors of society—such as the diffusion of new ideas, a gradual increase in agrarian productivity, the rise of manufacturing-type industries, and the gradual emergence of a division of labor—had been going on in Japan for decades. These changes were strictly internal, having no relationship whatsoever to the foreign impact. But they were not quite sufficient in themselves to create an industrial revolution and establish a modern state. Without foreign influence Japan might have gone the direction indicated by the dotted line in Figure I. But the historical fact is that the Western impact did come, thus accelerating the pace of social change. One might call it a process of imposition and adaptation. In other words, Japan had to find ways to respond to the challenge of the West in order to survive as an independent nation. Figure I is a simplified picture of Japan's place in world history. It was necessary for Japan to narrow the gap existing between its own and the West's "achieved industrial stage."

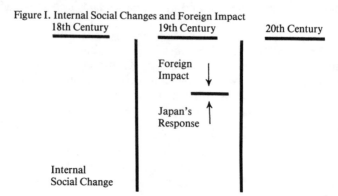

Figure I. Internal Social Changes and Foreign Impact

18th Century   19th Century   20th Century

Foreign
Impact

Japan's
Response

Internal
Social Change

The second point must be the assessment of the situation and decision-making under these circumstances. Though many documents have been written on the subject, several ideas held by one of Japan's important nineteenth-century political leaders are particularly helpful. His name was Okubo Toshimichi, a founder of the modern Japanese bureaucracy who was deeply interested in Western civilization. In 1871, he sent nearly the entire cabinet abroad for study. Upon their return to Japan, a report was submitted to the government, and Okubo wrote that although people tended to think that Western nations were basically similar to each other, that simply was not the case. One nation, the United Kingdon, seemed to him more similar to Japan than others for three reasons. The population of both was 32 million, both were island countries, and both had royal or imperial systems. In spite of these three similarities, however, the United Kingdom was wealthy and powerful while Japan was hardly independent. He attributed these differences to two major factors: the presence in England (and absence in Japan) of industrial revolution and political democracy. These were the elements that sooner or later Japan would have to achieve if she were to become a stable, modern state.

Okubo showed remarkable insights into the decision-making process as well as the differences between societies. He stated that in political decision-making, five factors had to be considered carefully: people, place, time, circumstances, and cultural background. The people with whom political leaders had to deal were Japanese, and the time was the latter half of the nineteenth century. The place was an island country, and the circumstances were difficult, in that Japan was struggling under great pressure from competing Western powers. Finally, there was the cultural background combining Confucian, Shinto, and Buddhist traditions. According to Okubo, all these factors had to be considered before any political decisions could be made.

Given these factors, it would have been difficult to achieve industrial revolution simultaneously with political democracy. In a society like Japan of a hundred years ago, it was understandable that a leader like Okubo feared that hasty adoption of political democracy might lead to confusion. He decided that industrial revolution was to be regarded as the primary objective of the country's efforts.

In his thinking, the establishment of a strong bureaucracy was a necessary condition for industrialization. He stated that if the British type "political-democracy-first" approach was called "orthodoxy," such an approach to industrial revolution would be called "heterodoxy." However, under the circumstances, he said, such an approach was necessary for the careful and responsible planning required to achieve industrial revolution in the shortest time possible. The second objective for Japan was to build up a strong defense force, mainly naval forces, because she was an island country. Political, economic, and educational structures were set up accordingly. Structurally, Western bureaucracy was copied to a great degree. In order to secure the loyalty of the population, however, the government decided to make much use of Confucian tradition, emphasizing seniority and authority. Thus, by combining Western-type bureaucracy with Confucian tradition, the absolute sovereignty of the state was confirmed.

It was impossible to establish popular sovereignty in the beginning years of modern Japan. An alternative was to assign sovereignty to some abstract being like the state, or to the Emperor. The conclusion that the government leaders reached in drafting the 1889 Constitution was to assign sovereignty to the state in which the Emperor was the ruler. The Emperor during the feudal period had been the symbolic center of the Shinto tradition and a large number of Japanese did not even know of his existence. In this sense, the Imperial political system was not traditional; rather, it was newly, though firmly, established at the time of the birth of modern Japan.

The third point is the relationship between the imposition of outside culture and the adaptation of the native culture in a developing nation like Meiji Japan. According to W. Ogburn, a sociologist, material culture changes more rapidly than nonmaterial culture. He referred to the gap between the two as "the culture lag." Ogburn's theory, however, does not seem to apply to all situations. If we call his theory "Cultural Lag Theory A," it becomes necessary to propose a "Theory B" to understand the culture change of a developing nation.

Figure 2. Two Patterns of Social Change

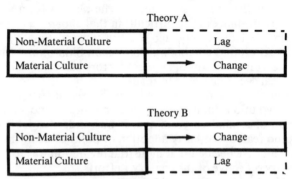

Source: William F. Ogburn, *Social Change*, (New York, 1966).

As Figure 2 shows, ideas borrowed from the West moved far ahead of such real changes in material culture as economic development and technological advance. One important leader, Hamao Arata, went to England and studied the system of craftsmen's schools. Upon his return to Japan, he stated that in the United Kingdom factories had been built first, before artisans' schools were established. But according to his view, in the case of Japan it was necessary to reverse this historical process, i.e., to build craftsmen's schools first with the hope that factories might be born later. Indeed, this was what happened in subsequent years in Japan and this is exactly what is meant by "Cultural Lag Theory B." Theory B may be applicable not only to Japan of a century ago, but to many other emerging nations.

It is important to point out that it was not too difficult initially, for Japan to meet the foreign impact, for Japan in the seventeenth century was not radically different from Europe of the same period. It was the presence or absence of industrialization that brought about the real differences between them. The gap that the Japanese had to fill was actually not very large. In comparison to the gap which exists between the development of emerging and advanced nations today, the Japanese task of a hundred years ago was far simpler.

By 1900, 96 percent of the people of Japan, including both men and women, were literate. Japan's educational development surprised the world. Again, it is important to remember that already by the middle of the nineteenth century about 40 percent of young Japanese males were able to read and write and about 10 percent of young women. To jump from 40 to 96 percent was not really such a surprising achievement, though these simple historical facts are often forgotten.

It was obvious that learning from the West was important in the beginning stages of modern Japan. However, some young Japanese intellectuals did not want merely to copy what was Western. If Westerners were capable of coming up with new ideas in the fields of science and technology, Japanese must be just as capable. The question of imitation and creation was discussed in the 1870s by Henry Dyer, a British scholar, who was then dean of the Polytechnical College of Tokyo Imperial University. Speaking to Japanese students, he said that their ambition to be creative was understandable, but given the circumstances it was urgent for Japanese to imitate Western culture as much as possible. Imitation, he said, was an indispensable learning process if Japan was to survive; the time would come much later when the Japanese could afford to think creatively.[2] The same words were spoken by responsible leaders of the time. In spite of these warnings, however, creativity may be inherent in human beings. It was in this very Polytechnical College of Tokyo University that so many creative scientists were born.

Now a final question, that of institutional rigidity, must be considered. Beginning in 1868, it took about forty years for Japan to achieve an industrial revolution. Before its culmination there occurred the Japan-China War broke out during the 1890s. Until that time Japan had never been at war with the Chinese. But the Japan-China War was the beginning of an unfortunate relationship. Japan grew overconfident from the victory over a great nation like China. Ten years later, she was faced with another war, this time with a Western nation, Russia. Again Japan won. At the same time, the industrial revolution became fully developed and economic growth continued. Prior to World War II, the economic growth of Japan averaged 3-4 percent annually. In my judgment, however, economic growth of itself says little about the development of a society. Because of Japan's success in economic growth after the beginning of the industrial revolution, a great navy and army were built and the Japanese became ambitious enough to compete with the greatest powers in the world, the United Kingdom and the United States. Her leaders also decided that Japan should expand into the Asian continent, sometimes to conquer and sometimes to develop those areas for the purpose of bettering the living standard of Asians. Those two goals were always delicately interwoven. What has happened since the industrial revolution in Japan cannot be described in detail, but as is widely known, the final consequence was defeat in World War II.

Most striking before World War II was the institutional rigidity in Japanese society. Land reform was not achieved, and the labor unions were fragmented and weak. Instead, monopolistic industries dominated. Had there not been such strong institutional rigidity, Japan in modern times might have walked a rather different path.

This institutional rigidity was the consequence of many factors, one of which was undoubtedly bureaucracy. Bureaucracy, according to Max Weber's definition, is supposed to be efficient and rational, but his is an ideal type of bureaucracy. What really existed was an irrational and inefficient organization. In addition, Japanese society is familial, with each person's status ascribed according to age and sex. When familialism is tied to bureaucracy, the structure becomes even more rigid. Another element which reinforced the rigidity was a strong coalition between bureaucracy and business. Although vertical social mobility is often considered a social force that facilitates the flexibility of social systems, it has another function of minimizing the strength of opposition against the establishment.

Universal education in Japan had precisely this double function of facilitating the vertical mobility on the one hand and minimizing the strength of opposition on the other. What was emphasized in primary school was, above all, practical learning—not freedom of inquiry. Another emphasis was loyalty to the state and respect for social hierarchy. At the university level, there was some emphasis on the freedom of inquiry, especially in the field of science and technology. Unless universities maintain a certain degree of freedom of inquiry, the society stagnates. If, on the other hand, all educational institutions are engaged constantly in the free exercise of intellect, the whole society may become unstable. This at least was the thinking of some important leaders of Japan at the initial stage of her modernization. Consequently every person was legally encouraged to climb the social ladder according to his ability. This was especially true in the military and normal schools, and to a certain degree in the Imperial Universities. Any persons who might by nature have remained in the opposition camp were thus absorbed into the establishment.

Let us ask finally whether the institutional rigidity was broken down after World War II. It is true that under occupation by the Allied forces, many reforms were achieved, such as land reform. the strengthening of labor unions, the dissolution of monopolistic industries, and the forming of a new constitution by which sovereignty resided with the people. However, one should not forget the simple fact that all this was done by the power of a double-headed bureaucracy. One head was the bureaucracy of the Allied forces; the other was that of the Japanese government working under the Allied forces. It was indeed an enlightened, authoritarian, despotic bureaucracy that brought about democracy in Japan. Such a political structure was undoubtedly helpful for quick economic growth and technological innovation. Since the end of the occupation, a new coalition of three major powers has emerged. They include the government, business, and the conservative party, which actually has not been a party but a branch of the government. For more than twenty years, no opposition has been able to stand against this great combination. And Japan's universal education on the whole has served the purpose of pulling people together under the leadership of this power system.

So, by and large, the major objective of the country since 1868 has been industrial revolution and—after the war—technological innovation and economic growth. Japan has been a nation obsessed for a century by the objective of catching up with advanced nations. In this sense the

United States and the Soviet Union, which also have developed as emerging nations outside of Europe, may be somewhat similar to Japan. It is important to note that in these three nations the percentage of those enrolled in higher education among the college age population is greater than anywhere else in the world.

However, as noted earlier, the major objectives of education in Japan have been the borrowing of ideas from outside, the application of these ideas to practical use, and the diffusion of ideas. Japanese scientists have been those who could select important ideas already developed elsewhere in the world that would be useful in Japan. Consequently, the standards of primary and secondary education are high. According to a 1964 UNESCO study, Japanese achievement in mathematics at the age of thirteen is the second highest in the world, following only Israel. But Japan's education is strong in quantity and weak in quality. Especially in the postwar society, universities have become very large and very much involved in the demands of society. Hence, it has become increasingly difficult for the larger universities to maintain genuine autonomy against outside political and economic interests.

Of course the relationship between science and technology on the one hand and social demands on the other is complicated. It is difficult to establish a hasty and causal relationship between these two elements. Many heterogeneous elements go into the concept of "social demands." And it is important to remember that scientists of our day live by paychecks and belong to large organizations. Though money comes from various sources, the military, political, and business demands seem to have priority. Sometimes the development of science brings about social changes and creates social demands. What really exists seems to be a feedback between the two elements. There are still many who wish to believe in the traditional folklore of the purity of science. However, in our day it is important to face social realities squarely and examine closely whatever really exists in the feedback relationship. The Japanese case suggests the importance of such an examination. Otherwise scientists and engineers could easily be trapped in the system and become victims of society rather than helpful contributors to it.

What I have tried to show in the foregoing discussion is that the Japanese case over the last hundred years has been one of successes and failures. Japan has been successful in her achievement of industrial revolution. That is what Rostow meant in *The Stages of Ecomonic Development* by his use of Japan as an example of a successful take-off.[3] But one should not forget that this same Japan suffered a terrible crash in World War II. Japan had her second take-off in 1945. And now some people in Japan are beginning to wonder whether she must not be more cautious lest another crash befall her. Some foreign observers are expressing a similar fear. At the end of November 1970, John Oakes of the *New York Times* wrote an editorial entitled "Can Japan Outlive her Success?" He pointed out the negative side of having the world's fastest growing economy, namely, the fastest growing pollution rate in the world. The air in Tokyo is now more polluted than that in Los Angeles.

The one experience of the Japanese which may prevent a possible disaster is that of the nuclear bomb. Japan is the only nation in the world to have experienced a nuclear bombing. For this very reason, people in Japan may be more suspicious than others of the value of science and technology. On this point, I am sure that the Japanese are rather fortunate. A large number of scientists argue in Japan that three principles must be observed in the process of scientific inquiry. They are peace, open exposure of any problem under study, and democracy in the sense that scientific inquiry is for the people. At the same time one must remember that the urge for economic development in Japan is still very strong. It is conceivable that we might be able to maintain in the future the kind of technological civilization that we have had in the past, the strong bureaucracy combined with business interest, the constant borrowing of ideas from outsiders even while creating some within Japan itself. But the prospects for this happening do not look bright. It will be necessary instead to build up a new culture in which science, technology, and economy are included in a larger, more comprehensive system of values. That is the reason I started this essay with a brief sketch of the continental influences over the Japanese in the early period. There is no doubt that the culture of Japan during the last century had been dominated overwhelmingly by science, technology, and economy. Not only Japan but the whole world may be at the turning point of history. Though people are uncertain as to the direction of history, some are in search of a new culture in which the realm of science, technology, and economy will be limited and in which the values of man and nature will be more highly esteemed.

The cultural influences which we received many years ago from the Asian continent may contribute to the construction of such a new culture. On a smaller scale, many nations in the past have gone through difficult times of socio-cultural changes within their own national boundaries. The seventeenth-century civil war in England, the nineteenth-century civil war in the United States, and Japan's Meiji Restoration of the same century were examples of such difficult changes. On a much larger scale, the whole world today seems to be faced with difficult socio-cultural changes. It is under such circumstances that each nation must find ways to build a new culture. As I have pointed out repeatedly, the inertia of economic and technological innovation is very strong in Japan. However, the negative results of supporting the world's fastest growing economy have become more and more evident in recent years. The institutional rigidity which has been created by Japan's single-tracked objective will likely come into conflict with those who attempt to bring about new systems in the society and culture. It is too early to predict what will be the course of Japan during the 1970's. Let us hope that the values of man and nature shall be re-established in Japan, in cooperation with those who are working toward similar goals in other nations of the world. Our traditions may be different from the Chinese, the European, and the American. But let us hope once again that we will all share more respect for the value of man and nature, and that the world culture of tomorrow will be one in which our offspring will be able to thank us for our efforts.

NOTES

This paper was written when the author was a member of the Asahi Shimbun Press. He was appointed Japan's Minister of Education, Science, and Culture in December, 1974.

[1] Engelbert Kaempfer, *The History of Japan* (Glasgow, 1906).

[2] Michio Nagai, *Higher Education in Japan* (Tokyo, 1971).

[3] Walt W. Rostow, *The Stages of Economic Development* (New York, 1971; 2nd ed.).

VII.

Identity Problems of Black Japanese Youth

By Hiroshi Wagatsuma

What follows is a synopsis of a Japanese television script.

A young man walks along the street alone; he is tall and slim with light brown skin and curly hair. A black American stops his car at the curb. "Can you tell me how to get to... ?" The question comes in English. The young man looks at the American, shakes his head and keeps walking. "Why should I know English?" he says to himself in standard Japanese.

Nobuo is a mixed-blood young man, the child of a black American soldier and his Japanese woman, neither of whom he ever knew. He grew up in an orphanage. Now he works at a small factory in the Arakawa Ward of Tokyo, where the other young workers are kind and friendly to him. On a spring day, as is customary in Japan, the factory workers charter a bus and go to a resort for a vacation. On the bus Nobuo happens to sit next to a young girl, Masako. When they arrive at the inn, the maid notices Nobuo's foreign features while he is talking with his friends. "He speaks such excellent Japanese! How long has he been in Japan?"

After a merry dinner at the inn, the factory workers, young men and women, go out for a walk. Masako returns alone, ahead of her friends. She sees Nobuo alone in his room, listening to his radio. "Have you not gone out, Nobuo?" "No, I did not feel like it." "May I come in?" "If you like." Masako, feeling sorry for Nobuo, talks to him and invites him to dance with her to the radio music. Two inn maids come along and see them dancing. "That young man, he is a mixed-blood child I heard," one says to the other. "No wonder he dances so well." "He certainly does. But look at his skin. So uncanny. I can hardly come close to that kind..."

After they have returned to Tokyo, Masako invites Nobuo to her birthday dinner at home. Her parents become upset by her friendship with a "black one" *(kuronbo)* and admonish her harshly. Feeling angry at her parents and guilty about Nobuo, Masako quickly intensifies her attachment to Nobuo. She invites him for an outing to a beach. They sit on the sand and talk. "While at junior high school I disliked English classes. I was once pretty good at English and my classmates said it was natural because I've got American blood in me. I stopped working hard then. In the world history class the teacher skipped the whole section in textbook on American slavery. Later when I was absent, my friends told me, the teacher went back to that section and spent an hour discussing it." Masako asks Nobuo, "Is it really bad to be black?" Nobuo answers, "I do not really know. People call me *kokujin* (black person) and *kuronbo* (black one). I used to cry with anger when I was a child. Now I have become sick and tired of my own body, this black skin, this hair, everything. I am sick of it."

Masako, feeling sorry for Nobuo, cries. Looking at her, Nobuo is suddenly caught by passion. He tries to embrace her. Masako breaks away and runs into the pine woods. Nobuo runs after her and catches up. Both fall down on the sand. Passionately they find themselves in each others arms.

Masako comes home rather late. Her worried parents ask her questions and finally she tells them what has happened. Her parents panic. "What is the matter with you?" asks her father. "Don't you know he is one of those products of irresponsible liaisons between black soldiers and Japanese prostitutes? Nobody treats them like humans." Her mother cries and wants to know why her daughter "became interested in *kuronbo*, while there are hundreds of nice Japanese boys." The father shouts, "Let us forget about the whole thing! It is like a traffic accident. What happened happened. It should never happen again."

Told by her parents to leave her job at the factory and never see Nobuo again, Masako runs away from home and goes to him. They find an apartment and begin living together. Their landlady complains to her neighbor. "At first the wife came to me alone and wanted to rent an apartment. So I said OK. Then she brings her husband later and he turns out to be black. I did not know what to do. But I could not possibly tell them to go away only because he is black." The neighbor agrees, "That is true. You would not do things like that. It would be racial discrimination."

Nobuo is called to his employer's office. The employer says that although Masako's mother came to ask him to do something about Nobuo and Masako, he decided not to interfere with their life. "Taking a broad view of the matter, I think it is not a bad idea after all that the mixed-blood products of the war marry Japanese women." The employer says to Nobuo, "If you were an ordinary Japanese worker you would have already been fired for causing such trouble. However, you have no other place to go and the mixed-blood children are the responsibility of the entire Japanese nation. Therefore, I am overlooking your behavior. You should understand it and work very hard. If you keep working hard, people might eventually accept you."

Masako works at a store but their life is financially hard. Masako asks Nobuo to find a better paying job. Nobuo visits a large factory for a job interview. Among several candidates only Nobuo is turned down. Masako learns of a program for training mechanics at a public institute for vocational education. She tells Nobuo to take the training every evening. He leaves the apartment but spends his time in pinball machine parlors. Masako asks him when the examination will be. Nobuo, not knowing, tells her a lie.

One day Nobuo visits the orphanage at which he was raised. The cage in which his favorite canary bird was once kept is empty. He is told that somebody opened the cage and the bird flew away. Nobuo says loudly, "What a foolish bird! Out of a cage he won't be able to live." A small half-black girl comes to him, crying. A half-white girl tries to soothe her. She tells Nobuo that children on the street shouted at the black girl and threw stones at her. Nobuo says loudly again, "What a foolish girl! Out of the gate she won't be safe. How many times were we told not to walk out of the gate? It is not safe out there!" Nobuo goes into the kitchen and sees a black Japanese girl of his age. They grew up together and the girl decided to work for the orphanage. "I have decided to work here. This is the best place for us, after all," she says. "What about getting married? If you stay in a place like this, you will be an old maid, like our director," Nobuo asks her seriously. The girl laughs, "You are a fool, Nobuo! I never want to marry. How could I? You should know that."

Masako attends her friend's wedding party. Looking at the couple receiving blessings, Masako suddenly feels sad and lonely. She recalls that it is the day on which Nobuo said he would be taking the qualifying examination to become a mechanic. She calls the institute for vocational training. She is told that the examination was held a week ago; Nobuo never went to the class. Masako returns to the apartment and confronts Nobuo, who sulkily protests. "What is the use of my receiving a license? Nobody hires me, anyway." Masako disagrees. "How can you say that? We never know until we try and find out." "You keep saying, 'try and try,' Masako, but there are things which mean nothing to you and give me dreadful pain. Do you know why I never go to a public bath house?" "Then what do you want?" Masako asks him. "What is going to happen to us? Would you suggest that we keep living like this forever?" "Why not? I do not want anything else. There is no point in trying anything else."

Masako blames Nobuo and tells him to have more courage. "If people stare at you, why don't you stare back at them? Why do you have to be so weak?" "It is easy for you to say it, Masako, but don't forget, it is not you but I who is black!" Nobuo suddenly leaves the room. He does not return home for days. A neighbor tells Masako that he saw a black man singing in a coffee-shop. She goes to the shop. Nobuo is imitating a black American, singing Japanese songs with a foreign accent. Masako asks him to come home. "Why do you have to imitate a foreigner? You sound silly, Nobuo." "It is easier to make money when I decide to be a black man. I shout, 'I am Japanese! I am Japanese!' and nobody listens. I imitate a *kuronbo* and act like one and I get paid for that! This is much better." Masako is not convinced. "Because you talk like that people feel contemptuous toward black people and people call you a prostitute's child. You are a coward. Why can't you be stronger?" Nobuo wants to be left alone. "I need no more pity from you, Masako. You must surely feel fine pitying me. We are through. If you feel your body has become dirty by sleeping with a black one like myself, you have my sincere apology!"

Nobuo and Masako sit on the wharf. The ship has already sailed. Nobuo says calmly, "Now I think it was I who was the most prejudiced and contemptuous toward the Negroes, more than anybody else in all Japan." What are they going to do? They have no concrete plan as yet, but they decide that Nobuo will go back to the factory and ask the boss to rehire him. They will go back to the apartment and live together again. "I am going to have a baby," says Masako. "It will be a really black baby. Is it OK with you?" Nobuo says, "Of course," and they begin walking away.

This television drama, "Harvest After Twenty Years," was written by Hirokazu Fuse, a well-known scenario writer, and broadcast on November 27, 1965. It was twenty years after the end of World War II and the beginning of the American Occupation of Japan. The "harvest" was the children born between American soldiers and their Japanese women. The part of Nobuo was played by a young black Japanese man for whom the drama became a successful start to a career as an entertainer-actor. Cheaply saccharine as the plot might sound, the drama accurately depicts Japanese prejudice and discrimination against mixed-blood children, particularly those with black parentage. Perhaps the drama should be criticized for its ending which is too unrealistic: one can hardly expect a happy ending for these unfortunate youths in a highly homogeneous and prejudiced society.

This essay illustrates attitudes which are antithetical to what the Japanese would have believed of themselves. Although they would claim to be free from prejudice, the numerous examples both in the television script and in the remainder of this article provide evidence that indeed they are prejudiced against blacks in general and against black Japanese in particular.

No one knows precisely how many of these "offspring of the Occupation" and those of the Korean War are in Japan now.[1] A recent estimate is that there are between 20,000 and 25,000 of whom probably one-sixth are black Japanese.[2] Over a thousand orphans of mixed parentage are believed to have been adopted into American families. Most of these children have grown up exposed to various forms of discrimination. They are stigmatized in more ways than one; most of them are illegitimate (which often prevents them from getting jobs and entering higher schools), and they are referred to as the "children of prostitutes." Whether or not their mothers actually were street walkers makes little difference in the mind of the average Japanese; preferring a foreign victor to a Japanese man was no better than prostitution.

Most importantly, they are physically different. As we pointed out elsewhere, the Japanese are often ambivalent toward the physical features of Caucasians and such ambivalence is often accompanied by conscious and semiconscious sexual fantasies.[3] Although they are ambivalent toward the Caucasian physical characteristics, the Japanese are unequivocally and unanimously negative toward the negroid features of black Americans and Africans. This negative feeling is frequently justified as a physiological reaction, that one's reasoning cannot control. Many Japanese associate Negroes with "animality" and this association is made in a number of contemporary novels written by noted Japanese authors. Many Japanese associate Negroes with the primitive tribes in the African jungle. This image leads to a widely held notion that contemporary black people, whose ancestors once danced to the sound of drums, inherently possess an excellent sense of rhythm and are, therefore, likely to be successful in musical careers.

Also, Japanese share with many Southern white Americans the notion that Negroes are sexually indefatigable. Such a notion is mentioned by a contemporary author, Ariyoshi, in her novel *Hishoku,* the story of a Japanese woman married to a black American.

> It is a popular opinion that Negroes are sexually stronger than whites and yellows. It was said that for this reason, those women who have married Negroes gradually become feeble-minded.[4]

Morishige, a well-known actor, seems to believe this when he offers his explanation why white American parents are opposed to having Negro boys attend the same school as their daughters.

> The parents know that if an adolescent girl once experiences a sexual relationship with a black boy, it almost always becomes difficult for her to free herself from the black boy. Blacks may not be particularly talented in sexual techniques, but they are certainly superior to whites in their sexual strength.[5]

Kajiyama, a popular novel writer, in his essay on human sexuality, does not fail to mention black sexuality.

Every evening at the apartment Masako cooks a meal for two, hoping Nobuo will return. He returns home occasionally and they go to bed, but without the love or understanding that used to bind them together. Masako's mother visits her daughter at the store where she works. The mother is worried and sad. Masako pretends that everything is fine and that she is happy. The mother offers her daughter some money. Masako refuses to accept it. "I do not deserve it, mother," she says. "After all, I have rebelled against my parents and married a *kuronbo*." The mother leaves. Masako suddenly feels sick and realizes that she is pregnant.

A letter comes to Nobuo from the orphanage telling him to see the director: an American family in California is willing to adopt him. Nobuo wants to go abroad. Masako tells him that she is pregnant. "What are you going to do about it, Masako?" Nobuo asks her. "I do not know," Masako answers. "Are you sure that you don't know? You must know what to do, Masako. Or do you want me to tell you what you already know? OK. Get rid of it!'' Masako murmers weakly, ''We are not good for each other any longer.''

Masako returns to her parents and tells them that everything is over. It was a terrible mistake. Her mother is happy that her daughter has come back to her. ''Let us forget about everything and start afresh,'' she says. Her father is also gentle to his broken-hearted daughter. Nobuo receives a passport and visa and stays at the orphanage until the day of his departure. Masako is taken to the hospital for an abortion but while waiting for the operation she hears the cry of a new-born baby. She runs out of the hospital without receiving the operation.

At the Yokohama pier, the orphanage staff and the mixed-blood children are singing hymns around Nobuo who is ready to leave. In the distance Masako tearfully watches them. Nobuo notices her and runs toward her. She runs away. Nobuo catches her and they find themselves again in each other's arms.

> Racially, blacks have the best one...the Japanese prostitutes told me that a white man's is soft, even though it is long, and a Japanese is hard, although short. A Negro's is long and hard. Once a woman experiences a long and hard black sword deep in herself, she loses interest in any other race.[6]

A short novel, describing the student unrest at the San Francisco State University, presents black students as capable of causing orgasms in women by inserting themselves deeply but without moving.[7]

Many Japanese believe that foreigners, e.g., Caucasians and particularly Negroes, have a strong body odor that is totally lacking in the Japanese. There is a notion held among the Japanese that close physical contact, and certainly sexual contact, with whites and especially with blacks, may leave its trace on a Japanese in the form of real or imagined body odor. In a novel the Japanese mother of a mixed-blood girl fathered by a black American soldier says,

> Would it be possible that my body acquired and retains the body odor of this girl's father? Do I display some sort of trace of my life with a Negro man? Something has permeated my body, and those people (Negroes) can sense that something as their own....[8]

Negative feelings among the Japanese toward black physical features are echoed in the results of some opinion surveys. In actuality, a number of black Americans, particularly the students who come in contact with Japanese, have experienced prejudice and discrimination in one way or another.[9]

The Japanese tend to feel the same ambivalence toward the Japanese children of white American fathers that they feel toward Caucasian physical features in general. However, they extend their unequivocally negative feelings toward African and American Negroes to the Japanese children of black American fathers. As if reflecting the Japanese ambivalence toward Caucasians, many children of white American fathers show a basic ambivalence toward themselves.

However, the Japanese children of black American fathers have strongly negative feelings about themselves and often express self-hatred.

For a small child of a black American man and a Japanese woman, the painful self- discovery, the realization that he or she is different from the Japanese around him, is often forced upon him by the ruthless comments of others. In *Hishoku,* the novel mentioned above, when the heroine takes her daughter to downtown Tokyo people around them loudly voice their reactions to her negro blooded child.

> "Look, the child of a *kuronbo.*"
> "Indeed, it is black, even when it is young."
> "She looks like a rubber doll!"
> "She must have taken only after her father. So black! Poor thing!"[10]

Quotations from other sources echo these reactions.

> As a small child, she (a black Japanese girl) was called *ainoko* (mixed blood), *kuronbo*, and *Indojin* (Indian). At school, her classmates refused to lend her a pencil, because "it will become black in the hand of a black girl."[11]

Hirano, a writer who has taken care of a large number of mixed-blood children, writes about one girl he has known.

> Kayo, a black Japanese girl, went to a nearby public school with other children of her orphanage. At the first physical examination at school she took off her dress and suddenly noticed that all the eyes of the parents visiting the school were glued to her body. She felt as if she were electrocuted and her face became frozen. Almost intuitively she felt that all those adults who were staring at her body did not like it. She overheard them whispering, 'Look at the palm and sole of the *kuronbo!* How stragely white they are!'[12]

In her autobiography, Keiko Ozeki, an orphan of a black American man and his Japanese mistress, adopted into a Japanese family, recalls that the neighborhood children would say to her,

> "Hey, you, *kuronbo.* Don't come closer to me. You are so dirty!"
> "Hey, Keiko. You piss here. Let us see if your urine is black."[13]

All the mixed-blood boys and girls interviewed reported some experiences of being called *kuronbo* or *kuro-chan* (both pejorative) or commented on their skin color and hair quality.

They also discover for themselves that they are different when they become aware of their physical characteristics, particularly their skin color. Which of the two happens first, the definition of their black identity by others, or the self-discovery of their physical characteristics, seems to depend on individual circumstances, However, many remember them happening more or less at the same time. A child with a dark skin and kinky hair growing up in an orphanage comes to notice a number of children with similar features. The child also notices the physical features of the children with white skin. It also sees those of the Japanese staff members. Then it wonders why there are these differences in physical characteristics and why its skin is so dark. When adopted by a Japanese couple, or raised by its maternal grandparents, such a child compares its skin color with that of its adopting parents or grandparents. This happened to Keiko Ozeki, the writer of the above mentioned autobiography. As a sixth grader, Keiko decided to ask her mother the question that she had long wanted to ask. Probably what she really wanted to know was the truth about her birth: why she alone was a mixed-blood child, while her parents were ordinary Japanese ("Am I really your child?")?

> One day, arriving home from school, I went to my mother and stood beside her while she was doing laundry near the outside well. I asked her, "Mother, why is my body black?" She stopped her hands, briefly glanced at me and said, "I ate too much *gobo* (burdocks) and *hijiki* (black sea weeds) while you were inside me." I asked my mother the same question several times. Her answer was always the same. She ate too much *gobo* and *hijiki* (both very common foods in Japan). Two other reasons were added later. "Those babies born during the day time have fair skin. Those born at midnight have dark skin. Keiko was born at midnight." "Keiko was exposed to too much sunshine while a small child and eternally sun-tanned." I had never learned such things at school but as my mother looked so annoyed and bothered by my question, I eventually stopped asking.[14]

Those youngsters with dark skin all tried to change their skin color. Keiko was no exception.

> My father had a cake of American soap and cherished it. He said it was very effective in cleaning his hands. I took it out secretly from his shelf one day and washed my body again and again, until the cake became a tiny piece. It was not effective at all. I even rubbed my face with *karuishi* (pumice stone—used on heels in Japan) until my face began bleeding....[15]

Many of them voiced the wish that they had not been born. Such a wish was often accompanied by expressions of anger toward their parents who not only gave them birth but often deserted them. An inmate of a correctional institution, discussing his feelings about his life, said,

> If I were not born, I would not have heard all these nasty comments. It is all my mother's fault. She could have chosen somebody other than *kuronbo*.

When asked whom she wanted to marry, a girl with a dark skin answered,

> I do not want to marry anybody. How could I? My mother made the mistake of giving me birth and I have to suffer. I do not want to make the same stupid mistake. I will not let my child suffer the same way.

Children in stable families of black American fathers and Japanese mothers must feel differently toward their parents. It so happened that none of the youngsters interviewed came from such families. Some of them remembered their fathers—black soldiers who stayed in their life only for a short period and slipped away forever. The children hate these figures in their memory. They hate the black Americans in general when they see them on the street. *"Kuronbo* are ugly," they say. "Because of them I have to suffer like this. I wish they never existed!"

A black Japanese deliquent boy in the Juvenile Classification Center in Kobe once managed to respond to ten Rorschach cards without ever using the word "black" (*kuroi*). Another black Japanese boy, whose only living relative was his younger sister, also half-black, talked about how close he was to his sister. It was almost as if these two unfortunate children were huddling together, protecting each other against a cold, rejecting, and hostile world. And yet, he would never go out with his sister because "she looks just like a real *kuronbo* and I do not want to be seen with her. People would think I am a *kuronbo* too!" (He seemed to think that his negroid features were so subtle that he could pass as an ordinary Japanese.)

Keiko Ozeki was deserted by her own mother and adopted by a Japanese couple. When she was fifteen years old her adoptive mother died and her foster father remarried. Keiko began quarreling with the father and, after a serious quarrel one day, she left home. Recalling that her real mother was living in Kyushu, she looked for and finally found her. At eighteen, Keiko met her mother, now married to a Japanese man.

I met my mother for the first time since I was born. No tears came out of my eyes. She was not excited either. I was surprised to see her that way. Doesn't this person care for me? Isn't she pleased to see her real daughter after eighteen years? Doesn't she feel guilty about having deserted her own child? Such questions flashed through my mind. I wished to hear her say, "Keiko, it must have been very painful. Forgive me." Instead, the meeting was almost like an encounter of total strangers. My own brother and sister had no kinky hair. They had white skin. For this simple reason I knew they were not my brother and sister. She was not my mother either. She was a stranger. I only 'borrowed' her womb.

Suddenly my mother said and laughed, "It was a mistake of youth." How could she dare to say such a thing? Why did she then give me birth? Who am I, the baby resulted from the mistake of youth? If it was a mistake, why did she not have an abortion?

Mother, why did you give me birth? Why did you not lose me by abortion? Once you gave me birth, then I am your child, am I not? Why did you not raise me with your own hands? No matter how poor we might have become, I wished that I was raised by my own mother. You deserted me and married another man and made a happy home. I no longer think you are my mother. Perhaps I should never have met you. I would have been happier.

The man who is my father, although I will never call him my father, you, as a member of an occupation army, took advantage of a Japanese woman. You simply had fun, without any sense of guilt. You were never serious. You played around and went back home. You think nothing of it now. You never thought of your own child who lives in Japan. You are no human. You are a beast!

Neither of our parents are human and yet, we, the mixed-blood children, are human and we are Japanese. At least I am Japanese. I was born and raised in Japan, eating rice.[16]

Ozeki's autobiography was entitled, *Keiko, a Japanese.* Repeatedly she writes that she is a Japanese and she blames Japanese for not accepting her as such.

I like Japan because I am a Japanese. I was born in Japan, dressed as a Japanese, learned Japanese geography and history. I have eaten rice and drunk tea. I wish I could be married to a Japanese man and have a Japanese home. I like Japan better than any other country. I love this country and yet nobody regards me as a Japanese. Nothing hurts me more. Nothing makes me madder.

My skin is darker than yours, indeed. My hair is kinky and my face looks different. But why do you have to be concerned with the physical appearance? There are tall people. There are short people. There are dark-skinned persons. There are fair-skinned persons. What difference does it make? My heart is no different from yours. Blood of the Japanese runs through my body. I wish I could cut myself open and show you inside myself to convince you that I am Japanese, pure and simple.[17]

And yet Keiko, a Japanese, married a black American.

I always wanted to get married like an ordinary girl to an ordinary Japanese. I always knew that it was not possible for me. That's why I told myself that I would never marry....I hate my own black skin. I wish I could peel my skin off my body with a sharp knife....

Although I am black myself, I always feel disgusted whenever I see a black person (*kokujin*) on the streets, probably because I hate my own father. A black person is a symbol of unhappiness. And yet, now, the same black person wanted to marry me....

I never liked the United States. Although it was called the country of freedom, the white people were discriminating against the blacks. The Americans took the trouble of coming all the way to Vietnam to kill. I never liked Americans, neither whites nor blacks. I did not know what I should do....

Then I thought of my own child. I would have a child of my own if I ever marry. My baby will be black, black like myself. It will be called *kuronbo* and will be laughed at as I always was in Japan. That is what will happen to my own baby if it were to be born in Japan. It is a sad fact that my baby will not be happy here in Japan, in my own country where I am not accepted....and my own child will blame me, like I blamed my own mother. If I marry a black American man and give birth to my child in the United States, the child will grow up among people of the same skin color. It will be much better than to be a black child among the Japanese. For the sake of my own child, I should leave Japan, the country which I love and yet which never really accepted me.[18]

Keiko tried to convince other Japanese that she was Japanese, without much success. However, many mixed-blood youngsters, both whites and blacks, do not feel that they are fully Japanese. Kazuko Kitayama, a half-black Japanese singer of Negro spirituals who uses the stage name Catherine Mine, once voiced her feelings about herself,

I cannot feel that I am fully Japanese. I cannot feel I am an American either. I try very hard to convince myself that I am Japanese and yet I cannot feel that I am fully Japanese.

Kazuko also said that marriage was an impossibility for her.

Suppose I meet a young man and we both agree to marry. Even when it is all right with us two, there are many other people around us, a grandmother, a grandfather, mother, uncle and others. Things can be quite sticky with the *Japanese*, you know. (She said the word "Japanese" as if she were a foreigner talking about the Japanese.) I think marriage is an impossibility for me.

Marriage was not an impossibility for Kazuko, after all. She too married a black American and moved to the United States. However, how many girls could have done the same, and what about the boys?

In recent years, because of their "exotic" looks and/or singing and dancing talents, a number of children of white American fathers and Japanese mothers, particularly girls, have been drawn into the limelight through appearances on stage and screen. Indeed, in 1966 and 1967 there was a so-called "mixed-blood boom" (*konketsuji bumu*) in the world of show business and fashion modeling. Weekly magazines published photographs of these "talents" of mixed-parentage and gossip columns were written about them. Altogether, however, such celebrities are only a handful. Notwithstanding the exotic careers enjoyed by the "elite", a great many youngsters, particularly those of Negro parentage, are harassed by the racial prejudice and social discrimination of the Japanese people at large. Most of them grew up in poverty, received minimal education, and, even in the absence of discrimination, would be ill-prepared for lucrative employment. Many grew up without much attention since their mothers worked, rejected or even deserted them. Added to these early experiences of deprivation was the pain and humiliation of being laughed at, stoned, or beaten by the neighborhood children. They are often emotionally insecure, immature, dependent, passive, or even apathetic, and lack persistence or harbor hatred.

It was mentioned before that the Japanese attitude toward Caucasian physical features is basically ambivalent. Many girls with white parentage said, when interviewed, that they were aware that they looked physically attractive to the Japanese eyes. Some of them, expressing their anger toward the discriminatory attitudes of the Japanese, pointed out the popularity of plastic surgery among young Japanese, especially to alter eye folds and to build up the bridge of the nose and the Japanese women's attempts to increase the actual or apparent size of their breasts by surgery or by padding. They said rather proudly that fortunately they "did not have to go through all this nonsense," seemingly trying to feel superior to the Japanese at least in this regard. Several white Japanese boys declared that they had "no difficulty finding girl friends to go to bed with." Upon further inquiry, however, those "girl friends" turned out to be mostly bar hostesses and their relationships tended to be brief and superficial.

The children of white American fathers and Japanese mothers often become the object of sexual curiosity among the Japanese. In their minds a chain association seems to form in the following way: white men are sexually more passionate and vigorous than the Japanese; these children of mixed-parentage must have inherited that quality from their white fathers; their Japanese mothers must have been unusual women as they preferred and could cope with sexually powerful white men; these children of mixed parentage must have inherited that quality from their mothers; *ergo*, they are sexually precocious, energetic, and enjoyable. The easiest form of employment a white mixed girl can secure is a position as a bar or cabaret hostess. Often she enjoys better wages than her purely Japanese counterpart.

One should emphasize, however, that the black Japanese boys and girls do not have even that much of an ego booster and that much of an opportunity for popularity. It is true that a very small number of young Japanese men and women with dark skin have been successful in the entertainment world but their number is insignificant. Although we do not know the exact number of these youngsters, neither do we know how they are living today. We are fairly certain about one thing: they could not possibly be leading very happy lives.

NOTES

No systematic, empirical research has been done on the Japanese children of mixed parentage. This essay is based upon a series of informal interviews and secondary materials the writer collected in Japan in 1966 and 1967. Admittedly, this essay is essentially impressionistic and allows in no way for generalization.

[1] Mixed-blood children are called in Japanese either *konketsuji* (mixed-blood child) or colloquially *ai-no-ko* (a child of mixture). The mixed-blood children themselves dislike the word *ai-no-ko*, as they feel it is derogatory. In the past another word, *haro-no-ko* (a child of hello) was used, which meant a child of an American GI. Recently the new word, *hahu* (Japanese pronunciation of an English word "half") has been used. The mixed-bloods prefer to call themselves *hahu*. Black Japanese are often called *kuronbo* (a black one) which is definitely derogatory, or *indojin* (Indian). Collectively, the mixed-blood children of Japanese women and American soldiers were referred to as *Amerika no otoshigo* (illegitimate children of the U.S.A.), *senso no moshigo* (children sent by the war), *kokusai koji* (international orphans), *unmei no ko* (children of fate). See Setsuko Takahashi, *Konketsuji* Mixed-Blood Children (Tokyo, 1952).

[2] Mainichi News, *Sengo no Konketsuji* (Mixed-Blood Children of Post-War Japan), (January 16, 1968).

[3] Hiroshi Wagatsuma, "The Social Perception of Skin Color in Japan," *Daedalus,* XCVI (1967), 407-443; "Some Problems of Interracial Marriage for the Japanese" in Lawrence E. Abt and Irving R. Stuart (eds.), *Interracial Marriage* (New York, 1972), Ch. 6; "Mixed-Blood Children in Japan," paper presented at the International Conference on Ethnic Relations in Asian Countries (Buffalo, 1972).

[4] Sawako Ariyoshi, *Hishoku* (Not Color) (Tokyo, 1964), 204.

[5] Hisaya Morishige, "Kokushoku kakumei" (Black Revolution), *Neingen no Kagaku* (Humanistic Science), I (1963), 34-43.

[6]Toshiyuki Kajiyama, *Ningen no Tanken—Sei no Hikyo o Hakkutsu Suru* (Adventure into Human Nature: Discovery of the Secrets of Sex) (Tokyo, 1969), 147.

[7] Masamoto Natsubori, "Sanhuranshisuko no haiboku" (Defeat in San Francisco), *Shosetsu Shincho* (October, 1953), 244-246.

[8] Ryuko Yasaki, "Me naki uo" (Fish Without Eyes) *Bungei Shunju* (August, 1966), 230-275.

⁹ Wagatsuma, "Mixed-Blood Children in Japan."

¹⁰ Ariyoshi, *Hishoku.*

¹¹ Tokyo Shinbun, "Yatto mitsuketa kofuku" (Happiness Finally Found) (Tokyo, 1966).

¹² Imao Hirano, *Nokosareta Remi Tachi* (Remi, Left Behind) (Tokyo, 1964), 65.

¹³ Keiko Ozeki, *Nipponjin Keiko: Aru Konketsu Shojo no Shuki* (Keiko, a Japanese: Autobiography of a Mixed-Blood Girl) (Tokyo, 1967), 15.

¹⁴ Ibid., 40-41.

¹⁵ Ibid., 42.

¹⁶ Ibid., 110-121.

¹⁷ Ibid., 190-192.

¹⁸ Ibid., 193-196. This remarkably revealing autobiography ends when the author moves with her fiance to California in 1966. Whether she has since overcome her self-hatred and negative feelings about the blacks while exposed to the constant efforts of the American blacks to restore their own pride in being black, we do not know.

VIII.

Being Chinese-American: The Reshaping of Identity and Relationships of One Generation

By Ai-Li Chin

What does it mean to be Chinese? To me, it is having a Chinese name and a Chinese face, or sometimes putting on a Chinese dress, or speaking Mandarin, my native Shanghai dialect, or haltingly, the Cantonese of my husband's family. It is a preference for home-style Chinese food. It means slipping naturally into a certain manner of greeting at a Chinese gathering, of showing deference and modesty, or the etiquette of *k'o-ch'i,* politeness. Being Chinese is experiencing pride for ancient Chinese art, an awareness of the special beauty of classical Chinese poetry, an admiring respect for the colossal Chinese civilization of the past. It is feelings of shame, hurt, and indignation over so much that has happened to China and in China since those distant days of greatness, yet also of exhilaration and amazement over what is happening in China now, of identification with China's new power and prestige, and with her suffering from the pain of natural and self-inflicted blows.

I came to this country from China more than thirty years ago, a young girl college-bound, and have remained here ever since, more and more deeply rooted in family and work. Yet, I feel kin to anyone of Chinese name or ancestry who does something noteworthy; I believe that the Chinese share a special wisdom that puts family unity over personal interest and requires elders to be treated with respect; and I feel regret over failure to live up to these demands. I am saddened that I have shifted allegiance from my native tongue to an adopted language and have allowed my Chinese to atrophy through neglect. I still feel a romantic or nostalgic attachment to the land of China and to remembered moments of my growing up there. All this adds to feeling not quite at ease in American society and to knowing that one's life is bound up somehow with the fate of all who are Chinese in America and, by effortless extension, with that of Chinese everywhere.

To others, being Chinese can mean all these and many other feelings in different combinations. The varieties of identity are all but innumerable, for among the 432,000 Chinese in America, there are those who came only recently, and those whose fathers or grandfathers came fifty, sixty, or even a hundred years ago. To the older, Cantonese-speaking immigrants, being Chinese still means holding on to the language, customs, and institutions of the established overseas Chinese communities and of confining their work and social life largely within these limits. To their American-born children and grandchildren, now ranging from second to sixth generations on the West Coast, it has meant a slow, often painful liberation from the conservatism of their elders and a gradual acceptance into American society. And in the last few years, some adults of this group have returned to the Chinatowns to take up leadership in new and urgently needed action programs. To American-born youth of Cantonese origin today, it means for the first time a new and wider range of identity choices. At one extreme are those who feel more or less integrated into American society, merging with non-Chinese in work and play. At the other, although more engaged in American social processes than were previous generations, are those who are forging a new Chinese-American or Asian-American identity, including some radical politics and militant tactics; but mostly this group is settling down to community activism, pitting itself from time to time against the American establishment, Chinatown power structure, and occasionally even against the liberal gradualists among their American-born parents.

The age-groupings and generations-in-America of the Cantonese families cut across each other to produce a mixed pattern, blurring the lines between groups. The reason has been the continued arrival of new immigrants, first in trickles, then in small batches of war-brides and other special groups during and after World War II, and finally the 20,000 or so a year since enactment of the new Immigration Law of 1965.

Still other immigrants began their lives in the United States only after the Communist party came to power in China in 1949, followed by the breaking of Sino-American relations. These include the original 5,000 or so students and scholars who could not return to their homeland because of the political split. They were joined during the 1950s and 1960s by more students, first a few hundred a year, and later a few thousand. A very large proportion of them have chosen to stay here. Their pattern of settlement, employment, and adjustment differs considerably from both the very new and the older Cantonese immigrants. The student immigrants, along with their American-born children, have formed a new Mandarin- or Shanghai-speaking Chinese group of about 50,000. There are clusters of such families in Ann Arbor, Detroit, and Chicago, in Cleveland and Pittsburgh, in Houston and Berkeley, as well as the larger groups in Boston, New York, and Washington, and around each major university.

For every Chinese in America, physical differences from non-Chinese make him stand out, locating him instantly at the margins where he lives. They signal all of the ways in which he may be different from the majority around him and evoke responses based not only on what he is or feels himself to be but also on his group's customs, manners, and morals, and on what others imagine that group identity to be. Yet, his life and his place in American society have been changing as part of the massive, wrenching transformation that has been taking place in patterns of racial and ethnic relations in America since World War II.

This transformation has resulted from the pressure of such world events as the end of Western empire and white supremacy in Asia and Africa, and from slower processes long at work inside American life itself. The many complex results of these processes have appeared most dramatically in the collapse of the previous patterns of American race relations, mainly between black and white, in the liquidation of many forms of legal racial discrimination, and in the emergence of an aggressive movement of American blacks to assert their worth and rights in white society. But the changes have also come in the status of members of other racial and ethnic minorities who had been denied their equal rights as citizens and been subjected to exclusion, discrimination, and in many cases bigotry carried to the point of violence. At a distinctly hastening pace through the 1950s and 1960s, for Negroes, Jews, Mexican-Americans, for Japanese-Americans, Chinese-Americans, and other minority groups, the old rules-of-the-game began to fall away. The old perceptions-of-others and perceptions-of-self began more slowly and with much greater difficulty to fall away in their turn. We now enter a period of confusion and reorientation in which groups are trying to find new self-definitions even as the society as a whole struggles to change itself.

In all of this, the immigrant Chinese and Chinese-Americans have shared in their own ways. This essay provides a glimpse of one small subgroup within the Chinese population as they go through this experience. I shall concentrate on describing the shaping of a Chinese-American identity among a parent generation in the Mandarin- and Shanghai-speaking group, basing my observations on interviews and discussions and my own experience as a member of this subgroup who came as students in the 1940s and 1950s and who are now in their mature years. Also, its distinct history and unique experience lend a measure of homogeneity to the group's identity, a major consideration in a short presentation. These reasons alone, and not the relative importance of this subgroup vis-a-vis any other, dictate the choice and boundaries of this essay.

"We are a dying breed..."

"What, in a quick first word, does it mean to you to be Chinese in the United States?" This question was put one evening in New York City to a dozen China-born, Americanized Chinese, all of them successful, some even distinguished, in their professions. They had come together at a dinner meeting to answer questions about themselves, and their first answers predictably skimmed the nearest surface. "Challenging," said an author and educator. "Creative," said a geography professor. "Adventurous," said his wife. More about both their individual successes and their lives in America came through in other answers: "It means to be popular," said a professor. "Enjoying an advantage," said a woman advertising executive. "Enjoying favorable discrimination," said a successful editor, also a woman. A professor of physics said that his life had been "enriched" and he did not mean only financially; another said that he had had to "try harder" but added that this had also meant "more fun."

Some responses cut a slice deeper. "It has meant becoming more and more Americanized," came one answer, but another: "It has made me turn more toward being Chinese." This revealed briefly a feeling common to almost all in this group: some sense of irretrievable loss of personal connection to a culture and a tradition. But they were all still "Chinese" enough to flit quickly past this dark spot and to convey, one after another, a solid sense of feeling quite settled in the United States or of expecting their children to be permanent members of American society. "This is home. Balancing the good and the bad, I am happy."

Much has happened to these and other members of this subgroup of Chinese. They lived their childhood in China during some of that country's most agonizing years of war and invasion. They were part of the elite selected to study abroad, became student refugees, and eventually found themselves reluctant immigrants. Or they fled China under the spurs of drastic political and social change and made their own way, by various routes, to America, where they began new lives. They all left behind the chaotic pieces of a country already shattered by Japan's invasion and soon to be even more shattered by civil war and revolution.

In the early 1950s, the uprooted students strongly shared the Cantonese "sojourner's" feeling—that of a stranger unsure of his welcome. Cut off from their families, their student visas expired, and with no other support in sight, not a few took on sojourner jobs, as dishwashers, for example, in Chinese restaurants. But liberalized legislation in the 1950s regularized their status as immigrants, and opportunities began to open to them in the American professional and industrial worlds. It was their good fortune to embark on their new lives precisely when American society itself was entering an era of unprecedented change. These Chinese emigres came to their American thresholds just as the shift in the color/race line occurred, slowly for the blacks, but—ironically, perhaps—more swiftly for others, especially the Chinese and Japanese, who were readier to seize the new chances offered, and for whom a readier acceptance was at hand. Thus, the Chinese grasped these opportunities and moved on to increasing levels of professional achievement while slowly sinking new roots, acquiring homes, raising families, and gradually accepting the fact that they had, as it turned out, come to America to stay.

Now, these Chinese look back on their experiences for the most part with a satisfaction qualified with certain misgivings. On the whole, most Chinese of this description have more reason to be glad of the advantages that they have enjoyed than resentful of any obstacles that they may have met along the way. Yet, they all reflect on what they have left behind, the past they have lost, the cost of the total and totally unforeseen transformations of their lives. What, some begin to ask themselves now, has become of their Chineseness as they have survived and competed as new Americans and proved their worth as scientists, engineers, and professors? What has come of their original destiny as elite carriers of a long tradition and how do they now relate to it? Most of all, what do they want for and of their children? How do they feel about their children who are merging socially and culturally—if not yet biologically—with the dominant American society? Do they want their children to retain something more than the physical marks of their origins? If so, which features, expressed how, and communicated by what means? Or must they accept the blunt and sombre statements of one adult that evening: "Let's face it. We are a dying breed."

"Americans are very friendly, but..."

The American experience of this tiny Chinese minority adds up to a success story, but like all minority struggles during these decades, it has its less successful past to overcome and some persisting limits. These Chinese know little, and that, only indirectly, of the brutal and often bloody history of American prejudice against earlier Chinese immigrants. As student refugees, they did have trouble finding housing and jobs. Nearly everyone whom I interviewed could recount some unpleasant episodes, most of them long past but some persisting in the hostile, condescending, stupid stereotypes which they encounter even now. But added up, they never seemed very important, very oppressive, or very damaging. The usual reaction was to shrug them off as part of the cost of living in an alien society. "We just laugh and forget about it," said one woman. "We treat it as a joke," added another. "They just don't know any better."

For the past two decades, these Chinese have been moving far into the academic world, and into the engineering, scientific, and medical professions, but barely into law, politics, or the big corporations, partly because of opportunities and partly because of inclination. But barriers are still sensed. "It is still hard for Chinese to move into some jobs in big companies," said one. "They don't often want a Chinese to be in an administrative job over others." "There are very few Chinese in executive positions." The evidence cited today, however, is less of gross discrimination than of subtler restrictions. In the professional environments in which they work, most have come to feel free, confident, and more or less equal to all others. Most believe that they now neither enjoy special advantages nor suffer from serious handicaps.

However, these students-turned-immigrants generally feel much less secure in their social settings. A certain sense of being different persists, a certain ambiguity intrudes into many of their personal relationships with other Americans. Some mix almost exclusively with other Chinese; a few associate mainly with non-Chinese. Between is the larger middle group which lives a double social life. Nearly everyone mentions the recurring reminders from their American friends that they are Chinese, in some way different and therefore not quite part of the common scene. Probably the most common has to do with Chinese food. As one professor said:

> In the middle of a professional meeting, someone will suddenly ask me, "Where is a good Chinese restaurant?" I will be reminded by this that he is thinking of me not as a fellow-scientist but as a Chinese who is supposed to know where the good restaurants are, even though we are both in another city far from home.

Another common experience, somewhat more flattering, is the assumption that one is an expert on all things Chinese—history, literature, art, geography, current affairs. Precisely because he is a little uncertain of himself in the American setting, the China-born Chinese will sometimes try to make the most of his unique background and his "expert" knowledge about such a special subject of interest to his American friends. But on the whole, this experience, shared by virtually all, is less painful than irritating or embarrassing. Since most Chinese do think "Chinese" *is* special in a positive way, the feeling is at least a mixed one.

But just beyond lies the feeling, also quite common among this group, that they do not quite belong, do not feel natural or comfortable in non-Chinese company. They participate in the usual social gatherings that go with their status—departmental or office parties, cocktail parties, and, less frequent, exchanges of dinner parties—but the China-born Chinese who takes part in this socializing is much more likely to feel "out" than "in,"no matter how well acculturated or adjusted he may appear to be.

This sense of not quite belonging does not often come from feeling unwelcome or unaccepted. Of all the Chinese in this country, this particular group has experienced least the pain of social or personal exclusion because of race or color. Had they tried in the 1950s to join certain clubs or circles, they would probably have suffered rebuffs, but few had wanted to. Now they are much more likely to remark that "most of the time most people are pretty nice," or "Americans are very friendly."

In the back of their minds, however, lies a private world, a social and emotional sanctuary. Herein exists the magnetic pull of what sociologists call the primary group, the mystique of some ultimate psychological homeland where one "really belongs." And so, when they want to relax without having to work consciously at fitting in with the group, they seek out their own. They take turns hosting Chinese dinners for each other, where they can talk without reserve about their own children and those of other Chinese families, and perhaps reminisce about this place or that person of their school days in China. A scientist in a technical institute in Troy, New York said: "If I want to relax and indulge in nonsense talk, I find it easier with Chinese. It's kind of easier to entertain Chinese without strenuous thinking." And an engineering professor shared his random thoughts:

> Our social contacts are still within the Chinese circle. It's hard to describe this. Our kids only know American friends, so we know their parents. I know colleagues at work too, but when we have social functions at home for Americans they are still the official kind. The casual things are done with Chinese. Occasionally we give a party for our neighbors.

> When old friends get together, we chat along about familiar traditions, etc., as we have common backgrounds. That's the only reason we still prefer to come together. I still find that I act a little differently when I'm with them. We don't have the same sense of humor as Americans. When Americans tell a joke I can't contribute to it and I feel awkward.... I'm beginning to feel that the Jewish people have the Jewish type of disposition and the English have theirs. So the Chinese are a little different. And each group can get lost in its own kind. When I'm with Chinese I have not a single care on my mind. I don't have to tune up.

Some who feel ill at ease in "mixed" social gatherings or do not find themselves invited frequently by other Americans to their parties remain content to move largely in Chinese circles. Said a Shanghai-born wife of an electronics entrepreneur:

> We belong to a close circle of Chinese—maybe ten to twenty families. *Ch'ing-lai ch'ing-ch'u.* We entertain back and forth. I feel at home here and Americans accept me, but I feel quite happy to live completely Chinese.

Parents, Children, and Respect

It is perhaps in their role as parents that this group of Chinese have been forced to move farthest away from their conditioning in China. They were born in China at a time when parental authority, indeed all authority, was being challenged, and the power of tradition was being weakened. The traditional system called for respect, for a hierarchy of authority that implied unquestioned obedience. It was assumed that the younger would identify closely with the will of the elders. The child was expected to follow his parents' wishes; if he did not know what these wishes were, it was his responsibility to find out. These precepts and practices began to crumble with the passing of the last Chinese dynasty and the onset of all of the confusions of modernization. The ideal of submission to authority and tradition, within and outside the family, was rejected as outworn by the seekers after a new society and dramatically flouted by the young revolutionists who set the tone for successive generations of Chinese in this century.

Except in extreme cases during the many upheavals of that time, the severance from the past was not total, was not made by some single great stroke. Certainly among those Chinese who came to America, and especially in the shaping of their self-image as parents, strands of these older beliefs and practices persist and memories of the Chinese past survive and even in some ways dominate. Those strands remain strong enough to block a full acceptance of American patterns and make up the elusive quality of being Chinese; they provide the thin margin of persisting difference. So these parents still measure their own performance as parents and judge the behavior of their children in terms of a dual reference—that of an idealized past and that of a demanding present. Some stress one more than the other, but both become inescapable burdens on the parental consciousness.

One result for this partially Americanized generation of parents has been the surrender of the stricture of unquestioned obedience. As youths, they had themselves managed to exercise considerable independence without openly challenging the forms of authority in the family, or breaking the structured inequality by which it was governed. In this way they acquired a much reduced sense of identification with the wishes of their elders. Now, they find that they have to make much more radical and explicit concessions than *their* parents had had to make, not only in substance but in form as well.

The underlying attitudes and pressures have also changed. One parent recalls that during his Chinese childhood, "little injustices were everywhere." Another remembers that "if I was unjustly scolded, I'd just go away and sulk or bang my head against the wall." But now, in their Chinese-American families, the process of change has meant tempering the ideal of "respect for elders" with a strong dose of egalitarianism, and stretching the ideal of family loyalty to leave ample room for individual rights. It has meant finding new ways of preserving "respect" at the expense of "obedience." Above all, it has meant opening channels for the release and expression of inner feelings. The way has been opened to conversational give-and-take between the generations— something most of these parents never experienced in their own youth— allowing the children to talk back, to argue. The parents recognize, painfully and reluctantly, that this is an inescapable part of the living style of their American children, and, indeed, is also a way of enlarging the capacity of everyone in the family to live the American life.

For the parents, however, there is almost always a persistent discomfort, an ambivalent wish that they could somehow rescue and preserve the "respect"—more, the respectfulness—which was part of Chinese family life for such a long time. A certain note of unhappy retreat is heard in the remarks of some fathers:

> It's not a question of allowing them. They *do* argue back. It depends on what you mean by argue back. But as long as they're reasonable, as they're able to reason, it's all right.

To give up obedience while trying to preserve what is called "respect" raises some sharp issues about the inner nature of the whole relationship, as is evident in this mother's account of the instructions that she gave to her daughter before the teenager left to visit her grandparents:

> I want respect to elders as a general trait. Respect is of course quite different from obedience. In fact, I told my daughter she did not have to obey her grandparents. She could try to get away with things, just be smart in doing so. I would be satisfied if she just showed respect.

This is more of an echo of the youthful experience of the mother's generation than most might be willing to admit, for, as they are learning from their own children's behavior, the step from lip-service respect to the absence of any special form of respect is a small one. Many parents end up by subscribing to neither the old codes nor their outer forms:

> My parents' generation was very traditional. They talked about *hsiao* or filial piety and they talked about respect for their elders. They also talked about supporting their elders. We don't think about *hsiao* and we don't think about having our children support us, or show respect for elders. We just tell our children to study hard.

Still, it is hard to surrender remembered values that, feebly as they might have been practiced, still seem to have been somehow better than the confusions now offered in their place. In this, Chinese parents in this country are sharing with all American parents a certain pain in the discovery that their age and experience count for so little with their young. For China-born parents particularly, the decline of parental roles and prerogatives means the further crumbling of what they have seen as the once-mighty fortress—the classical Chinese family. Its two prime features, respect and family loyalty, are still seen as distinguishing the Chinese from all other peoples. These parents wish that somehow they could hold on to this uniqueness, especially because it still seems a better way of discharging their responsibility as parents.

The trouble is that most of these parents feel that they have not tried hard enough. They see the gradual, inevitable dissolution of authority, respect, and traditional propriety in the family as a loss for which they are mainly responsible. This loss, already irreparable in China, they fear, is being compounded by the disintegration of the Chinese family style outside of China. And it adds a certain anguish which can be felt in the statements of a father of three and a mother of four:

> Unfortunately, the relationship in our family is quite American. They don't have the Chinese respect for parents or obedience. They are quite independent. I didn't try to instill Chinese traditions, such as respect for parents and obedience...I knew it wouldn't work. When I was young I was very scared of my father. But of course these Chinese ways are not necessarily the best.

> The upbringing of our children is all mixed up—probably more American than Chinese. They don't know the Chinese language. We sent them to language school for four or five years, but they quit each year and didn't learn very much. They like Chinese food though. We eat half-and-half—sometimes Chinese, sometimes American. We don't give them any systematic education in Chinese culture, and we don't enforce any manners. Our living is the same as American living.... With my children there are a lot of conflicts about dating. How do we settle them? They just go

ahead and date. You can't make them do anything. We have a couple of arguments, but there is no pattern of settling these differences. Sometimes they win and sometimes I win. I can influence them in subtle ways but I have no authority over them.

There is still another facet to the paradox, because most of these parents do not really want to base their authority over their children merely on an appeal to tradition. I have heard them. in conversations with their college-age sons and daughters, insist on citing their own youthful idealism and rebellion. Most would not resurrect the old Chinese family system with its repressions and its smothered emotions; many prefer the more open, freer life that has come with liberation from the old styles. At the same time, the new styles repel them, so they do not know what, after all, they really do want. Without being able to identify it, they cling to whatever it is to be Chinese. In all of the ways that they yearn after it and try to impress their children with the value of preserving it, their efforts become in most cases an expression of an undefinable longing for a lost past.

"Our Chinese Children"

Even after so many years in this country, many Chinese parents, when speaking in English about their American-born children, will call them "our Chinese children," but when speaking in Chinese among themselves will more or less jestingly call them *wai-kuo-jen,* "foreigners." Between these two contending thoughts lies a small but uncharted sea. All immigrant groups in America have had to cross it, and the Chinese are no exception in believing that they are buffeted by higher winds and deeper currents than other newcomers, feeling tossed by storms, certainly, that affect no other group in precisely the same way. Chinese often hear it said by others that they have no identity problem, that they know who they are. But this says too little and too much, for most of them do not know *where* they are, culturally speaking, and are painfully unsure of what will be the result, in their children, of their own mix of Chinese and American experience.

Most of these Chinese began their families after coming to America; hence, the mark of American culture is perhaps felt most heavily in their role as parents. As young couples they were cut off from the more common family network in which they probably would have stayed at home in China—relatives and elders always willing to lend a hand, to interfere, to instruct, to criticize, to set norms. Instead, these young parents were taught by American pediatricians how to take care of their babies. They learned from American neighbors how small children were supposed to be disciplined in this society and were counseled by American teachers and guidance personnel on how to lead the young.

One mother who herself grew up in a family of three generations living together, described her own parental experience in this way:

I used up three copies of Spock in raising our children. I also read Gesell's books and someone else's called *How to Play with Children.* If I had older relatives here I wouldn't bother about these. But as there are only two of us we go by the book for everything. If the children want to keep a dog, first we read a book. If we want to go camping, we read a book. We also have weekly family meetings.

This example of "going by the book" may be somewhat unusual, but the absence of elders and relatives clearly made an enormous difference to this group of Chinese, a difference not usually shared, incidentally, by American-born parents of Cantonese origin, whose elders and other relatives are seldom very far away. The total separation of the Mandarin- and Shanghai-speaking groups from their families left them free to discover American ways of bringing up children. Yet, inevitably, and in most cases unconsciously, they brought to their lives with their own babies everything that they had acquired in their own rearing at home in China. All of the beliefs, practices, notions, habits, all of the holdings of the past surfaced at the call of their own parenthood, but in a setting so different from that of their childhood in China.

Much less complicated was the problem of formal education. For the most part, this defined itself. Unlike an earlier generation of Cantonese immigrants, these Mandarin- or Shanghai-speaking parents showed little or no impulse to send their children back to the available China-substitute schools in Taiwan or Hong Kong. On the contrary, although they floundered uncomfortably in that uncharted sea of cultural cross currents, they resolutely set their young on educational courses that would lead them directly to successful careers in America.

With only rare exceptions, these parents made no provision for turning back, either for themselves or for their children. They gave full support to the Americanization of their children, calling American education "the great equalizer," "a shortcut to security," "a license to a job." All during the 1950s and 1960s, they concentrated on making their own way successfully and seeing to it, as far as they could, that their children would do likewise. This consisted of prodding their young to do well, or simply expecting that they would do well naturally. A high proportion of the children distinguished themselves in high school and entered leading universities. Their parents felt proud of this record, glad to see their children carrying on what they considered to be their tradition of learning. There were some, of course, who did not do so well, and others who did not do well at all.

Although these parents tended to choose the scientific and engineering fields as sure roads, different patterns are turning up among their children. As with other immigrant groups that have made their way in this society, the new generation that goes on to higher education tends to move also toward the humanities, the social sciences, and the arts. Many parents disapprove of this trend, although most hesitate to insist upon their preferences. Some take a more relaxed, optimistic view. One such parent, impressed and amused that a friend of his had agreed to let his daughter major in dance, commented cheerfully: "As long as they are in America, they can choose what they like, and no matter what they choose, they can get jobs."

To be Confucian or To be Free?

"We have changed," said an East Coast professor. "We have changed so much that we don't recognize ourselves anymore." Then he added: "But we will never cease to be Chinese." It was not possible for him to explain exactly what he meant, but he was describing the dilemma of remaining Chinese in a non-Chinese environment. "To be Chinese," said another, "is to be in a strait jacket hard to get out of. Externally, we are Confucian; inside, we all long to be free."

To be "Confucian" or to be "free"—a difficult choice, all the more so because the meaning of either is not clear to anyone. To those now living far from China and in an adopted society, being "Confucian" seems to mean carrying on the spirit of traditional China, some of the essence of the Confucian ideal, but without the support of surrounding Chinese institutions, styles, rituals, and formalities. In more personal terms, it means the spirit of deference and self-restraint, of reverence for the past, of order and hierarchy, seeing the self primarily as a prescribed series of duties and obligations and only secondarily as an individual with separate, inherent rights and needs. These traits they are proud of and would like to pass on to their children.

Their view of "tradition," however, is accompanied by a certain resistance to the Confucian ethic, especially its restraints and constraints. In older, more traditional terms, an escape was offered through Taoism. Its transformations and combinations with Buddhist beliefs resulted in a flight from worldly pressures and demands toward nature and the spirit. As far as life's realities are concerned, fatalism and withdrawal were combined, the former being translated into an acceptance of things, and the latter into a style of avoiding hard conclusions or decisions, of tolerating ambiguity, of rationalizing action, and of letting circumstances dictate one's course of life.

In real life, however, this choice was for most people neither obvious nor readily available. At best, one performed one's public roles while nurturing private thoughts. To become effectively free of constraints and obligations was possible only for those who chose the role of recluse or some other life at the fringes of society. In modern times the choice of styles has persisted in a way—especially in the gap between public behavior and private thoughts or feelings—but as a guiding philosophy of life, it has been churned up by the turmoil of a society forced to transform itself.

All Chinese have gone through some part of this experience—the choice between being "Confucian" or being "free." But for those who have been cast into the role of immigrant in American society, the choice took a new turn. "Freedom" became not a flight into a spiritual or poetic fantasy or withdrawal, nor even "freedom" from some of the myriads of old-style familial and related obligations. Rather, it became "freedom to feel free." As one man at the New York discussion said, "Here in the United States I can be my own man." He was alluding to some subtler form of emotional release, a sense of freedom to choose and to put his very individual stamp on everything he touches.

Those Chinese who try now to puzzle out this whole question, to reconcile the outer with the inner life, the rational with the emotional, are already more Western than they are Chinese, certainly as far as this effort is concerned. Introspective self-scrutiny of the questioning sort rather than in the spirit of self-rectification is not one of the more obvious legacies from any older Chinese tradition. In our present group, it is much more a product of their American experience. To be outspoken, to dispense with excessive formality, to be more expressive and to show emotions—these are some of the more personal ways of experiencing release from Confucian restraints. To be more aggressive in work, to be willing to face open conflict, to be ready to press demands on one's own behalf or on behalf of a group, to join some outside cause, to enter into political life in American society—these are the more public expressions of this release. But for the China-born, even those raised in a modern, urbanized setting, a self-conscious feeling of constraint and inadequacy may still remain. This is "our" inheritance from "our" remnant of both Confucian training and Taoist resistance to it.

The legacy of Confucian ethics resulted in submersion of self and in perseverence. It also produced a reverence for protocol and a reliance on elaborate codes of etiquette to facilitate interpersonal relationships and soften the clash of competing interests and incompatible needs. Knowing these codes gives the individual immersed in Chinese society a sense of security, and adhering to them fits him into the well-worn paths of customary relationships. A professor of architecture, being partially liberated from these old constraints, observed:

I know how the typical older Chinese behave and I react accordingly. Chinese show a lot of courtesy to others, sometimes false courtesy. For instance, you're supposed to offer someone something three times and they are insulted if you don't repeat your offer after the first time. But since I know this, I won't offend people. It's nice to be able to turn it on and off like this. I know how to behave correctly with my family. At times, you have to do things you don't want to or don't believe in. You do them to please your parents. Sometimes, maybe you have to lie a little here and there.

Inner restraint and outward conformity can hamper maximum adaptation to certain new situations. These characteristics, when taken out of a Chinese context, produce what some called "excessive politeness, touchiness" and "making things kind of embarrassing for everyone." Virtues in one social setting are thus viewed as a handicap for adaptive living in another. One scientist thought the modesty of Chinese made them socially uninteresting:

The Chinese are afraid to show up. They are such perfectionists they won't try new things. Americans will try anything, and if they fail it's okay. It doesn't mean they are going to entirely lose face. For instance, if Americans sing a song and hit a sour note, well, it's all right. But the Chinese would be so embarrassed. So when the Chinese get together they do the safe thing: it's bridge and mah-jongg.

A scholar well versed in classical learning summed up this general tendency:

> Our individual free will is restricted by the pressures of conformity. We usually take a second or third choice in jobs. Many things we just won't do—or take a long time before we decide—in fact we might end up driving our wives mad.

Love and Chineseness

The families that our group grew up in lavished a great deal of attention and open affection upon the very small child. They fondled him, carried him about, and enjoyed him for what he represented and for the enrichment he gave to family life. Whether in an old-style large household or in a conjugal family, the small child was the object of much indulgence—and also much teasing—from parents, grandparents, relatives, and servants. But this relatively free and carefree phase ended when the child began school. Then the distance widened between parent and child, brother and sister, old and young. Most kinds of physical contact also ended, along with much of the show of affection and direct praise. Growing up meant learning to do with indirect signs of approval and love. The highest reward was to be called a "good child," meaning a well-controlled child. If he felt anger, he learned at an early age to curb it; if he met injustice, he learned to accept it; and if he found joy in something that he accomplished, he learned to confine it well within his private thoughts. This shaping and containing of the emotional life of a child held true even when the traditional extended family broke up and its splintered units moved away to cosmopolitan cities and treaty ports.

The relationship between older children and parents focused more on the dimension of respect, esteem, and caring, than on the dimension of affection based on fondness. This was less true in relationships between mother and child, where personal emotions had more room for play. But, as a rule, one simply suppressed personal feelings when it came to relations with one's parents.

In young adulthood, most in the educated, socially privileged circles firmly believed that marriage should be based on love rather than on family arrangement. But the freedom to love, and to marry for love, was only fought for and won by members of the generation preceding them—a small, educated group of "revolutionaries". This was part of the tumultuous beginnings of twentieth century China. By the time this generation was growing up, love and love marriages were already in the air, at least in the urban centers of rapidly changing China and on the college campuses. Thus, before taking up their second life as adults and parents in American society, they had already been exposed to the Western ideas of love through translated literature and films, and from pioneer Chinese examples. Yet, the love ideal as it took root in China, acquired a somewhat different, "Chinese" quality or character. Love became associated first with the struggle for freedom from the shackles of the traditional family, with the right for personal development and individuality. The search for an ideal mate became not a mysterious process of romantic love, sufficient unto itself, but a matter to some extent of finding someone who met proper "qualifications"—qualifications involving "worthy" careers, "proper" attitudes toward social and political problems of a modernizing nation, and a "serious," nondecadent view of life. Love thus was somewhat hedged by a host of rational and practical considerations—or else it slipped into the easy slickness of the Chinese imitations of Hollywood.

During the flowering of the New Literature in the 1920's and 1930's, Chinese authors wrote of this freedom to love as a social protest and as the birthright of the modern Chinese. This literature, which our generation was brought up on, can give us some glimpses into the conceptions of love that influenced the soon-to-be emigrants. Love in this fiction, as in real life, was strongly colored by concern with self-determination, but the stories reveal a negative side as well, a fear of excess and loss of control, the limits of self-determination. Love was recognized, accepted, and favored by these authors as a harbinger of the new China and the passing of the old order. Despite the hesitancies and envisioned pitfalls, modified forms of romantic love began to take hold and to flourish among the more privileged classes of young men and women, and dating and courtship styled after the Western fashion became more accepted as the foundation of marriage. Love in its various shapes and meanings gradually took the place of family arrangements, edging out duty to the lineage as the cementing force for new family life. Of course, love and devotion also had their place within the traditionally arranged marriage, but were not a necessary condition. One usually did not look to marriage for sex and romance, but rather to other practices such as concubinage for those who could afford it, or extra-marital alliances. It was only among modern-minded young people, including those who became student-emigres, that love became a definite precondition for marriage, and fulfillment of sexual needs was brought within the confines of the conjugal relationship. For the first time, love and duty became one.

As students in America, they brought ideas about love and courtship that are Western in form but infused with special Chinese expectations and associations, hesitancies and vulnerabilities. It is a gentler, more controlled version of Western love—containing more mutual esteem and compatibility and less passion. Love between husband and wife among these transplanted Chinese rests heavily upon a sense of mutual commitment to duty—duty as husband and wife, and duty as parents. Self- control continues, as individual needs and wants are subordinated to this generalized sense of duty and propriety. Floodgates of private feelings are locked. What then is conjugal love in the Chinese family in this country? At its best, it is a kind of mutual caring, it is respecting each other's rights, interests, and personalities, it is striving to achieve harmony through complementary roles, all of which speaks for stability and minimizes surface frictions.

However, roles themselves do not remain stable. In their lifetime of migration and change, their sense of well-being and fulfillment is in flux.

How then is this balance to be reestablished and harmony maintained? How does a wife show the love and esteem that she feels for her husband when the old style of solicitude over his personal needs conflicts with her own sense of personal dignity? How can a husband hope to be gratified when he expects his wife to be both the main builder of the "close Chinese family" and also a modern and adaptable spouse? How, in fact, can he tell his wife of his love and appreciation when he is uncomfortable in the vocabulary of praise and the more direct gestures of love? How indeed are differences cleared up or true harmony restored by this transplanted generation when surface calm is valued, emotions are trained to remain under control, and the verbal communication of feelings does not come easily or naturally, if it comes at all? This sense of selfhood, this curbing of individual needs and private emotions for the sake of family unity are the price of stability.

In both the old and the new Chinese milieus, it is a parent's duty to spur his sons and daughters on to high moral and scholastic attainment. Chinese parents do so more by exhortation than by praise or demonstrative love, expecting children to turn out well but with little outward reward or recognition. One of the mothers whom we interviewed described her growing up years in a large, traditional family in which everyone, including the servants, would tell the children: "Your father scolds you only because he cares about you. You have to be worthy to be scolded." This same mother has now discovered to her chagrin that parents can no longer expect their American-born children to know parental love and concern without more direct signs, or to know that a reprimand is a sign of worthiness. When she asked her college-bound daughter, "Do you think when we scold you that we reject you or are ashamed of what you've done?" The girl, assuming that one individual was being pitted against another, said simply, "We think you are mad at us." Some parents explain that praise would spoil children or make them conceited. (Chinese modesty often goes with a certain trained inability to feel, or at least to display cockiness.) Said a father of two college-aged children: "Praise and punishment should be sparingly used; otherwise they lose their effectiveness." Many other parents acknowledged their own sense of inner restraint: "I can't praise directly."

Chinese parents also try to withhold words of anger, but his is partly a class-bound phenomenon. The educated man in old China maintained his self-control under all conditions;his contemporary counterpart finds it difficult to depart too far from this model. As an example, a China-born man who has spent the last twenty-five years in the United States said he was angered at the sight of his son's defiantly long hair and yet described his overt reaction as mild: "I'm likely to say nothing, or maybe I'd say something too soft to be heard. I have too much Chineseness in me." And so parental dignity is maintained, open clash avoided, and it is the father who now has to regain his inner balance.

Yet, immersed in the American milieu, those with a Chinese childhood have had to try to learn the more spontaneous and open expression of emotions toward their children. Though hardly anyone is able or willing to change completely, another layer of protocol is slowly being stripped away in Chinese family relations. The ideal of the self-contained, distant father is giving way to the good listener and ready counselor, ever prepared to receive, even exchange direct expressions of feeling across the generations. And the ideal of the dutiful and compassionate mother is being edged out by the understanding confidante. No longer are expressions of emotion a one-way street: parents who as children were expected to watch their parents' moods and to strive to please them now have to learn to watch and try to respond to emotions in their own children.

The affection a parent feels for his children is of course independent of whether he shows it outwardly or not. Traditional parents had a repertoire of indirect indications of affection. But here we are talking about adoption of different group-sanctioned ways for demonstrating feelings. China-born fathers who are quite Americanized in their professional life still believe in restrained show of affection or approval toward children; they simply find outward display unnatural. Revealingly, in the Chinese language the expression *ni-ai* means "too much parental love"— literally, to drown someone with love. Doting parental love is seen as undermining, not strengthening, the family.

We asked members of the New York meeting if they "hug and kiss" within the family. This created a palpable stir in this modern urbane group, a nervous laughter, and obscurely, a cerain titillation. The answers were themselves brief and not very informative: some said no; others said yes, "but awkwardly." For all, it was obviously a subject on which no one had questioned them before. All were just a little amused and flustered about the novelty of the topic, but became thoughtful about the meaning of the change.

Central to another difference between the Chinese parents and the American families whom they associate with is the belief that the Chinese family, even in its modernized, Americanized version, possesses some unique strength. It follows that building the "good Chinese family," especially for those living abroad, is central to self-esteem. When a science professor said to his sociable, outgoing wife, "Your children are your life," he voiced a sentiment of many Chinese fathers, and, with greater ambivalence, of many Chinese mothers, even after two or three decades on American soil. This belief in the Chinese family is part of the Chineseness that parents seek to pass on to their children.

Belief cannot be long maintained without practice, and in practice, the love which these Chinese parents feel for their children is perhaps weighted with a strong sense of identification with their children for a longer period of time. Parents assume the prerogative and responsibility of shaping the habits, interests, and natural bent of their children with greater persistence than do American parents, and past the age when the latter would think such overt interference either possible or desirable. The identity of Chinese parents, then, has a closer tie with the achievement of their children, academically and in other respects. This sense of duty and identification is derived from their Chinese past but is sustained in part by their present circumstances of having to ensure the children a solid place in American society. When transmitted to children, this means parental love entangled with expectation of performance from them. To the extent that parents are successful in getting compliance from their young, the result is that special brand of family closeness which binds the generations together. It is no longer the same kind of unity found in traditional Chinese families by which children incorporated the will of parents without question. Now the center of gravity has shifted; it is the parents who anxiously watch the will of their children in the hope of shaping it.

A logical question follows: As the traditional Chinese parent was unable to "love" the child who was disobedient and disrespectful, how well in America can he love the child who fails to live up to expectations of achievement? Can the parent say, "My son is doing something he likes. He has found himself—I am happy"? Or, "My daughter is marrying someone she loves, and he happens not to be a Chinese—I am happy"? The tension between high expectations and eventual reality is a special vulnerability of these parents. Compensating for Chinese over-concern with parental duty and expectation is the avoidance of a kind of pitfall sometimes found in American families: emotional domination of parents over children through or in the name of love. This type of tyranny, the product of overstimulation of individuality, takes its toll in the emotional life of the American child. This is rarer among Chinese or Chinese-American families.

Yet, even some of these thin margins of difference in the uniqueness of the Chinese-American family in the United States are rapidly vanishing. Take, for example, a working woman who has struggled to be a dutiful wife and mother for twenty years here and now asks: "Have I been wrong in putting duty first? Maybe my first duty as wife and mother was to be happy, and the rest would follow." And reflectively she says, "I must not only take care of my children's needs and make sure that they study hard; I must also *like* them." She then voiced surprise that she should have to make a conscious effort to "like" her own children. Back in China, such doubts would not have arisen. Another mother, a physician, was hurt and desperately at a loss as to why her teenage children turned out to be "rebellious." In despair, she said she has always tried so hard to *teach* them to be good Chinese children. Perhaps Chinese parents have to learn that in this land where young people jealously fight for independence so early, to be dutiful parents to one's American-born children is not enough. It is not easy for parents who have tried their best to be good parents only to discover that their children are turning away from them or even against them. Some may eventually stumble on the key question: Is it possible to be good Chinese parents and also to like one's children, simply to enjoy them? How many parents of older children can recapture the pure joy they felt when they carried them as babies in their arms and loved them for what they were, for just being part of their lives? How many experience the urge sometimes to hug impulsively their older children but find themselves unable to do so?

Today, to be dutiful Chinese parents in the United States may mean to be less rigid or righteous, and more open and approachable, than Chinese parents of a generation ago. This introduces a new aspect to the meaning of family closeness. "We are educated and we are reasonable," said a research scientist and father of three, hoping to maintain closeness in his family by being open-minded. "We are *k'ai-t'ung*, enlightened, and we try to close the generation gap," said another father. But many still find it difficult to enter into a new kind of closeness, the closeness that comes from being "pals" with one's children. At an early stage of interviewing for this study I remember how taken aback I was when a China-born mother said that the relationship she most wanted to achieve with her teenage daughter was that of "friends." Many interviews and many months later I was surprised to discover how anxious I too was that my two teenage daughters should regard me as a "good friend," how relieved or pleased I was to be treated with a new kind of liking or acceptance as a person, sometimes even with a dash of teasing disrespect. I came then to realize that the special Chinese bond of closeness is shifting, and that the parental conviction that duty is everything is giving way to doubt, helped perhaps by the discovery that respect and obedience in the Chinese family are already too thin to carry the weight of parental influence and discipline. This is a new turn in parental love and family closeness for these families in the United States.

In the summer of 1972, I revisited my homeland. To me then, China meant first of all that tiny spot that was "home" even after an absence of more that thirty years. It meant returning to the house that I had grown up in, and reuniting, if briefly, with my father, who is now old and retired. For a few days I sat with him each morning as he practiced his daily calligraphy. It meant seeing my brothers and sisters, all with families of their own, and eager to show me their own homes, as if physical impressions could make up for some of that void left by years of separation. It meant tasting long-forgotten dishes from childhood and walking the familiar yet strange streets in the neighborhood. It meant recalling childhood games at the familiar sight of small boys crouching on the sidewalk in front of cracks in the cement wall and waiting to catch crickets.

Seeing China included, of course, visiting fabled Peking and being in the presence of the splendor of imperial palaces and treasures and the solemnity of more recent accomplishments. It included marvelling at prehistoric excavations and new architechtural monuments such as the Yangtze River bridge at Nanking. But there were also more private moments. For me, there was also the search for cloth-sole shoes, the kind which my grandmother used to make, and peasant blue cloth, a vanishing handicraft that I had long admired. There was a memorable meeting with an old master craftsman whose traditional dough figures were exquisite creations of art, and there was the chance encounter in the street with a grey-haired working woman, whose new-found dignity prompted her to call me her friend and to invite me to visit her home, a gesture unthinkable in the old society. Most of all, it was an experience of renewal to be considered one of their "own people" by strangers in a remote, interior city in China, thousands of miles from my old Shanghai home. To me, to be Chinese away from China is a little like being a spirit detached from its body, still part of it, yet not encompassed by it, linked with it in fate, yet standing apart, watching it from afar.

What I have described are but some aspects of the newly reshaped identity of a tiny minority of Chinese-Americans—those aspects concerned with relationships, but not others having to do with physical appearance, history, and civilization, or with China itself.

China is a massive presence on the mental map of every Chinese. It is part of almost everyone's common "Chineseness" to think of it in the perspective of its centuries, a continuous political entity and unique civilization deeply encrusted in time. Despite tensions and ambiguities, no Chinese can dissociate himself wholly from what happens in his homeland. Its failures and humiliations are his failures and humiliations, its triumphs and its prestige are his triumphs, his prestige. In some degree and in some fashion, the continuity of China is preserved as a large certainty in the minds of all, retaining intact much of what it always stood for, its long history, its sophisticated culture, its large population. China is to the Chinese abroad like an anchor to a ship, loosely and invisibly secured, but holding it to the limits beyond which the ship cannot drift without entering foreign waters.

IX.

Sons of the Soil Migration, Ethnicity and Nativism in India

by Myron Weiner

There is much talk these days about the "sons of the soil." The advocates and op-
ponents of this theory do not seem to agree among themselves. Perhaps, the following
classification might solve the problem of those involved in the controversy.

First, we must not accept the present division of states and districts as they are political
and man-made. When we swear by the soil, we must adhere to the natural, geological
divison. Our earth has been clearly divided into different kinds of soil regions: alluvial,
volcanic, etc. It is but natural that sons should work only in their respective mother
soils. For example, only those born in the alluvial soil can work in the alluvial region.
They may call themselves "alluvians" and proclaim "Alluvial soil for alluvians only."
People of other soil regions may form similar groups. People may be given identity
cards with the name of their soil clearly printed on it.

To solve the problem of babies born in the air (planes), they should be employed as
pilots and air hostesses. Nobody except the sons and daughters of the air should get
these air jobs. They could be allowed to stay on earth in a non-classified soil region
when they are off-duty.

S. Pushparaman
Tiruchirapalli
Letter to the *Times of India*,
January 28, 1973

To the outsider most of the societies of Southern Asia and Africa
are multi-ethnic, diverse mosaics of tribes, linguistics groups, religious
sects, races and cultures. To the insider, to the dweller of a village, small
town, or urban neighborhood, the community of residence is itself often
homogeneous, a familiar terrain where people speak the same language,
share the same religious beliefs, and practice the same customs. To the
outsider the "problem" is one of integrating diversity into a single nation
and an orderly political system; to the insider the "problem" is often one
of preserving the community against the encroachments of outsiders.

Many of the ethnic groups that make up the multi-ethnic societies of the Third World have a territorial base, a geographic, not simply a cultural community. India, for example, is a multi-lingual society with a dozen major languages and countless minor languages that are the official languages of their own state. Most individuals in India, as elsewhere in the Third World, live on the land among their own people; they speak of the soil, the hills, the rivers and lakes, and the forests with a sense of community proprietorship that transcends private ownership. People speak of "their" land, though they may "own" (in a legal sense) none of it. An individual Bengali peasant or landlord may own some farmland, but the land occupied by Bengalis "belongs" in a psychological and cultural sense to all Bengalis. Individuals may buy and sell land, but the land itself is a collective birthright that cannot be alienated to outsiders. Among the bitterest conflicts experienced by mankind are those between ethnic groups laying claim to a land that each considers its exclusive birthright.

The nationalist upheavals of early twentieth century central and eastern Europe were political movements by ethnic groups to carve out an exclusive political turf in which culture, territory and state sovereignty were conterminous. This was not so in many Third World countries where independence meant freedom from European colonial domination, but where states were made up of diverse people who shared national political power while maintaining their own territorial exclusiveness.

Internal migration has undermined that territorial exclusiveness. In a single country with diverse cultures but a common citizenship, people move from one locale to another in search of education, land, and employment. The shift of emphasis from agriculture to industry, transportation, communication, and services is accompanied by a movement of people from rural to urban areas. Regional disparities—the availability of irrigated lands in one region but not in another, industrial growth that is more rapid in one region than elsewhere, and the development of extractive industries and plantations—provide still another incentive to population movements. As new occupations and new opportunities are created, individuals see migration as a way of improving their well-being. With the expansion of opportunities and an increase in social (and hence, spatial) mobility, people become less attached to the soil, and more oriented toward their job than their geographic community.

Most migration is from countryside to town and city within the same cultural region, but, increasingly, migrations are over longer distances and across cultural-linguistic boundaries. In Nigeria, for example, Ibos along the coast moved northward to create businesses and find jobs in areas where the Fulani and Hausa reside; in Indonesia the Javanese move from their densely packed island to nearby Sumatra; in Pakistan Punjabis move to Karachi in the province of Sind; in India Bengalis move to the surrounding regions of Assam, Orissa, and Bihar, while Malayalis move to Madras, Bangalore, Bombay and as far north as Delhi and Calcutta.

In much of Southern Asia and Africa the process of culturally diversifying towns, cities and, less often, the countryside through internal population movements is well under way.[1] To the extent that individuals are free to move, the process is likely to continue. Only governmental intervention, aroused by political demands, is likely to slow or arrest this process.

Indeed, in many regions opposition to culturally alien migrants has already arisen along with demands that government intervene to halt internal migration. In Nigeria the tensions that arose between Ibo migrants and local populations were no small element in the strife that led to the civil war. In Malaysia, the Malays speak of themselves as "Bhumiputras" or "sons of the soil" in opposition to migrant Chinese, demanding that they be given special rights in employment, education and land. And in India opposition to migrants has developed in the city of Bombay, in the Brahmaputra districts of the state of Assam, in the western region of the southern state of Andhra, in portions of southern Bihar, and in the city of Bangalore—political movements that also go by the name, "sons of the soil."

This paper examines the development of such organized movements against inter-cultural migrations within India, the world's largest multi-ethnic state. I will explain why opposition to migration has developed in some areas of India but not in others, why such sentiment is strong among some classes and ethnic groups but not among others, and why opposition emerged in the late 1960s and early 1970s though inter-cultural, inter-regional migrations in India have taken place for a long time. And most fundamentally I will explain why anti-migrant or "nativist" sentiments are a particular form of ethnic politics, one of several types of ethnic politics.

I. Nativist Political Movements: India and the United States

Let us first describe several anti-migrant political movements in India and show how they are similar to or different from anti-migrant nativist movements in nineteenth and early twentieth century America.

In Bombay, a city known for the wide variety of its linguistic, religious and cultural communities, a political party called the Shiv Sena has demanded that jobs in the city not be given to migrants from other Indian states. The Shiv Sena has been particularly hostile to the Tamil migrant population for occupying the middle class jobs sought by the local Marathi-speaking population. Within two years of its founding in 1966, the Shiv Sena became the largest single opposition party in the Bombay municipal elections, supported by a majority of the Marathi-speaking people in the city.

India's northeastern state of Assam has been torn by clashes between the migrant Bengali Hindu community and the indigenous Assamese over what should be the state language, and whether Bengali should continue to be used in schools and colleges. In early 1973 the disturbances became so severe that the central government in New Delhi found it necessary to send the army into the major towns of Assam to restore law and order.

In the south Indian state of Andhra conflict has arisen in the western districts of the state, a region known as Telengana, over the migration of people from the prosperous agricultural delta districts in the east. The people of Telengana have expressed anxiety over the entrance of migrants into the state administrative services, their purchase of housing in the capital city of Hyderabad, and their "colonization" of land in the countryside. In an effort to reduce migration, Telengana has successfully pressed for the establishment of preferential rules for the employment of local people. The people of the eastern districts have responded by agitating for the bifurcation of the state, a demand which became so violent in late 1972 and early 1973 that the state was temporarily placed under the jurisdiction of the central government.

In the industrial belt of southern Bihar, in the region known as Chota Nagpur, the native tribal population, a poor, illiterate, predominantly rural people belonging to four large tribes and countless smaller ones, has been overwhelmed by waves of migrants who have been settling in the region over the past century. The migrants dominate the steel and mining industry, a heavy engineering plant, many large and small industrial establishments, and the region's schools and colleges. Today the indigenous tribesmen are a minority, living in a region whose administrators, teachers, factory owners, lawyers, and merchants come from outside. Unable to cope with these changes, many tribesmen have turned to messianic cults, secessionist movements, and radical politics. The tribals have their own political party, the Jharkhand party, which advocates the creation of a separate tribal state that would restrict the role of the non-tribal migrants and limit future migration into the region.

In the late 1960s a small political party emerged in the south Indian city of Bangalore, known as the Kannada Chaluvalagars (the Kannada word for "agitators"), calling for restrictions against Tamil, Malayali and Telugu migrations into the city and demanding that employment preferences be given to the local Kannada-speaking population. The party won several seats in elections to the municipal corporation in a city widely regarded throughout India as a model of linguistic harmony.

In each of these political conflicts a section of the local population has expressed antagonism toward a linguistic or cultural migrant community that is distinguishable from the local population and has sought protection against the migrants in competition for employment. Each of these conflicts is an example of the phenomenon known in the United States as "nativism."

In American historical and social science literature "nativism" refers to an intense opposition to internal minorities because of their foreign origins. At different times in American history nativists have had varying antagonists—Roman Catholics, Celts, the new migrants from Southern and Eastern Europe, and the "hyphenated" Germans and Japanese. At times nativists were concerned with the volume and character of migration as these affected the rate at which newcomers culturally and politically assimilated into American life. At other times nativists expressed avowed racist views, dwelling on the special racial qualities of Anglo-Saxons on the one hand, or of Orientals, Southern Europeans, or Slavs on the other. Nativism in America also took a variety of organizational forms—the Know Nothing Party before the Civil War, the American Protective Association at the end of the nineteenth century, and the Ku-Klux Klan in more recent times. But whoever the antagonists, and whatever the tone, or the organizational form, nativism always has been linked to various concepts of American national identity.

Anti-migrant movements in India can also be seen as nativist phenomena; that is, they represent the response of emerging "nationalities" (a term which requires special explanation in this context) to internal minorities with foreign connections. In the Indian context, the emerging "nationalities" are regionally, linguistically, and tribally defined; and the "foreign" minorities or migrants are defined as people who speak the language and share the cultural beliefs and identities of those who live in other regions of India. It should be apparent, of course, that in one fundamental respect the Indian case differs from the American: the nativist reaction in India is not to foreign migrants from another country, but to so-called "foreigners" from other cultures within the same political system. In this respect, however, the Indian experience is more typical of what is found in many other developing countries where plural conceptions of nationality (or what may be more precisely called "regional cultural identities") are often emerging within a single political framework.

The nativist phenomenon in such societies is particularly complex since various conceptions of nationality or of regional cultural identity are in the process of being formulated and nativism is often a way of defining the boundaries of one's own culture in relation to others. It is in this context that we can ask what the conditions are under which nativist movements arise and why some migrant groups are defined as alien while others are not.

II. American Theories of Nativism

Since social scientists concerned with understanding and explaining the nativist phenomenon first looked at the United States, it is only appropriate that we first turn to theories derived from the American experience. At the risk of oversimplification, we can classify the various theories under five general groups: (1) economic competitive models which explain the rise of nativist movements in terms of employment fears, especially on the part of the working class; (2) status mobility models which emphasize the threats posed by migrants to the social status of the upper and middle classes, especially to New England Anglo-Saxons; (3) political interest models which stress the fears of certain social classes to the political threat of migrants to their interests, as was the case in the reactions of the ante-bellum South to the demand by migrants for homestead legislation, and early twentieth century urban elites to the growing political power of the new migrants in urban areas; (4) psychological models which emphasize the relationship between frustration and aggression and the importance of displacement, particularly as exemplified by the hostility often expressed by one minority group against another; and (5) demographic models which suggest that the rate and volume of migrants into a given social space may pass some optimum threshold of tolerance by the native population.

The most common sense explanation is one which points to cultural differences as a determinant of native-migrant conflicts. It is useful, therefore, to consider first to what extent cultural differences explain the rise of nativism.

The cultural-difference explanation holds that People A (the local people) and People B (the migrants) subscribe to antagonistic cultural norms: People B eat beef or pork, while People A consider such food practices counter to their religious sensibilities; People A respect cleanliness (or orderliness, or punctuality) in contrast with the slovenliness (or disorderliness or indifference to time) of People B; People A admire the arts, while People B prefer business activities to aesthetic pursuits; People A are warmhearted and generous, while People B are clannish and aloof to strangers; People A believe in one God, People B are polytheistic; People A worship their God directly without intermediaries, while People B have elaborate rituals and a hierarchical priesthood; People A are attached to the land, while People B prefer urban life; People A prefer leisure to work, while People B are thrifty, hard working, enterprising; and so on.

The Indian experience suggests that a cultural explanation of conflict is inadequate in three respects. First, there are numerous instances in India of people with widely different cultures living side by side without conflict. Indeed, in India's agglutinative society it would be difficult to find a rural district or an urban settlement in which there were not people speaking different languages, subscribing to different religions, differing in cultural beliefs and social practices. All of India's large cities are multi-lingual, multi-cultural, and have large migrant populations. But while Bombay, Hyderabad, Gauhati, Bangalore and Ranchi have nativist movements, Delhi and Calcutta do not. Moreover, two communities with cultural differences may clash in one locale, but not in another. There is, for example, nativist sentiment in Bihar and Orissa against Bengali administrators, teachers, office clerks, and lawyers, but no significant nativist sentiment in Calcutta against Oriya and Bihari workers.

Secondly, there are innumerable instances of conflicts between our hypothetical People A (the locals) and People B (the migrants) when the cultural differences between these two groups are not as great as between People A and People C (another migrant community). Whenever there is a clash between the local population and a culturally different migrant community, one can often point to another migrant community with whom the local people do not clash, but with whom their cultural differences are at least as great. The nativist movement in Bombay opposes Tamil migrants but pays little attention to the more numerous Telugu-speaking migrants, though both are equally alien people from the south. The local population of the city of Hyderabad is hostile to migrants from the eastern part of the state with whom they share a common language, culture and religion, but there is little resentment against Marathi, Kannada, and Tamil-speaking migrants from other states with whom the cultural differences are far more substantial.

Finally, the cultural-difference theory does not explain why nativist movements have arisen in the past few years, although in most regions there have been no major increases in inter-regional migration and cultural differences are no greater now (and in some instances are reduced by an increase in bilingualism) than a few years ago. Why did nativist movements emerge in the 1960s and 1970s in the towns all along the Brahmaputra valley of Assam, and in the cities of Bombay, Hyderabad, Bangalore, and Ranchi? Why are there fluctuations in nativist movements in India over time? For example, in its various guises nativism was a political force in Chota Nagpur at the end of the nineteenth century, declined for several decades, and became important again in the late 1930s. In Hyderabad, nativism was important in the 1920s for several years but then remained dormant until the 1960s. And Bangalore had no history of nativism until the Chaluvalagar party emerged in the late 1960s.

In short, there are many instances in which migrants and natives with substantial cultural differences do not conflict, instances in which cultural differences appear to be slight but conflicts are intense, and instances when cultural groups are currently in bitter conflict though at other times their relationship was either cordial or indifferent.

But if cultural differences are not causes of nativist hostility to migrants, they surely accompany such conflicts. It is a distinguishing feature of nativism that its adherents emphasize differences, no matter how slight, between the culture of the native and the culture of the migrant, for nativism defines who is local in cultural, not territorial terms. Local people, the natives, or what Indians call the "sons of the soil," are defined by the tribe to which they belong, their mother tongue, or the ethnic community with which they identify, rather than the locale of their birth. The Marathi-speaking person, for example, who migrated to Bombay from a town in Mysore state may be considered local by the nativist, but not the Bombay-born Tamil whose parents or even grandparents came to the city decades ago.

Nativism magnifies cultural differences precisely because it is a way of defining cultural identity. In Hyderabad, to give one pointed example, supporters of the nativist Telengana Praja Samiti, who advocate restricting the employment of "outsiders" in the Telengana region and in the capital city of Hyderabad, have attempted to define a Telengana cultural identity that would distinguish them from the Telugu-speaking people in the rest of the state. They emphasize small differences in food habits (Telengana people drink tea, while the people in the eastern districts drink coffee), language (there are more Urdu words used in the Telugu spoken in the Telengana region), and clothing (the men in the east wear a characteristic scarf not worn by men from Telengana). Much is made of small nuances in manners, gestures, attitudes, and accents, most of which reflect the historic domination of the Telengana region by the Muslims. Yet little more than twenty years ago, when there was a movement for uniting the Telugu-speaking people into a single state, the political movements in Telengana sought to minimize the importance of Islamic culture and to emphasize the similarities of all Telugu-speaking people. Here again we see how political movements attempt to define cultural identities.[2]

In short, nativist movements convert cultural differences into cultural conflicts. Cultural conflicts should be viewed as the effects, not the determinants, of nativism. What then are the determinants? Are there factors that must be present when there are nativist political movements and which, conversely, can never be present in the absence of nativist movements?

III. Conditions for Nativist Movements in India

This paper attempts to specify a set of conditions for nativist movements in India. First, we shall ask what conditions are present in each of the regions and cities in India that have nativist movements which are not present in locales without nativist movements; and secondly, we will ask what changes have taken place in each of the regions preceding the emergence of nativist movements that may explain why at a given time these movements emerged. Since in several areas there have been nativist cycles over a period of decades, whatever variables account for the rise of nativist movements must also help explain their decline.

We shall draw our analysis from the five cities or regions where in recent years there have been major nativist movements: Bombay city, the Brahmaputra valley of Assam, the Chota Nagpur region of Southern Bihar, the city of Bangalore, and the Telengana region of Andhra.

In four of these areas there are explicitly nativist political parties: the Shiv Sena in Bombay, the Jharkhand party and the Birsa Seva Dal in Bihar, the Kannada Chaluvalagars in Bangalore and the Telengana Praja Samiti in Telengana. In Assam, nativism informs the sentiment of the governing Congress party, but there is also a loosely structured nativist movement known as the Lachit Sena. The focus of this analysis will not be on the parties themselves, but on the social context within which these movements emerged.[3]

In three of these areas nativism is not a new phenomenon. In the former princely state of Hyderabad, in which the Telengana region is located, a movement against outsiders, or as they are called, "non-mulkis", developed shortly after World War I when the local educated population expressed its opposition to the government policy of recruiting Muslims from northern India into the state administrative services. The present movement against "non-mulkis" is now against migrants from the nearby Telugu-speaking regions of eastern Andhra.

Similarly, the anti-Bengali movement in Assam began in the mid-nineteenth century when the Assamese protested the domination of their educational system and administrative services by Hindus who had migrated from Bengal. At that time Assam, along with Orissa and Bihar, was part of a single province known as the Presidency of Bengal with its capital in Calcutta.

Finally, in Chota Nagpur the hostility of tribals to non-tribal Bihari settlers was a central theme of the major political movements and upheavals in the region in the middle of the nineteenth century, culminating in the great Birsa rebellion in the 1890s calling for the "restoration" of tribal lands.

What are the conditions shared by these diverse contemporary and historical situations? The first condition is that each area with a nativist movement has migrants from outside the cultural region. The number of migrants and their descendants can even be greater than the local population. The extreme case is the six districts of the Chota Nagpur region of Bihar where the indigenous tribal population, the Santal, Munda, Ho, and Oraon tribes, now constitute a minority of 33 percent. Only in two districts, Ranchi and Singhbhum, are the tribals a majority with 2.3 million out of a total population of 4.2 million, or 54 percent.

In the six districts that make up the Brahmaputra valley of Assam (population in 1961, 9.1 million), 73.3 percent report themselves as Assamese-speakers, 7.4 percent speak indigenous languages other than Assamese, amd 19.3 percent speak migrant languages. But in the urban areas of the valley 350,000 people are Bengali out of an urban population of 913,000 (38 percent), as against 304,000 Assamese (33 percent). (Another 13 percent are Hindi-speaking migrants, and the remainder a mixture of migrants and some local tribals.)

In Bombay the Marathi-speaking population in 1961 also constituted a minority, 42.8 percent of the population. Similarly, in Bangalore the local Kannada-speaking population in 1951 had dropped to 23.8 percent, for the first time falling below that of the Tamil-speaking population (Table 1).

Table 1. Changing Language Composition: Bombay

Marathi Speakers

1911	53.7%
1921	51.4%
1931	47.6%
1961	42.8%

Changing Language Composition: Bangalore

	Kannada	Tamil	Telugu
1911	33.3%		23.5%
1921	33.6%	21.1%	25.6%
1931	32.5%	22.6%	23.0%
1961	23.7%	31.7%	17.8%

Of the five cases, the Telengana region has the smallest migrant population. According to the 1961 census, migrants comprise one-fourth of the population of the city of Hyderabad—a smaller proportion than that of many Indian cities. And for the Telengana region as a whole, in-migration from other states and from other parts of Andhra is considerably smaller. But since 1961, only a few years after Hyderabad was made the capital of the new state of Andhra, there has been a substantial influx of migrants from the eastern districts of Andhra to take jobs in the administrative services and open small businesses.[4] There are now many "Andhra" housing colonies (as the migrants from the eastern districts are called) in or close to the city.

In each of these five cases, the migrant population and its descendants belonging to "alien" ethnic communities constitute anywhere from a fourth to two-thirds of the population, perhaps somewhat less in the Hyderabad case, though the recent figures are not yet available.

Without an alien migrant population, there cannot be a nativist political movement.

A second condition is that there must be some perceived cultural differences, no matter how small, between the migrants and the local community. These differences can take any one of many forms: language, religion, preferences in food and dress, and belief systems. But above all the native community must have some awareness of a cultural identity by which they distinguish themselves from the migrants. The litmus test for such a separate cultural identity is the use of a distinguishing name.

In three of the five cases the names are linguistic. In Assam the distinction is between the Assamese (those who speak Assamese as their mother tongue), and the non-Assamese Bengalis, Marwaris, Nepalis, Biharis, etc. In Bombay it is the Maharashtrians (Marathi-speakers) as distinct from the Tamils, Telugus, Gujaratis, Sindhis, and Hindi-speakers. In Bangalore it is the Kannadas (sometimes called Kannadigas or Mysoreans) as distinct from the Tamils, Telugus, and Malayalis.

In Chota Nagpur the tribal people group themselves together as "adivasis", a term used by Gandhi to mean the "original" people; outsiders are called "dhikus", a word with perjorative overtones.

In Telengana the term "mulki" is used to refer to people originating from the region, irrespective of language and religion. The term was initially used before Andhra was created to refer to anyone born in Hyderabad state; it implied that one was a citizen of the state or, more properly, a subject, for the state was, until 1948, governed by a monarch. When the Telengana region was merged with other Telugu-speaking districts of South India to form Andhra, the term was used more narrowly to mean the people who lived in the Telengana region (one of several regions that formed the old state of Hyderabad). The term, originally intended to specify who was qualified for employment in the state administrative services, is even now used in that sense. Someone who is not qualified, an outsider, is called a "non-mulki."

Although all nativist movements are by definition anti-migrant, not all anti-migrant movements should be called nativist. A community or government may want to slow or halt the rate of in-migration for a variety of reasons: overcrowding of schools; inadequate urban services, such as sewerage facilities, water, electric supply, and mass transportation; concerns over the environment; general anxieties concerning overcrowding; and so on. A community may also be hostile to the class composition of migrations: well-to-do communities often want to keep out the poor.

The characteristic feature of nativism is its ethnic selectivity. It accepts or rejects migrants (and their descendants) because of the ethnic community to which they belong and with which they identify or can be identified. *Without perceived cultural differences there cannot be a nativist political movement.*

A third condition of nativism is that *in areas with a nativist movement, the local population is likely to be immobile relative to other groups in the population.* Out-migration from Assam, Maharashtra and Andhra is below the national average, Mysore is at the mean, and Bihar is above average. But statewide census figures are an unsatisfactory measure of mobility on the part of the native population; for one thing, it is more relevant for our purposes to know whether there is out-migration from the region, district, or city in which the nativist movement thrives; for another, it is more relevant to know whether the native ethnic group is mobile or not, not simply how much out-migration there is from a locality. State-wide out-migration figures, therefore, are a crude index (Table 2); regional out-migration figures are better, but still not adequate; a linguistic dispersal table indicating what proportion of the people speaking a given language lives outside of the region in which the language is spoken provides us with still a third crude measure (Table 3).

Table 2. Migrant Dispersal Table

State	Number (000)	%
Assam	116	1.0%
West Bengal	505	1.5
Jammu & Kashmir	78	2.0
Maharashtra	867	2.2
Madhya Pradesh	824	2.5
Orissa	471	2.7
Andhra Pradesh	870	2.7
Gujarat	734	3.0
Kerala	624	3.4
Mysore	794	3.4
Madras	1,095	3.5
Uttar Pradesh	2,583	3.5
Bihar	2,041	4.5
Rajasthan	1,132	5.6
Punjab	1,318	6.5
Delhi	183	7.0
India	14,641	3.3

Migrants by state of birth, 1961.
Percentage represents proportion of the total population born in each state residing outside of the state.

By any available measures the Assamese are among the least mobile linguistic group in India. Only 1 percent of those born in Assam live outside the state—and some of these migrants are not ethnically Assamese. Only 19,000 Assamese, or 0.3 percent of the total Assamese speakers in India, can be found outside Assam, according to the 1961 census. Even within Assam there is relatively little movement of Assamese from one district to another or from rural to urban areas within the state. Only 3.5 percent of the population of Assam lives outside the district of birth, and this figure includes both the non-Assamese and Assamese-speaking people born in the state. Assam has one of the highest in-migration rates of any state in India, but the Assamese themselves remain a predominantly non-mobile people in a status-based society.

The linguistic dispersal index is unsatisfactory for measuring out-migration among the Marathi and Telugu-speaking people since state boundaries have been drawn in such a way that substantial numbers of speakers of both languages are found in districts bordering the state. Both states, however, are among the lowest (along with Assam) in the proportion of population living outside the state: 2.2 percent for Maharashtra and 2.7 percent for Andhra. The census also reports low out-migration from the Telengana districts, including Hyderabad, into other districts of Andhra.

Table 3. Linguistic Dispersal Table
(1961)

Language	% Speakers In Home State	% Dispersed In Other States	Number of Speakers In Other States
Assamese	99.7%	0.3%	19,000
Kashimiri	99.0	1.0	18,000
Bihari*	97.8	2.3	364,000
Hindi#	96.5	3.5	4,323,000
Malayalum	94.5	5.5	929,000
Gujarati	92.9	7.1	1,434,000
Marathi	92.3	7.7	2,534,000
Marwari	92.6	7.4	460,000
Oriya	92.5	7.5	1,175,000
Tamil	93.0	7.0	2,129,000
Kannada	88.8	11.2	1,944,000
Bengali	87.1	12.9	4,346,000
Punjabi	84.5	15.5	1,531,000
Telugu	82.2	17.8	6,710,000
Rajasthani	76.2	23.8	3,547,000

Note

Bihari includes Bhojpuri, Maithili, and Magahi including their variant forms.

#The major variants of Hindi—Awadhi, Baghelkhandi, Chhattisgarbi, and Khariboli—are not included here, but in each instance more than 99% of these languages are spoken in their home state. The home states of Hindi are here defined to include Delhi, Bihar, Madhya Pradesh, Punjab, Rajasthan, and U.P.

India's other major languages do not have a "home" state and are widely dispersed. These include Urdu (23,323,000), Santali (3,247,000), Bhili (2,439,000), Gondi (1,501,000), Konkani (1,352,000), Kurkh/Oraon (1,141,000), Pahari (1,004,000). One other language with more than a million speakers, Kumauni, is confined (99.8%) to U.P. Two non-Indian languages, Sindhi (1,371,000) and Nepali (1,021,000) are widely dispersed.

Out-migration from Bihar is of less importance for this analysis than out-migration from Chota Nagpur which has a long history of tribal out-migration to the tea plantations in Assam and northern Bengal. The 1891 census reports that as many as 421,000 persons born in Chota Nagpur had emigrated. The number rose to 707,000 by 1911, and 947,000 (to Bengal and Assam alone) by 1921. Out-migration figures are not available thereafter, but we have some evidence to suggest that out-migration dropped sharply in the 1930s when the tea industry was no longer expanding. There may have been a small increase in the 1940s when some tribals found employment in Assam, since the British and American armies were engaged in constructing roads, airports, and other military installations. In the 1950s and 1960s migration out of the area appears to have declined. The period between 1900 and 1931 is thus the major period of out-migration; tribal emigration evidently provided an alternative to political unrest, for there was a marked decline in tribal political protest between 1900, the year of the death of Birsa Munda, the leader of the most famous tribal rebellion in the region, and the 1930s when the nativist Jharkhand party was formed.

While the evidence for this condition still remains incomplete, there is data to support the inverse condition; that is, *states or regions with a high in-migration and a high rate of emigration tend not to have nativist movements.* Neither the Punjab nor West Bengal have nativist movements, though both have the largest migrant populations of any states in India, 14.2 and 15.7 percent respectively. The Bengalis and Punjabis are also among the most mobile people in India. 15.5 percent of all Punjabis live outside the Punjab and Haryana (in 1961), and 12.9 percent of all Bengali-speakers live outside West Bengal.

The quantity of out-migration is a surrogate for another variable: the ability of a people to compete in the labor market. *A competitive employment situation locally may be tolerable if there are employment opportunities outside the region. This leads us to the fourth condition: the rate and pattern of unemployment.*

There is no town, city, or region in India that does not have a high and growing unemployment rate. It is officially estimated that in the early 1970s there were 7-1/2 million unemployed in India, apart from disguised rural unemployment and seasonal unemployment, but all unemployment figures either for the country as a whole, by region or by city, are likely to be imprecise, since not all job seekers register at the Employment Exchanges. The Employment Exchanges do, however, report an alarming increase in the number of people seeking employment. In 1961 there were 1.8 million registered at the Employment Exchanges, and in 1970 the number was up to 4 million. The sharpest increase occurred after 1966, reflecting the slowdown in industrial growth and, for much of Indian industry, an actual decline in employment. In Bombay, for example, the number of workers employed in factories rose from 505,000 in 1961 to 572,000 in 1966, and then declined thereafter to 551,000 by 1969.

Raj Krishna, in his presidential address to the Indian Society of Agricultural Economics in 1972, estimated that if one includes in the unemployed those who are severely underemployed and available for additional work, nearly 21,500,000 workers are unemployed, of whom 19.3 million live in rural areas and 2.2 million in urban areas, or approximately 9 percent of the labor force.[5]

The growth of unemployment in India is associated with the following factors:

1. There has been an accelerated increase in the size of the labor force in the mid-1960s as a result of the declining death rate of the previous decades. Infant mortality has substantially declined, and survival rates for all age groups have improved so that the "drop out" rate from the labor force through mortality has declined while the entry rate has increased. The growth in the labor force between 1951 and 1961 was greater than in the previous fifty years:

Labor Force 1901-1961 (000)[6]

1901	110,712
1910	121,301
1921	117,764
1931	122,168
1951	139,890
1961	189,190

It is estimated that additions to the labor force now total 4.8 million annually, increasing each year so that by 2007 the annual increase will exceed 7.5 million; changes in the birth rate will have no impact on the annual inflows into the labor force until the 1990s.[7]

2. Increases in employment have not kept pace with the expansion of the labor force. Between 1961 and 1969 factory employment rose from 3.9 million to 4.77 million, an annual increase of 2.5 percent, about equal to population growth. But employment in mining has grown at only 1 percent per annum since 1956 and India's plantation sector, which employs about a million and a quarter workers, has actually been declining. According to the National Commission on Labour employment in the private sector actually decreased by 1.9 percent in 1966-67 and by 2.4 percent in 1967-68, reflecting the impact of the economic recession that emerged in 1966-67.

The number of employees in the entire organized sector in 1968 was 16.3 million, about the same as the previous year, for while employment in the private sector declined there was a slight increase in public sector employment from 9.63 million in 1967 to 9.8 million in 1968. It should be noted, incidentally, that state governments, with 3.8 million employees, are the largest employers, followed by the central government (2.72 million), local bodies (1.8 million), and quasi-government establishments (1.48 million).[8]

Why the demand for labor has not kept pace with the growth in the supply of labor is a complex matter that need not concern us here except to report that the rate of investment, according to Raj Krishna, has been declining or stagnating since its peak of 13.4 percent in 1965; for the last four years (1968-72), reports Krishna, it has been less than 10 percent.[9] "In a poor developing economy," he notes, "investment growth and employment growth are highly complementary."

3. A rapid expansion of the educational system since independence, particularly at the matriculation and college levels, has substantially increased the number of young educated people seeking employment, especially in urban areas.

Since independence there has been a tendency for the higher levels of education to expand more rapidly than the lower levels. The proportion of children attending middle school increased from 12.7 percent in 1951 to 31.7 percent in 1965-66, while there was a more than three-fold growth in secondary school enrollment (from 5.3 percent to 16.8 percent) and an even greater growth in undergraduate enrollment, from 1.89 percent to 6.38 percent.[10] The proportion of expenditure going to higher education grew substantially from about 23 percent in 1950/51 to 29 percent in 1965/66.[11]

Paradoxically, an important incentive for the expansion of college enrollment has been the growing unemployment of secondary school graduates. As unemployment increases, parents send their children to college with the hope that additional education will increase their chances of securing employment.

Defining the educated unemployed as those who have completed at least eleven years of schooling and are totally without any employment but seeking work, Blaug, Layard and Woodhall estimated that conservatively there were a half million educated unemployed in India in 1967, and if all educated people registered with employment exchanges are counted (including those who work part-time), as many as 900,000 were unemployed.[12]

The expansion of higher education has tended to transfer[13] unemployment from rural to urban areas, from the unskilled to the skilled labor markets, and from the laboring classes to the middle classes. As unemployment increases, the rate of unemployment among the educated appears to increase more rapidly than among the uneducated. India's growing unemployment in the late 1960s and early 1970s has been accompanied by a sharp increase in the numbers of educated registered at the employment exchanges.

But unemployment rates, even if they were accurately measured by registrations at employment exchanges, are an unsatisfactory index of competitiveness between migrants and the local population. There are many jobs that local people do not want even though unemployment is high. Educated Bengalis do not seek work in the jute and textile mills near Calcutta, where the labor force is largely from Orissa and Bihar. In Assam neither the urban educated nor the uneducated peasantry sought employment in the tea industry when it was expanding, preferring instead to see tribals take the jobs as tea pickers. In Bombay Marathi-speaking workers seek employment in factories, but generally do not compete against unskilled Rajasthanis for jobs on construction projects, or against Telugu migrants for jobs as dock-workers.

A high degree of occupational specialization by ethnic group among the working classes in India tends to reduce, though not wholly eliminate, competition within the labor force among ethnic groups even when unemployment levels are high.

However, for middle and lower-middle class positions—defined broadly as non-manual occupations irrespective of salary levels—there is far less ethnic specialization. Within every large ethnic group in India there are substantial numbers of people seeking middle class jobs as office clerks, typists, teachers, office messengers, clerks in retail shops, etc. Probably no social class has grown in size more than India's middle classes; in every state the most rapidly expanding occupational category has been employment in government services, including employment in the educational system. The entrance requirement for middle class employment in India is a matriculation certificate or college degree.

A locale in which there is a high level of unemployment among the indigenous middle class (middle class in education and aspirations, but often not yet in employment and income) *and a substantial proportion of middle class jobs are held by culturally alien migrants, is a likely candidate for a nativist political movement.* In Gauhati, Hyderabad, Bombay, Ranchi, and Bangalore, most of the lower-middle class positions are held by migrants and their descendants, while in each of these cities—as in other cities of India—the number of educated registered at the employment exchanges has sharply increased. Other cities also have high levels of educated unemployment—cities like Calcutta, Canpur, Lucknow, Allahabad, Trivandrum, and Madras—but in these cities the middle class jobs are already held primarily by the native population.

A fifth condition is that *areas with nativist movements have experienced a rapid growth of educational opportunities for the lower-middle classes.* In four of the five regions with nativist movements, the local population were historical late-comers to education. While the Bengalis and Tamils were among the first communities to be exposed to the British-created system of education and hence were among the first to produce a substantial middle class, the Assamese, the Marathis, the "mulkis" of Telengana, and the Munda, Santhal, Ho, and Oraon tribesmen of Chota Nagpur are among the most recent groups to become educated.

In Assam prior to 1947, the middle class was almost entirely Bengali Hindu; teachers in the schools and colleges, a substantial portion of the state administrative services, and most of the professionals were Bengali Hindus. After 1947 the newly independent government utilized a considerable portion of the state's resources to expand educational facilities, especially for the local Assamese. The number of students in Assam increased from 934,000 in 1950 to 3,154,000 in 1965. There was a proportionately even larger educational explosion in the secondary schools and colleges. The number of students attending colleges and universities in Assam almost doubled every five years:

1950	8,601
1955	14,595
1960	28,226
1965	45,387

Thus there developed in Assam an educated class that aspired to become middle class before it achieved any of the occupations and materials standards of middle class life. For this aspiring Assamese middle class, the Bengali Hindu middle class stood as an obstacle to advancement.[14]

A similar situation obtained in Bombay. Though the Marathi-speaking population was by no means as educationally late as the Assamese, they tended to lag behind the Parsis, the Gujaratis, and the Sindhis in Bombay. The proportion of Marathi-speakers in semi-skilled and middle class positions in Bombay was substantially below the proportion of Marathi-speakers in Bombay. A study conducted by Lakdawala of Bombay University in the early 1950s reported that 4.9 percent of the Marathis earned more than Rs 500 monthly, compared with 17.3 percent of the Gujaratis and 10.1 percent of the South Indians.[15]

According to estimates made by Mary Katzenstein, there has been a sizeable increase in the number of matriculates throughout Western Maharashtra. In a study of the social composition of the nativist Shiv Sena party in Bombay, Katzenstein reports that almost all of the party workers surveyed belong to the lower-middle classes. "The list of specific jobs," she writes, "reads like a directory of lower-middle class occupations—including on the one hand neither professionals (teachers, doctors, or lawyers), big businessmen, nor simple, unskilled laborers or menial workers on the other hand. Rather, the job descriptions— accounts clerk, bookshop owner, salesman in bookshop, clerk in bank, towing operator, assistant supervisor in auto workers, inspector in municipal corporation—suggest that Shiv Sena organization leaders are predominantly of middle and lower-middle class backgrounds."[16] Katzenstein goes on to report that the elected Shiv Sena members of the Municipal Corporation are less educated (26 percent have college degrees compared with 53 percent of the two Congress parties and the Praja Socialist party municipal councilors), and more often in the lower- middle class (42 percent are clerks or skilled and supervisory factory personnel, as compared with 25 percent for the other three parties in the corporation).[17] The Shiv Sena is the party of a new, expanding, lower-middle class of Marathi-speakers in competition with the non-Marathi middle classes.

Few communities in India are as educationally backward as the tribal population. Until recently few of India's 35 million tribals had achieved higher education. In 1961 only 9,532 tribals in the entire state of Bihar (with a tribal population of 4.2 million, most of whom live in Chota Nagpur) had matriculated (the equivalent of a high school education) or attended college, and of these only 231 had completed college. Though more recent data are not yet available, there has evidently been a marked increase in tribal education within the past decade.

In 1970 there were 1,590 "educated" tribals registered for employment at the exchanges, of whom 945 were matriculates, 224 had some college education, and about 400 were college graduates. Though education among the tribals still remains substantially below that of other communities in Bihar, for the first time there is now emerging among the tribals a young, educated, largely urban group seeking middle class employment.

The Jharkhand party is still the major nativist political movement among the tribals, but in recent years a new organization, the Birsa Seva Dal, has won support among young tribals in the major towns. The organization achieved public recognition in 1968 and 1969, when it launched violent attacks against non-tribal landlords and led mass demonstrations in the streets of Ranchi demanding the creation of a tribal state. Although the size of the Birsa Seva Dal is not known—in any event it does not appear to be a well-organized membership organization—it is generally agreed that many of its supporters are matriculates who have had difficulty finding employment, for they are neither skilled nor educated enough to qualify for the technical jobs or the senior administrative posts that have opened in the new public sector industries, and they are too educated to seek employment as day laborers. Some jobs in the state and central administrative services are reserved for tribals, but no such reservations exist in the public sector enterprises, many of which have sprung up in and around Chota Nagpur. The unemployed tribal matriculates constitute not just a reserve labor pool, but a reserve political pool as well.

Telengana, our fourth case, is educationally the most backward region in the state of Andhra. In 1960-61 only 40.6 percent of the 6-11 age group in Telengana (which includes the city of Hyderabad) attended school as compared with 61 percent in Coastal Andhra (north) and 85.5 percent of Coastal Andhra (south).[18]

Even when Telengana formed part of Hyderabad state it was educationally the least developed region. For Hyderabad state as a whole literacy in 1949 was only 9.2 percent, but for each of the Telengana districts (excluding Hyderabad city), it was typically only 6 or 7 percent.[19] When the Telengana region was joined with the Telugu-speaking areas of the neighboring Madras to form a single Andhra Pradesh, there was considerable anxiety within Telengana that their small, but also growing, educated middle class would lose out in the competition for employment in the state administrative services and in the state educational system. A "Gentlemen's Agreement" was reached between the political leaders of the Telengana region and those of the rest of the new state of Andhra which provided that "future recruitment to services will be on the basis of population from both regions", and that "some kind of domicile rules, e.g., residence for 12 years, should be provided in order to assure the prescribed proportion to recruitment of Services for Telengana area."[20]

Even in 1956, when the new state was formed, the Telengana middle class feared that they might lose out in competition for employment unless some legal safeguards were created. Since Telengana, including Hyderabad city, has a small industrial base and a small private sector compared with Bombay, the concerns were mainly over employment in government, or "services" to use the Indian term. In 1966 there were 663,000 persons employed in the public sector of Andhra: 137,000 worked for the central government, 231,000 for the state government, 101,000 for quasi-government establishments, and 194,000 for local bodies.

A decade after the state was formed, the Telengana political leadership complained that the Gentlemen's Agreement had been violated, and that non-mulkis were taking positions in the state services that should rightfully go to the mulkis. There were protests from the Non-Gazetted Officers' Central Union, the trade union of lower-middle class government employees, that the Public Employment (Requirement as to Residence) Act of 1957 which specified the rules for employment of mulkis and non-mulkis had been violated. This was accompanied by similar protests from the major student organizations in Hyderabad, particularly the Osmania University Students Union. "The growing acute unemployment, particularly since 1966 owing to the slackening of the tempo of development, agitated the minds of the students and the lapses, though minor, in the implementation of the Public Employment Act, 1957, only enraged them,'' wrote one local observer.[21]

In one important respect the Kannada-speaking people of Bangalore—our fifth example—are not educationally backward compared with the migrant communities that have settled in the city. Mysore state has for some time been well-advanced in engineering colleges, technical institutions, and polytechnics. The major private firms in Bangalore (e.g., Kirloskar Electric Motors, the Indian Tobacco Company, Mysore Electrical, and International Instruments) and the public sector firms (Indian Telephone Industries, Hindustan Machine Tools, Hindustan Aeronautics, and Bharat Electronics) all have a substantial number of Kannada engineers and managers. Moreover, many educated Kannadigas have successfully competed for high level appointments in public and private firms outside of Mysore state. Although out-migration from Mysore is not high (it is only 3.4 percent), Mysore does have a larger and more mobile managerial and technical class than many states.

Nonetheless, Mysore's educational development still remains below that of her neighboring states of Tamilnadu and Kerala, two states from which migrants come. 31 percent of the Mysore population is literate, as against 39 percent for Tamilnadu and 60 percent for Kerala. Literacy in Bangalore is 59 percent, as against 62 percent for Madras city, 63 percent for Madurai, and 65 percent for Coimbatore, the largest cities in Tamilnadu, and literacy rates are near 70 percent for Kerala cities.[22]

Mysore experienced a rapid growth of its educational system between 1957 and 1968, as these figures of school enrollment reveal:

Table 4. Educational Enrollment in Mysore

Enrollment	1956-57	1967-68	% Increase
Primary school students	1,727,000	3,662,000	112%
Secondary school students	178,000	510,000	185%
College students	30,000	86,000	183%
Technical institutions, polytechnics	9,000	32,000	240%

Literacy: 19.3% (1951), 25.3% (1961), 31.5% (1971).

Support for the Kannada Chaluvalagars, Mysore's nativist party, comes neither from the most educated sectors of Kannada society, nor from the working class, both of whom have found a place in the industrial and managerial sectors, but from the secondary school graduates.[23] The leader of the Chaluvalagars is a young man, born in 1942 in a village twenty miles from the city of Mysore, whose father was an agriculturalist and small shopkeeper. He went to school in his village, then attended secondary school in Mysore where he matriculated. He started but never completed college in Bangalore. He created a weekly Kannada newspaper, ran for the Bangalore corporation and, in 1967, successfully won a seat in the state assembly. He formed his own party which won six of the sixty-two seats in the Bangalore municipal elections in 1971. His active party workers are sociologically similar to those of the Shiv Sena and the Telengana Praja Samiti; they are young, often below voting age, matriculates, and have jobs in shops, restaurants, cinema halls, or are unemployed. Their dress is distinctively lower-middle class: bushshirts, trousers, and chaples (sandals). The Chaluvalagar election symbol is the bicycle, which effectively identifies the social class and the age group that gives it support, as well as the way the lower-middle class moves about.

Unemployment has become increasingly acute among secondary school graduates. The live registers of the Directorate of Employment showed that while 175,000 registered themselves for jobs in the state in 1967, the figure rose to 304,000 by mid-1972. The Kannada Chaluvalagars single out the five major Government of India firms in Bangalore—who together employ about 60,000 people—for failing to hire Mysoreans. The state government claims that more than 75 percent of the middle income staff positions are held by Mysoreans, but the Chaluvalagars argue that the government has not properly defined a "Mysorean," for they include anyone who registers for a job in the state, including resident Tamilians and Keralites. "Grievances against the Central undertakings are mounting, as hundreds of 'luckless' Mysorean candidates throng ministerial chambers for help and intervention. Probably 50 percent of callers on ministers in a day are candidates who are unsuccessful in getting jobs."[24] In arguing for a system of preferences in employment for "sons of the soil," the Chief Minister of the state declares,[25] "can you name any state which does not prefer its own people?"

IV. Social Mobility versus Spatial Mobility

The cities and regions with nativist movements analyzed here share the following characteristics:

the locale contains a substantial number of middle class migrants belonging to culturally distinguishable ethnic groups originating from another section of the country;

—there is a native middle class, expanding under the impetus of a growth in secondary and higher education;

—there is a highly competitive labor market in which the native middle class seeks employment in private and public sector firms and in government where middle class positions are already held by migrants or their descendants;

—there are limited opportunities for the native middle class to find employment outside their own locale.

These conditions suggest a single proposition: *nativism tends to be associated with a blockage to social mobility for the native population by a culturally distinguishable migrant population.* To the extent that ethnic specialization, rather than migrants, tends to block either social mobility or lateral occupational changes, the industrial labor force and peasantry are less affected by nativist sentiments.

This proposition explains why, in India at least, nativism is largely a middle class sentiment, not a movement among the industrial labor force or the peasantry, even though there are culturally distinguishable migrants in the industrial labor force in many cities and in some rural areas. Should India's native urban working classes seek employment in industries and in job categories currently held by alien migrants, we can anticipate that nativism will also become a working class phenomenon. This proposition thus explains why nativism tends to emerge even when there is no noticeable change in the rate of migration; of greater importance are social changes within the native community that change job aspirations.

Were the labor market in Indian cities expanding more rapidly, then there might be a niche both for the migrants and for the growing native middle classes, but under conditions of slow economic growth the labor market is correctly perceived by job seekers as a zero sum situation in which employment for the local population depends upon restricting employment for the migrants. Nativism in India is fundamentally a protectionist movement whose tariff walls are domicile regulations for employment and whose population is like an infant industry seeking protection against competitive foreign imports.

Nativism in India is a movement toward ethnic equality. Nativists believe that by pursuing a policy of favoring the native inhabitants over migrants they can equalize their income, their occupation, and their class position in relation to the migrants. If this analysis is correct, then the question of how close the migrant population is to the language and culture of the native population—and by inference, how much it assimilates—is less important in shaping the attitudes of native populations toward culturally alien migrants than the question of how effective the local population is at competing against migrants for the jobs they both want in a labor market of few opportunities and a plentiful labor supply.

Nativism in India is a political response to conflicting forms of mobility: the spatial mobility of migrants (or their ancestors) and the aspiring social mobility of a social class within the native population.

V. Nativism as a Variety of Ethnic Politics

How does nativism differ from other political expressions of ethnicity, and particularly from other kinds of regional movements?[26] Is there a theoretical difference between nativist political movements and other ethnic movements in India—such as the Akali Dal, a political movement in the Punjab, the Dravida Munnetra Kazhagam (D.M.K.), the regional party that governs the southern state of Tamilnadu, or the various political movements that agitated for linguistic states in the mid-1950s and early 1960s, the Andhra Mahasabha and the Samyukta Maharashtra Samiti? In what sense can we call the Jharkhand party nativist but not the Akali Dal, or the Telengana Praja Samiti but not the Andhra Mahasabha? Why the Shiv Sena but not the Samyukta Maharashtra Samiti? Is nativism not simply a logical extension of regionalism in India, a short leap from demanding a separate state for one's people to demanding that alien migrants from other states be excluded and even expelled?

To answer these questions let us first consider what differences there are between nativist and regional movements, then turn more generally to consider how nativism might be viewed as one of several alternative types of political expressions of ethnicity.

What are generally referred to as "regional" movements in India are political movements by ethnic groups to create or govern states organized around an explicit ethnic identity: hence, the Akali Dal (and what was more broadly known as the Punjab Suba movement) demanded the creation of a Punjabi-speaking state; in Assam's hill areas various tribal parties agitated for the creation of a tribal state known as Meghalaya; and the Samyukta Maharashtra Samiti called for the creation of a Marathi-speaking state. After these and other ethnically (mainly linguistic) defined states were created, regional sentiments persisted and deepened. In each state the governing party expressed (some would say used or even exploited) regional sentiments in clashes with the central government or with neighboring states. Moreover regional, but particularly linguistic sentiment, affected state government policies concerning the choice of language in education and administration, and the adoption of a variety of cultural policies.

The development of either a regional or national identity—both expressions of a sense of ethnicity when "ethnic" becomes synonymous with "region" or "nation"—is a precondition to the development of nativism, but nativism is not its inevitable consequence. Nativism is that form of ethnic identity that seeks to *exclude* those who are not members of the local or indigenous ethnic group from residing and/or working in a territory because they are not native to the country or region: nativism is anti-migrant. To the extent that the D.M.K., the Akali Dal, the Andhra Mahasabha, and the Samyukta Maharashtra Samiti were not anti-migrant, they should not be classified as nativist. In contrast, the Jharkhand party and the Telengana Praja Samiti are regional parties that are *also* anti-migrant, i.e., they are nativist.

Nativism is thus one form of ethnic politics. Sub-national ethnic movements seeking to create a state, either within or apart from the country, are still another form. When the ethnic group identifies itself with a given territory within the country, we generally speak of *regionalism*; when it seeks statehood outside, we describe the movement as *secessionist*. If the ethnic group believes that people of the same ethnic and linguistic heritage should belong to one state or nation and makes claims upon the territory of a neighboring state because it contains the same ethnic group, we speak of the movement or demand as *irredentist*. Then there are ethnic groups that make specific interest claims and engage in coalition politics to achieve their objectives, a pattern common in the interest group politics of the American political system. All of these forms—nativism, regionalism, secessionism, irredentism, and interest articulation—should be understood as varieties of demand-making on the part of ethnic movements, as varied as the forms of demand-making among class-based political movements. All these forms of ethnic group politics can be found in India.

To the extent that an ethnic group is characterized by a high degree of solidarity, demand-making on the part of one class within the ethnic group may become adopted by the ethnic group as a whole. Thus, while nativism may first develop within one class—in the Indian case, within sections of the middle class—nativism may become widely accepted by most politically participant members of the ethnic group. The electoral results demonstrate that in several regions described here nativist parties won support that extended well beyond the social class which initiated the movement.

Moreover, each of these nativist movements tends to have multiplier effects. When nativism develops in one region, it is not long before other regions soon develop nativist movements as well, although the same proximate causes may not be present. The hostility to migrants in one region creates a counter-hostility in another. Thus, anti-Tamil movements in Maharashtra give rise to anti-Marathi sentiments in Tamilnadu, and anti-Bengali sentiments in Bihar and Orissa stimulate anti-Bihari, anti-Oriya sentiments in Bengal. A new set of determinants begins to operate quite apart from those propounded in this paper. The *diffusion* process has a dynamic of its own independent origins. It is thus only in the early stages of the development of this form of ethnicity that its determinants can be understood. The same elements of cohesion and diffusion may similarly affect our understanding of the determinants of other types of ethnic politics.

Finally, we need to consider whether nativism need be the only political response to blockages to social mobility. Can there be a secessionist response or even a revolutionary, class-oriented response? Anyone who has witnessed the political responses of the middle classes in neighboring Sri Lanka or Pakistan to blockages to their quest for power, status, and wealth must recognize that there can be a variety of alternative responses, depending upon whose gains are blocked, who is doing the blocking, and the political context within which the response takes place. Indeed, when one considers the alternatives, nativism may well be among the least destructive choices, both for the political system and for individuals within it—for in one sense nativism contains within it the seeds of its own destruction. As nativism within a multi-ethnic society spreads from one region to another, as each region creates barriers to migrants from other regions, each ethnic group must ask whether it gains when all regions behave in the same way. Like economic protectionism, when practiced by a few there are gains, but when practiced by all many of the gains are cancelled out. As the principle of reciprocity serves to diffuse nativism, so too does it suggest the means by which nativist restrictions can be brought to an end.

Notes

This study was made possible through a grant from the Behavioral Sciences Research Branch of the National Institute of Mental Health.

[1] While there is a large literature dealing with migration in developing countries, relatively few studies focus explicitly on the heterogenizing effects of ethnic migrations. Among the exceptions are W.J. Hanna and J.L. Hanna, "Polyethnicity and Political Integration in Umuahia and Mbala," in R.T. Daland (ed.), *Comparative Urban Research: The Administration and Politics of Cities* (Beverly Hills, 1969); J.C. Caldwell, *African Rural-Urban Migration: The Movement to Ghana's Towns* (New York, 1969); M.A. Cohen, *Urban Policy and Political Conflict in Africa: A Study of the Ivory Coast* (Chicago, 1974); W.A. Hance, *Population, Migration and Urbanization in Africa* (New York, 1970); W.J. Hanna and J.L. Hanna, *Urban Dynamics in Black Africa* (Chicago, 1971); H. Heisler, *Urbanization and the Government of Migration: The Interrelation of Urban and Rural Life in Zambia* (New York, 1974); H. Kuper (ed.), *Urbanization and Migration in West Africa* (Berkeley, 1965); W.A. Schack, "Urban Ethnicity and Cultural Process of Urbanization in Ethiopia," in A. Southall (ed.), *Urban Anthropology,* (New York, 1973); E.W. Soja, *The Geography of Modernization in Kenya: A Spatial Analysis of Social, Economic and Political Change,* (Syracuse, 1968); Howard Wolpe, *Urban Politics in Nigeria: A Study of Port Harcourt* (Berkeley, 1974).

[2] For an excellent discussion of how the political process determines which ethnic ties become politically salient, see Paul R. Brass, *Language, Religion and Politics in North India* (Cambridge, 1974). Brass quite properly rejects the notion that ethnicity is a "given" to which the political system responds. His theoretical perspective is close to the viewpoint expressed here.

[3] For accounts on some of the nativist movements discussed here see Ram Joshi, "The Shiv Sena: A Movement in Search of Legitimacy," *Asian Survey,* X (1970), 967-978; Mary Fainsod Katzenstein, "Origins of Nativism: The Emergence of Shiv Sena in Bombay," *Asian Survey,* XIII (1973), 386-399; K.V. Narayana Rao, *Telangana: A Study in the Regional Committees in India* (Calcutta, 1972); Myron Weiner, "Socio-Political Consequences of Interstate Migration in India," in W. Howard Wriggins and James F. Guyot (eds.), *Population Politics, & The Future of Southern Asia* (New York, 1973) 190-228; Myron Weiner, "Assam and Its Migrants," *Demography India,* II (1973), 314-349; Hugh Gray, "The Demand for a Separate Telengana State," *Asian Survey,* XI (1971), 463-474; Hugh Gray, "The Failure of the Demand for a Separate Andhra State," *Asian Survey,* XIV (1974), 338-349; S.C. Sinha, Jyoti Sen, and Sudhir Panchbhai, "The Concept of Dhiku Among the Tribes of Chota Nagpur," *Man in India,* XLIX (1969), 121-137.

[4] More than half (52.7 percent) of the growth of Hyderabad between 1961 and 1971 was due to migration, the remainder from natural population growth. It should be noted that of India's twenty largest cities, in five more than half of the growth was due to

migration: in addition to Hyderabad, Madras (65 percent), Bangalore (52.6 percent), Jaipur (53.7 percent), and Surat (56.6 percent). Other high migration cities included Greater Bombay (47.4 percent), Poona (46.4 percent), Indore (48.5 percent), Madurai (48.3 percent) and Jabalpur (48.9 percent). In Ranchi, the other city with a nativist movement dealt with in this study, 75.7 percent of the growth was due to migration. In most Indian cities, however, growth is more by natural population increase than through in-migration.

In contrast, a larger proportion of the urban growth of African cities is the result of migration than natural population increase. For data by region and by country see Kingsley Davis, *World Urbanization, 1950-70* (Berkeley, 1971), I, esp. 141-160 (Table D).

[5] Raj Krishna, "Unemployment in India," reprinted in *Teaching Forum,* 38 (1974), Agricultural Development Council, New York.

[6] J.N. Sinha, *Census of India, 1961,* I, Monograph No. 11, *The Indian Working Force: Its Growth and Changing Composition,* 23. The 1971 census estimates the labor force at 227 million, but comparisons with 1961 labor force figures are difficult because of changes in the criteria for measuring participation in the labor force.

[7] John C. Cool, "The Dynamics of Indian Population Growth," paper presented at the Wingspread Conference on the Social and Cultural Responses to Population Change in India (1974).

[8] *Report, 1968-69,* II, Employment and Training, Government of India, Ministry of Labour, Employment and Rehabilitation, (New Delhi, 1969), 8.

[9] Krishna, "Unemployment in India."

[10] Mark Blaug, Richard Layard, Maureen Woodhall, *The Causes of Graduate Unemployment in India,* (1969), 44. This study provides an excellent account of the uncontrolled expansion of secondary and higher education in post-independence India.

[11] Ibid., 47.

[12] Ibid., 1.

[13] The word "transfer" may be misleading, for we are not suggesting that the growth in education is increasing unemployment, but simply that the unemployed are more educated, more urban and more middle class than if there had been a small expansion of secondary school and higher education. As Blaug et al. note, "the rate of unemployment among the uneducated turns out to be a much better predictor of educated unemployment than the proportion of educated people in the state labour force...over a third of the variance in matriculate unemployment is associated with the unemployment rate of those below matriculation" (93-94).

[14] For a more detailed analysis of the relationship between the Bengali Hindu migrants and the Assamese middle classes, see Myron Weiner, "Assam and Its Migrants."

[15] D.T. Lakdawala, *Work, Wages and Well-Being in an Indian Metropolis,* (Bombay, 1963), 281, cited by Mary Fainsod Katzenstein, "Political Nativism: Shiv Sena in Bombay," unpub. draft of Ph.D. diss. (M.I.T., 1975).

[16] Katzenstein, "Political Nativism," Ch. VI, 18.

[17] Ibid., Ch. VII., 7-8.

[18] K.V. Narayana Rao, *Telengana: A Study in the Regional Committees of India,* (Calcutta, 1972), 232.

[19] Ibid., 70.

[20] Ibid., 82-83.

[21] Ibid., 336.

[22] Literacy figures are from the 1971 provisional census.

[23] While a substantial part of the industrial labor force in Mysore is Kannada, employment in Mysore's plantations and in construction is largely non-Kannada; here, again, is an example of ethnic specialization, for neither construction nor plantation employment is sought by the Kannada working class. In the large scale construction projects Tamils are generally employed for "earth work" and Telugus for "stone work." Plantation workers generally come from Kerala, and forest operations—that is, cutting loading and trucking—are also mainly carried on by Kerala laborers.

[24] *Times of India,* Oct. 7, 1972.

[25] Ibid.

[26] I am grateful to Paul Brass of the University of Washington, Seattle, for probing me on this issue.

X.

The Search for Identity in Southeast Asia

By Robert Shaplen

Some men are more at home than others in the century in which they live—we still can't choose when to be born, though a chromosomal computer may yet arrange it. I doubt that Harold Isaacs, were he offered the option, would have chosen a different period, for the twentieth century has been wonderfully suited to his inquisitive mind. As a journalist, author, scholar, and teacher, he has sifted and winnowed the multifarious confusions of our time and framed his unique observations and judgements. If they haven't always consoled us, it is a tribute to his probing curiosity and to his deep social conscience that he has sought out the root causes of evil and inequality in the world and, sometimes with anger but more often with compassion and remorse, has begged our better comprehension.

Unlike many youthful ex-radicals who become disillusioned and drift in later life into compromise and conservatism, and often grow embittered in the process, Harold has never despaired of humankind, though he has spent a good part of his life taking it to task for its shortcomings. He is still a revolutionary at heart and in spirit, rebelling against the inanities and the inertia of a world in which millions are deprived of decency. In a new introduction to the 1966 edition of *No Peace for Asia*, which he had written twenty years before, he placed himself in true perspective when he wrote: "I am still refusing to accept things as they are, but I do accept more than I did then. I still reject despair, but I do so more doggedly even than I did then. And I am still asking questions in what I know better now than I did then is a world without answers."

As he built up his shelf of studious, reflective books and articles primarily on politics and ethnic themes, Harold Isaacs never ceased to ask questions, and he has provided answers that have often been as disturbing as elucidating, stirring our own consciences and arousing our further curiosity and concern. Following his early classic, *The Tragedy of the Chinese Revolution*, which dealt with what he felt were the multiple betrayals and historical implications of that momentous event, and *No Peace for Asia*, which prophetically portrayed the setbacks suffered by the post-war nationalist movements fighting both recrudescent colonialism and their own factionalism, he moved slowly into the larger themes of race and of the complex web of inter-personal and inter-ethnic relationships. Speaking, again in the same 1966 introduction, of "the shift in preoccupation and change of focus" that marked his later work, he aptly summed up his more difficult task: "I began to move from the study of the large political process as such to the examination of the impact of political change on the group identity patterns of people caught up in its great swirls. This carried me down from the large dimensions of nationalist and power politics which had engaged me so fully for so many years to the more intimate and more elusive matters of the mutual images and self-images of groups of people, the meaning of their cultural, national, ethnic, or racial identities, and the way these interweave with the patterns of political power. The pursuit of these matters before long led me out of the world of journalism in which I had worked for twenty-five years and into a no-less lively but more permissive academic environment in which I could more readily follow my own bents wherever they took me."

There is no need here to summarize Harold Isaacs' books. Instead I will indulge myself in some personal reminiscences of my long association with him and, as a fellow journalist and author, offer some comments of my own on subjects, primarily Asian, that have preoccupied us both.

The passage of time has blurred some of my images, but, as I recall it, I first met Harold during World War II when we were both war correspondents for *Newsweek* and were home on leave. He was covering the China-Burma-India theater and I was assigned to the Southwest Pacific. Perhaps we met earlier, at some Socialist gathering in New York before the war. I certainly knew *of* him before then because, aside from our mutual involvement in Socialism, he had known my father, Joseph Shaplen of *The New York Times*, himself a lifelong Socialist and a father confessor to several generations of young reporters who passed through the sacrosanct city-room of that paper. (I myself grew up, journalistically, in the far more raucous and rangier halls of *The New York Herald Tribune*.)

My father was a Menshevik, a Social Democrat, and he felt strongly about the betrayal of the Russian revolution, as Harold did about the Chinese revolution, and, for different reasons, about the Russian revolution as well. He had as little use for Leon Trotsky, who wrote the introduction to the original edition of *The Tragedy of the Chinese Revolution,* as he did for Stalin and Lenin. I have no record of those early conversations of my father with Harold and other ex-radicals, except that, through the years (my father died in 1946), a number of them have told me that they came to believe in the validity of his moderate Socialist views and subsequently understood better his staunch opposition to totalitarian Communism. I cannot speak for what Harold felt at that time, but I do know that these city-room discussions were heated and controversial. Harold was still an ardent and articulate protagonist of revolutionary *causes*, however vitiated and corrupted some of them had become, and, being as forceful and persuaded of his beliefs as my father was of his, Harold probably felt that Shaplen *pere* was too "right-wing" or even "reactionary."

They undoubtedly had their differences as well about the defence of Trotsky, which was coming to a head during those days. They also differed about the future course of world socialism, and about the role that the radical movement in the United States should play. The mellowness with which Harold and other young men and women regarded my father, and have since remembered him, was based more generally on his passionate concern for human freedom. And they have all recalled his ardent willingness to help those who were younger than he understand more about both journalism and life, including the need for genuine reform which, in those depression and post-depression days, was the passionate concern of us all.

After our introduction in New York, Harold and I next met in Manila where I was temporarily based as *Newsweek*'s Pacific correspondent and as publisher of its new Pacific edition. The war would soon be over and we discussed the future and our plans. I wanted to establish a bureau in Shanghai, and we talked about China, which Harold knew so well and I only dimly sensed. My own premature anti-Communism and my support of America's alliance with the Kuomintang Chinese during the war made me far more sympathetic to Chiang Kai-shek than Harold was—in fact, he was to be banned from post-war China. He sensed sooner than I did that the Koumintang held no promise for the future of China and that the upheaval which had been partially submerged during the anti-Japanese struggle would soon be surging toward an inevitable denouement. As for Southeast Asia, his skepticism about the success of the nationalist movements, which he had not yet examined in detail, was scarcely restrained by his paramount disdain for the stubborn attitude of the colonialist countries, and their reluctance to surrender their imperial perogatives. All of this served as a useful introduction for my own subsequent experience in that beleaguered area. When I did open a Shanghai bureau in 1946, and saw what an insurmountable mess the Kuomintang was making of the already complex post-war situation, I soon lost my earlier sympathy for Chiang Kai-shek and the men around him. In the two years I spent in China, at a time when it was possible, because of the presence of the Marshall mission seeking a formula for peace between the Communists and the Kuomintang, to travel widely, it did not require much prescience to see that the Communists would eventually win out over the corrupt and totally disorganized government.

As I write this, I have been re-reading parts of *The Tragedy of the Chinese Revolution* as well as Harold's introduction to *Straw Sandals*, a collection of Chinese short stories of the 1918-1933 period which he edited. Looking back to some of our earlier talks, and some of our subsequent ones as well, many things come into fresh focus across the wide expanse of the last four decades. In the introduction to the stories Harold describes his own early days in China, beginning in 1931, when he was twenty years old. He was still involved with many Communist friends, and was living a semi-underground life as the publisher and editor of a magazine called *China Forum* after having worked as a reporter and editor on *The Shanghai Evening Post* and the *China Press*. His few autobiographical pages vividly describe how he collected the left-wing stories of youthful martyrs and how he began to break with the Communists whom he had known as their own intricate plots and betrayals became clearer to him. Beyond that, these pages depicting the Shanghai of the 1930s evoke for me memories of that fabulous city a decade later and of my association with some of the people Harold knew; among them was Madame Soong Ching-ling, the widow of Sun Yat-sen. In the 1940s when I knew her, she was still sponsoring the China League for Civil Rights and living a charmed life under Kuomintang pressure as she now leads a remote and honorific one under the Communists in Peking. I have often wondered, as Harold has, what her private thoughts, at the age of 80, must be.

When I did my own traveling around China, including visits to Manchuria and one to Yenan where I had a lengthy interview, in October 1946, with Mao Tse-tung and long talks with other top-ranking Communists, I began to understand more clearly, even though I had no ideological or political sympathy with them, how easy it must have been in the 1930s, let alone in the 1940s, to admire their dedication, zeal, and absolute conviction that they would conquer China. Like other correspondents and the more forthright and realistic government officials, such as John Paton Davies, Jr., who were later pilloried for their views, I felt and wrote that we had better prepare ourselves for a Communist take-over, whatever alternative we preferred. In those days the Communist leader we met most often was Chou En-lai, who was the principal liaison man in Nanking and Shanghai with the Kuomintang and the Americans, under General Marshall, as distinguished an American as any I have known. Our meetings with Chou usually took place in the evening at a house in the old French concession area of Shanghai, which had hardly changed in the decade since Harold left it, except perhaps that it was no longer quite the haven for political conspirators and gangsters that it had been earlier. Even then, Chou, a handsome man of infinite magnetism and charm, understood more English than he pretended and would often correct his interpreters, one of whom was Chiao Kuan-hua, recently China's Foreign Minister, and known as Chiao Mu. Our discussions frequently stretched into long debates over countless cups of hot tea that would last until long past midnight.

Thirty years later, as I regard China from my perch in Hong Kong, it is impossible not to feel twinges of nostalgia for those exciting days when, as Harold had earlier, we felt ourselves on the front-lines of an historic revolutionary struggle. It was apparent to most of us, almost from the start, that Marshall's painstaking efforts, conducted with great patience and dignity, would have slight chance of success. There was a brief period in 1946 when a breakthrough appeared possible before the right-wing members of the Kuomintang persuaded Chiang that he did not have to make compromises with the Communists because the Americans were sure to back him anyway. Short of thirty American divisions, whatever support we might have given Chiang would have failed to "save" China, and I doubt that even that many divisions could have done it. Such an expeditionary force would have been a forerunner of the Vietnam disasters we were to perpetuate in the mid-1960s. History of course is full of tragic ironies: today, as we seek to pursue our still tenuous detente with Peking, Vietnam, which has occupied most of my attention over the past ten years, seems an even greater mistake in the light of our present China policy. One of our principal reasons for entering the Vietnam War was to curb Chinese-supported insurgency throughout Southeast Asia and rally the nations of the region into an anti-Communist bloc. Insurgent movements are still active, and are supported by Peking. With the exception of Indonesia where the Communists were crushed and killed by tens of thousands after the failure of the 1965 coup, our intervention in Vietnam has made little difference in the area as a whole, and if we did not altogether misread Chinese intentions we surely exaggerated their importance. The paramount concern of the Chinese remains the establishment of a new rational domestic order—and of course the containment of the Russian threat. The Chinese revolution, different phases of which Harold and I witnessed, is still by no means over, and it sometimes seems to me that the revolutionary dynamic is something the Chinese thrive on, as necessary to their survival, after all these years, as is the air they breathe. Whatever catharsis they find seems destined to be reached through the seeds of chaos.

I have always envied Harold one of the many radical friends he knew in Shanghai in the 1930s. Then named Nguyen Ai Quoc, he later became famous as Ho Chi Minh. At the time he was living underground in the International Settlement area, though Harold says he met him quite often at the Chinese YMCA. Some eight years later Ho would form the Indo-Chinese Communist Party, and, in August 1945, enter Hanoi with his few thousand guerrillas to establish the government that still rules North Vietnam today and has just achieved its thirty year old dream of conquering the South. Unfortunately, I never met Ho—when I got to Hanoi, in 1951, five years after my first trip to South Vietnam, Ho was back in the jungle fighting the French, and I was unable to return to Hanoi after his triumphant return there in 1954. Harold preceded me to Saigon immediately after the war, in the fall of 1945, and one of the finest chapters in *No Peace for Asia* deals with the chaotic situation in the south at the time, when the French were just returning and the short-lived Vietminh government that briefly held parts of the city had been dispersed back to the countryside. We have always shared an intense hatred for all forms of colonialism, but perhaps particularly for the French variety, which was the least compromising of all. The United States made its first big mistake in Vietnam by lending the French its support during the eight long, futile years from 1946 to 1954 when they struggled to maintain their imperial hold on the country.

I say "first" mistake, but there was one that preceded it, though our leverage to pursue it was limited: that was to try to come to terms with Harold's old Shanghai friend Ho, in effect to "pre-Titofy" him. Many of us thought then, as we still do now, that this was a gamble we and the French should have taken; certainly it stood as good, if not better, a chance of working as our attempt to force a coalition government in China. The crisis came to a head in the summer of 1946, when I was in Saigon, and Ho had gone to France to determine what sort of bargain he could drive. It was then that the returning *colons* on the scene in Cochin-China (now the southern part of South Vietnam) made clear their intention of hanging on. Though Ho had told Harold, who had managed to re-establish contact with him, that he was willing to accept help from the West and co-operate peacefully in return for independence, his mission to France was subverted by what was happening back home. As I made clear in one of my own books, *The Lost Revolution* (New York, 1965), I never had any illusions that Ho was not a Communist, but he was a nationalist first, and highly independent-minded despite his earlier Comintern connections. That he was serious about wanting to reach a compromise with the French was attested by the criticism he received from his own extremists during the crucial summer of 1946, when he returned to Hanoi; there is some evidence that, for a period of two months, he was even under a mild form of house arrest.

The untried gamble with Ho would have been more or less in keeping with Harold's post-factum prescription for avoiding disaster and violence throughout Southeast Asia at the close of the war. He felt then and later that the United States, with "its power paramount, its physical and moral authority unlimited, could have written the beginnings of a new dispensation" simply by "temporarily freezing the political status quo, and requiring that any new changes in the status of these (SEA) countries come about through international negotiations as part of the settlements ending the war."(*No Peace for Asia*) The formula seems to me a bit simplistic. I doubt that, even with our authority supreme, we could have frozen the status quo in the area as a whole, if only because events moved too swiftly, including the fledgling, and in some cases not so fledgling, nationalist rebellions. But we certainly could have done more than we did, which was next to nothing, to arrest the return of the colonial powers and we should have refrained from offering them our moral as well as physical support. Had we lent our support instead to the true nationalist movements throughout the area, even if some of them were tinged with Communism, it is possible that we not only could have avoided unnecessary bloodshed in Vietnam but could have averted what has since become, and remains today, with the momentary exception of the democratic experiment in Thailand, a trend toward increasing authoritarianism throughout Southeast Asia.

It may be, however, as I have recently come to suspect, that those of us whose imaginations were captured by the exciting events in Southeast Asia thirty years ago overestimated the importance, or at least the efficacy, of nationalism at the time and allowed our own euphoria to carry us away. In many ways, nationalism was a somewhat blunted weapon, blunted or weighed down by the past it sought to unshackle. Nothing in that past warranted the supposition that the new nations would be able to develop overnight, or even over a matter of years, into Western-style democracies with neat, well-ordered parliaments and a proper division of executive, legislative and judicial functions and powers. In fact, the history of the area was one of authoritarian control going back to pre-colonial times when various waves of religion and commerce moved across from the subcontinent, sometimes peacefully and often violently, and autarchic dynasties rose and fell. Subsequently, the imperial powers simply superimposed their own systems and laws on the cultures and civilizations that existed before and, for their own economic purposes, created new mechanisms of authoritarian rule. Then the Japanese moved in, cruelly and ineffectively, with no understanding of the local cultures, and at the end of World War II, ironically, sought to stimulate the new nationalism as a kind of eleventh-hour pan-Asianism. At the same time the returning Western nations, including the Americans on the scene, employed the Japanese troops to help "keep order." It was pure travesty, but, unfortunately, also a deadly serious game.

Under the circumstances, it was to be expected that the post-war course of new nationhood was extremely uneven. The ironies kept multiplying. Surely there was a sad and even wicked irony in the contradictory role the Americans played in the Philippines and in Indo-China. In the former, our own colony, we granted independence so rapidly, and without sufficient planning, in 1946, that the Filipinos created a caricature of democratic government, imitating many of the worst features of American democracy at the same time that they added a few touches of their own oligarchic past; it wasn't long before the new native oligarchy took over, political life became a mockery, and social and economic disparities grew wider and wider. And then, in a sense, events came full circle, and President Ferdinand Marcos imposed his martial law rule, with the pretense that rigged "citizens assemblies" represented a "new" form of democracy. At this moment, early in 1976, to compound the ironies, Marcos is fighting a Communist insurgency which has Maoist backing at the same time that he has recognized Peking, and is facing a severe racial challenge from the Muslims in the south which might have been avoided if successive Catholic governments had ameliorated sooner the lot of the Muslims and put a stop to Christian land-grabbing in Mindanao.

In Indo-China in 1946, in contrast to our policy of de-colonizing the Philippines, we went out of our way foolishly to support the continuation of colonialism. In so doing, we had an ulterior motive that didn't work out: we wanted the French to support what was then called the European Defense Community, but they reneged—as years later they would renege on the North Atlantic Treaty Organization—and left us, or more specifically left John Foster Dulles, holding a dead colonial cat by the tail in Vietnam. We produced Ngo Dinh Diem, hopefully nursed him along for two or three years of delayed nationalism, and ended by help-ing overthrow him in 1963. At that point, or shortly after, we made the fatal mistake that we had not made twenty years earlier in China; we engaged in a major land war on the Asian mainland.

This is no place to deal with the Vietnam War, which I have done in various books and many articles. But I would like to make a number of points about the war because it brought me in conflict at the outset with a number of my old friends at home, including Harold. Having failed, through our own lack of persuasion, to move the French to grant the South Vietnamese their independence, I felt that we had an obligation after 1954 to do what we could, belatedly, to help preserve some kind of order in the country, and, once it became apparent that the Geneva ac-cords were not going to be implemented, to encourage South Vietnamese freedom and reform. In my view, under the increasing Communist threat from the north and from within the country as well, we were justified in supporting the South Vietnamese economically and militarily, including building a functioning counter-insurgency movement. Once it became ap-parent that the reforms were not forthcoming, that the Diem regime was becoming more dictatorial, we should have ceased aiding it sooner than we ultimately did and perhaps thereby forced him out in a less violent way than became inevitable. After the coup, neither we nor the Viet-namese had any real comprehension of what was going to happen, or what should happen, and the deadly drift through coups and counter-coups began. It was at this point, in 1965, that we made the mistake of entering the war full-scale and of bombing North Vietnam. Having failed to use our political leverage properly, we should simply have withdrawn from the scene. Once over-involved, we not only continued our political failures—and under circumstances of even far greater leverage—but taught the Vietnamese to fight the wrong kind of war while fighting a wrong war ourselves.

As I look back at the long Vietnam experience, and our parallel ex-perience in Cambodia and Laos, it surely cannot be said that what was, at best, an effort to delay the ultimate Communist victories in those countries was worth the cost in human lives, and in money and misery. If we had played our cards differently from the outset, a more limited American involvement might have served a more useful purpose, but we were neither sophisticated nor wise enough to follow such a course. Both in Vietnam and in Cambodia, our lack of political judgment proved catastrophic, while the military path we followed was even more disastrous. In Laos, perhaps, we acted more subtly, though we made our mistakes there too, and the end result has been the same.

I was in Saigon when it fell to the Communists. Though like everyone else I was surprised by the swiftness of Hanoi's victory, few of us had come to expect anything but an eventual Communist take-over. During the first few months of 1975, it appeared that Hanoi was still will-ing to accept a political solution, one that would be in accordance with its wishes as set forth in the Paris agreement of January, 1973, with the government placed in a defensive position. But starting in January, 1975, the alternative of moving toward a military option began to be made clear. When the Communists captured Phuoc Long province in the first week of January, and the United States demonstrated that it was no longer in any mood to give the South Vietnamese military aid, the leaders in Hanoi started to move more sharply down the military road. When the highlands collapsed in mid-March, the die was cast, and with the capture shortly thereafter of Hue and Danang in the northern tier of the country, and the ensuing collapse of the whole chain of coastal provinces, it quickly became obvious that the end was near.

Though long beset by many problems of their own, including those of poor internal morale and reconstruction in their own country, the North Vietnamese had never forsaken their dream of capturing the South. One way or another, they were destined to make their influence predominant. In retrospect, the more recent turning point was Paris. By forcing the Americans out of Vietnam, and by winning the argument over keeping their own troops in the South, the North Vietnamese knew they had finally established the foundations for victory. From the American point of view, it seemed justifiable enough to remove our troops and obtain the release of our prisoners, but the Paris pact did little to help end the long fratricidal conflict. I know for a fact that our highest officials never expected any more than that out of Paris. For the South Vietnamese, as I wrote at the time, it was a "cruel agreement," which accounted for their resistence to signing it. In the weeks before and after the agreement went into effect, we continued to pour military aid into South Vietnam, but as the months dragged on, and the mood of Congress and the American people became more jaundiced and uncaring, we slackened that aid, and at the end were no longer even replacing lost or destroyed military equipment on the so-called one-for-one basis that the Paris agreement stipulated. Hanoi no doubt made a highly plausible assessment of the situation early on: it told its cadres to be patient, while it prepared itself for the final attack. Then, late in 1974 and in the first three months of 1975, when the Russians quadrupled their aid to North Vietnam, the attack was launched. If need be, Hanoi was still ready to negotiate—on its terms. But the need never arose, and the path to Saigon soon lay clear.

What brought about the fall of Vietnam, and what was wrong with the overbearing American involvement? In past writings I and others have analyzed the conditions that seemed to seal the country's doom, but they warrant a brief recapitulation. There was never, to begin with, a valid and persuasive nationalist force in the South. The country's regional and religious difference made this difficult, in contrast to the North, but the development of a more cohesive sense of nationalism need not have been impossible, had the southerners, as early as 1954, determined to resolve their political animosities and differences, and set about rationalizing their social and economic system. Instead, the divisiveness among them grew, and they developed a peculiar lemmings-like compulsion for self-destruction. When the 1963 coup against Ngo Dinh Diem took place, with the support of the United States, there seemed some hope for a brighter future, but the successive governments revealed an even greater incapacity to govern than had Diem and his tyrannical family. Corruption became even more rampant, lack of leadership in the armed forces more apparent, and there was no real attempt, despite the vast amount of lip-service and experimentation, to create a new fabric of society that could both cope with the continuing war and offer the South Vietnamese people anything more than an individual chance for survival, each man on his own terms.

The Americans simply never understood the Vietnamese psychology, and instead of trying to teach them in ways that, as Asians, they could comprehend, we sought to superimpose our Western ways and methods on their Oriental society. It was bound not to work. Politically, they were not prepared to adapt themselves to Western democratic forms. Militarily, we made the mistake of fighting the war for them, wreaking vast destruction on the country and the people, and we never trained them properly to fight either a conventional *or* unconventional war. All our paraphernalia of imposed panaceas—strategic hamlets and Phoenix programs to kill Vietcong agents—were the products of our "think-tank" approach and were masterminded from the White House basement without sufficient consideration of Vietnamese social and economic mores. As the North Vietnamese mounted their major offensives in 1968, 1972, and in 1975, the social planning went awry, and our lack of political judgment, or use of leverage, led us time and again to back the wrong leaders because they were amenable to doing things "our way," no matter how ineffective and corrupt they and their entourages were.

Toward the very end, when it was too late, I saw some signs, similar to those of 1945-46, of a new nationalist sentiment—both anti the government of President Nguyen Van Thieu and anti-Communist. The Buddhists and the Catholics, for example, appeared to demonstrate a belated desire to cooperate in getting rid of Thieu. But, once again, aside from the lateness of the hour, the various political and religious elements allowed their differences to preclude strong united action. At the same time, the Americans, finally grown weary of supporting Thieu, moved too slowly to bring pressure on him to resign sooner. Had that happened, and had a new government willing to negotiate been created, the worst might have been avoided, and at least a more graceful and dignified surrender might have been possible, one that might have allowed the southern leaders some role in a new Communist-dominated regime. But as things turned out, the North Vietnamese clearly judged the emerging picture and, with the military odds all in their favor, made the decision to go for broke.

Now that they have all of Vietnam in their grasp, what will the North Vietnamese do with it? It is of course too soon to draw any firm conclusions, but one can make some preliminary estimates. In economic terms, the South will undoubtedly be utilized as a breadbasket, particularly for rice, and as a source of raw materials, perhaps including valuable offshore oil which was in the process of being explored and developed when Saigon was taken. Politically, the outright capture of the country by Hanoi's troops and cadres will enable the northerners to subjugate or use the southern Communist elements of the Provisional Revolutionary Government (P.R.G.) as they see fit. It may be presumed that Hanoi will now work more directly through the apparatus of the People's Revolutionary Party (P.R.P.), the direct southern adjunct of the northern Laodong (Communist) party. This does not mean that such southern leaders as Huynh Tan Phat and Nguyen Huu Tho, the top P.R.G. and National Liberation Front leaders, will play no role, but it probably does mean that their actions will be carefully monitored if not directed by Hanoi and the P.R.P. hierarchy. The tough northern leaders, led by Pham Hung, a prominent member of the Politboro and long the leader of the war effort in the South, will in all likelihood move slowly and carefully at first to superimpose their plans and desires, but within six months or a year, in my estimation, the pattern of government the North wishes to establish will become clear. Although I hope that there will not be a major bloodbath, and do not expect one, it seems to me inevitable that considerable numbers of people, especially long-time anti-Communist leaders and former petty and corrupt government officials, will in one way or another be dealt with "harshly," as Hanoi has steadily warned. Unfortunately, since we primarily extricated our own Vietnamese employees as refugees, many of the bona-fide anti-Communist intellectuals were left behind. They are bound to have trouble.

It has seemed apparent to me for some time that the North Vietnamese would dominate all of Indo-China, though it also seems inevitable that they will come into some conflict with the Chinese, who have had their own direct lines to the P.R.G. and who were not overjoyed by the massive North Vietnamese victory. To a lesser extent the Russians were also not overjoyed. If the Americans have enough sense to adjust to the situation, render aid without strings to the new Vietnam, and repair some of the immense damage we wrought, we might yet play a salutary role in the area. As I write, the coalition government in Laos, whose sole chance for survival lay in a political solution in South Vietnam, has moved toward a government of complete Communist domination, although it is experiencing some continuing resistance. All three major powers—Russia, China and the United States, for their separate reasons—have looked upon Laos as a potential buffer state. The desires of the powers to neutralize the country in some fashion may restrain the Vietnamese from going too far, and eventually this might make it possible for a native Lao nationalism to survive, but it will at best be a thoroughly left-wing nationalist-Communist type of rule.

Cambodia, at the moment, even after the Khmer Rouge victory, remains in a state of near-total chaos. The Communists, who variously look to Hanoi, Peking, Moscow, and, to a lesser and evermore waning degree, to Prince Sihanouk, are likely to continue their battle for supremacy among each other. The leaders who seem most likely to emerge as the true strong-men are Ieng Sary, who looks to Hanoi, and Saloth Sar, who looks to both Hanoi and Moscow, insofar as we know anything about him. The Khmer, all but obsessed with their desire to cling to what little remains of the old Khmer empire, so far have exhibited a degree of tough, no-holds-barred handling of the people, pushing thousands into the countryside to live on the land and be "re-educated," and eliminating, probably by execution, the top men of the old regime, as well as at least 300,000 lesser officials and ordinary citizens in what has indeed been a bloodbath. How long this harsh policy of repression and widespread movement of people will continue is impossible to judge, but it does not augur well for a peaceful, prosperous new Cambodia. Sooner or later, as in Vietnam and Laos, the Cambodians will require some foreign assistance, though they have rejected it during the first year of the takeover. The chances are that the French will be among the first to return to Phnom Penh, just as they will also play a role, to their advantage, in Vietnam and to a lesser extent in Laos. There is ample irony in all this: more than two decades after the rejection of French colonialism (which the Americans so abysmally backed during the period from 1945 to 1954, in Vietnam above all), it will be the French who may well benefit most from the Communist victories.

The period between 1965 and the Communist Tet offensive of 1968 in Vietnam was a new time of transition in the rest of Southeast Asia. This was when Lee Kuan Yew, the Prime Minister of Singapore, set forth the "timed gained" theory—that, by keeping Vietnam from being overrun by Communism, the Americans were affording the rest of the Southeast Asian nations time to set their own houses in order. There were some, both Asians and Americans, who were persuaded that, finally, some proper democracy-building could take place, but, for the most part, too many American policy makers thought in terms of building a solid bloc against further Communist expansionism. As things turned out, neither was accomplished. There was some hope in Indonesia, after the failure of the 1965 Communist coup, that the new Suharto regime would not only clean up the economic mess left by Sukarno but would also move toward political liberation by allowing the old secular and religious Socialist parties to participate once more in political life. The hope soon proved illusory. Economically, Indonesia made progress; inflation was stopped, or greatly reduced, and the nation's shattered infrastructure was gradually improved. But today, unfortunately, Indonesia is sunk in fresh corruption on a level far greater than before, with foreigners deeply involved as they seek, in post-colonial ways, to participate in the "development" of the nation's rich resources. Virtually nothing has been done to improve conditions in the impoverished villages, and everywhere the gap between the rich and the poor grows greater. In January 1974, riots and demonstrations took place, ostensibly against the new Japanese imperialism, but, in fact, expressing mass discontent over the failure of social and economic development by the Suharto regime. Politically, the regime has created a sham framework of democracy while the military rules the roost and authotitarian control increases.

Elsewhere in the region the growth of authoritarian governments offers little hope for reform. At present, Thailand alone stands out as a democratic exception, but I have grave doubts that this latest attempt to create and sustain a constitutional government will prove successful. There are no real political traditions in the country, simply a plethora of ambitious parties with no outstanding leaders. The student-led revolution of late 1973 that overthrew the military dictatorship was a healthy phenomenon, but corruption and deep social and economic inequalities have not been dealt with, though perhaps it is too soon to make judgments. If the political vacuum is not satisfactorily filled, there will be an unavoidable return of military rule, perhaps more benevolent than before under the gentle but persuasive eye of the esteemed monarchy, and that will pave the way for the Communists.

Malaysia remains caught in deep racial conflicts that, although held in check since the riots of 1969, could readily explode again. The tenuous effort of giving the Malays more political power while permitting the Chinese their economic superiority is a difficult path to pursue. Here, too, no solutions have yet been found to bind the racial wounds of the past by improving conditions for the poorer Malays. One wonders whether the deep-seated problems of race and society, which have monopolized Harold's attention in recent years, are really solvable politically. Only a strong authoritarian hand, backed by the police, so far seems to have controlled the situation in Malaysia, despite the use of democratic electoral trappings.

In neighboring Singapore, which became a republic after being ousted from Malaysia in 1965, Lee Kuan Yew has demonstrated little effort to permit greater political freedom. His one-party city-state has prospered economically, but for those of us who looked upon Lee, the highly intelligent ex-Marxist who knew how to deal with the Communists, as the most far-seeing statesman in Southeast Asia, he has proved a deep disappointment. In his obsession with economic progress, he has scarcely used the "time" he once spoke of "gaining" through the Vietnam War to encourage freedom in his small domain. Labor unions and newspapers have been suppressed in the alleged interests of maintaining a calm atmosphere—and of drawing more foreign investors. As the Chinese leader of a predominately Chinese island pocket in a Malay sea, Lee admittedly has racial problems to contend with, but he has allowed his own phobias, including racial ones, and his obvious fear of Chinese Communist influence in Singapore, to lead him far from his earlier Socialist tenets toward his own harsh form of authoritarian rule.

In looking back, thirty years after I first came to Asia, it seems to me that the questions of race and identity which so much concern Harold have, if anything, grown more complicated and difficult to analyze. Partly because of the Vietnam War and the destruction that it wrought, and partly because of post-colonial economic imperialism and the new influence of money and power, including corruption, I note a general or at least partial loss of identity. There are some obvious exceptions: Most notable is Japan, where the historically homogeneous society still prevails, and a foreigner, or *gaijin,* feels his solitude impinging upon him like a cold shroud. The Koreans, despite the unfortunate bifurcation of their country after World War II, still retain a very positive sense of their racial identity, quite different from that of the Japanese; they are at once more outgiving and tougher. (It is interesting that, although they remain supremely proud of their Japanese-ness, the Japanese today are deeply engaged in what they refer to as an identity crisis, though there is no Japanese word specifically defining identity. This search for identity is the result, in part, of their injured sense of pride over being called "economic animals" and their loss of social awareness. The search, like so many fads in Japan, may simply prove a passing fancy, but it is a current and often amusing pursuit.)

The Vietnamese, who, historically, have had a strong sense of identity, have had it blurred by the American impact more permanently, I fear, than we may suspect. Where the much longer influence of the French created a series of subtle changes in the Vietnamese character, the blunter and harsher shock of the American presence has been a more disturbing factor. One saw the effects in the behavior of the children and youth as well as in the new attitudes of the older generation. What the Communists called "a just war" in which a believed cause, whether right or wrong, served as a stimulant and enhanced identity, sometimes to the point of chauvinism and suicidal madness in battle, had the opposite effect when the war proved to lack a common denominator of patriotism, or, if you will, nationalism. It then served to diminish the sense of identity, which became splintered by the various social and economic forces that came into play. Eventually, as the war in Vietnam dragged on, it built up pressures that caused the moral disintegration of the society. Survival and opportunism, and, of course, corruption, became a way of life in themselves, and the identity of those caught up in such a grim welter was all but lost. Thus, while we speak of the traumatic effect of the war on the United States, the Vietnamese trauma went far deeper. The Communists will not find this easy to cope with or to rectify. In fact, even in their far more controlled society of North Vietnam, they have suffered some of the same problems of moral disintegration and loss of identity, as their exhortations and articles, replete with self-criticism, increasingly have revealed.

The Chinese identity is so many-faceted that I hesitate to comment on it; moreover, until I spent a week there with President Ford in December, 1975, I had not been in China since 1947 so cannot speak at first hand of the identity changes wrought by two and a half decades of Communism. But from all one reads, the changes have been many in the altered family structure alone and in the whole new world of the communes and collective factories. It is hard to imagine that the traditional Chinese society could, in so short a time, have undergone so many drastic, if enforced, changes, but, for better or for worse, the Communists seem to have altered it. I think that it is probably too soon to tell how much the new Chinese identity can be defined, since, along with the continuing Chinese revolution, it is still undergoing so many transformations as the Chinese leaders keep re-defining the identities of their heroes and villains. My own experience with the Overseas Chinese throughout Southeast Asia has been greater and I have noted some changes among them. For one thing, while remaining Chinese, they have become less chauvinistic and are more willing, when they are given the chance, to blend into the societies of their adopted countries. This is certainly true in Thailand and the Philippines, and even in Malaysia, but less so in Indonesia, where the anti-Chinese hangover from the 1965 coup slaughter remains strong. Throughout the area, the loss of identity has derived from the increase in change of family names from Chinese names to names native to the country in which they live.

This rather pessimistic, rambling essay of reminiscence and reflection has been primarily designed to update Harold Isaacs and myself with the times and events that we have shared and experienced separately. No more than Harold would I have wanted to miss the adventures of Asia which remain a constant challenge, ever-surprising and always worth exploring in their multiple ramifications and mutations. There are still no answers, as Harold said years ago, and, if anything, there are more questions to be asked than there used to be, as Asia, like the rest of the world, becomes more complicated. Most of us have become more aware of the problems, and are not as prone as we once were to put too much faith in over-simplified panaceas or causes, including the cause of independence, which remains an elusive one. Independence from what and for whom? This is one of the new questions being asked in the wake of our disappointment not only with political events, but also with what has happened to the revolution of rising expectations and even to the green revolution. Too many people, not enough food, poor management—these are the paramount problems, and no one has yet begun to solve them. Freedom, as a concept, means very little when millions are starving, as in Bangladesh, one of the newest of the "free" nations. The imbalances of poverty and wealth have grown rather than diminished in the years that I have been in Asia. A desperate chance to survive becomes the sole legacy of war, of racial strife, of natural disasters, and much of Asia is engaged in that day to day struggle without much strength or will to think of anything else.

One cannot "retire" from the interests pursued all one's life, and I cannot imagine Harold Isaacs retiring from anything. I visualize him, years hence, wandering with his questions through Africa or Asia, through the urban jungles of America, weighing the answers that he gets against the vast experience and knowledge which he has gained. His quizzical mind is made to be scratched—and he may yet write a book called *Scratches on My Mind* as an autobiographical sequel to his *Scratches on Our Minds* which dealt with American images of China and India. The multiple scratches that he has already passed on to us have helped us understand the basic conflicts of our time, the dreams that failed, the hopes that went awry, and the multifarious personalities of different peoples and races and their ever-changing interactions on each other. May he scratch away, and continue to be scratched, and tell us more.

Epilogue: Echoes of the Present

by Arnold R. Isaacs

It is a bizarre twist in our family history that I am writing these lines now, having just returned (via a US Marine helicopter one day before Saigon's surrender) from covering the last months of the Indochina war. Almost exactly thirty years earlier HRI had witnessed the beginning, or at any rate one of the beginnings, of that long conflict when, as a *Newsweek* correspondent, he reported on the French return to Indochina after the end of World War II and the start of the Viet Minh resistance. He was no great optimist about human affairs even then. But I wonder what he would have said if someone had suggested, amid the crackle of those early firefights around Saigon in 1945, that three bloodsoaked decades later his son would be there to hear the next-to-last shots of the war.

The parallels go beyond the coincidence of a father's and son's reporting careers having spanned both ends of the Indochina conflict. For HRI was in Saigon then, he has written, because the turnings of another war had barred him from China, the country that had filled his career until then. And so during those strange days aboard ship on the South China Sea after my evacuation from Saigon the thought of HRI and China sounded somewhere in my mind like an eerie echo. The circumstances were different but now I too had been cut off from the Asian country that had played a large part in my own career. As HRI was, I also had been plucked from my front row seat and dumped outside the theater like a disorderly patron, unable to see the actors any more in a great drama I had been concerned with for several years, no longer hearing anything more than a muffled thump or indistinct voice as the play went on without me.

I imagine HRI must have felt then somewhat as I do now, all those years ago when he was pushed out through that one-way exit door from China. It is like an anchor rope snapping, a sudden weightlessness. One is abruptly detached from large absorbing events, from small personal links, from crowded sensations and emotions, from the sheer sleepless busyness of trying to see and grasp and write about it all. The door shuts on friends, on familiar places, on the scenes of large and small happenings that taught important lessons about war, death, power, humanity (and self). A chapter has been chopped off in mid-sentence; a piece of one's life has been lost, left behind in the smoke and fire of one or another bit of history. Though perhaps that isn't quite the right way to phrase it, because it is really a little more like that tired old gag about the Indian grumbling in the darkness: "Me not lost, wigwam lost." For it was not just that we disappeared from certain places—HRI from China, I three decades later from Vietnam—but that the places we left were disappearing too, the knowns becoming unknowns, remembered scenes changing into new ones with new sets and new actors. It is odd that these sensations too should have come round from father to son in these thirty years.

I should not leave these musings without noting, ruefully, one other parallel—that the instinct for timing does not seem to have improved much with the passage of generations in the Isaacs family. HRI was writing about his Asia long before Americans were listening; I am writing about mine when most Americans have stopped, if they ever listened at all. So our lives, which fell into such a curious pattern of echoes this year, have also the same question mark: we have something to say, or think we do, but who is there to hear?

What to make of all these echoes? On one dimension, certainly, that the human race has not made much progress toward sanity during HRI's lifetime. The reporter's notebooks now are filled with the same scenes as his were. On some pages blasted homes, rivers of refugees, peasant boys blown to bits in one uniform or another, children dead from shrapnel in Vietnam or from starvation in Bangladesh. On others glimpses of presidents, commissars, generals, diplomats and their courtiers, bathing in ego and cynicism and self-righteous talk, flashing past in sleek limousines or sitting fatly in conferences, indifferent and conscienceless. In HRI's younger socialist days the dream of a more humane world still seemed possible to him, but that dream has been shattered by bombs and drowned in an ocean of blood. No political orthodoxies remain, just a frail helpless faith, somehow not shaken off, that it is still worthwhile to try to understand and communicate.

If history and politics played their part in the recent echoing of HRI's life in mine, so did smaller more personal factors. I am here, after all, partly because I had known from childhood that one day I would travel to Asia, find new crowded lands, see places with melodious names like Luang Prabang or Balikpapan or the Karakoram Mountains, eat wondrously, and have adventures. Where did I know that from if not from the atmosphere and talk as I grew up in HRI's family. And I became a reporter, a trade I have followed for thirteen years now, surely because of the years in which I absorbed from HRI a curiosity about the world and a desire to see and write about it.

Reporting was his trade too, and with all its limitations I think he would agree that it has its values. It teaches clarity and directness of language, respect for fact. These HRI brought with him to the more reflective work he has done since moving from journalism to academia—still a reporter, in a sense, but focusing not on perishable headlines but on more enduring questions of persons and groups grappling with a changing world. I doubt if his quest down these roads has led to any greater hopefulness than his earlier travels in the world of political events. HRI's work of the last twenty years has not brightened any promise of humans becoming freer of fear, hate, suspicion, or division. Much of it has chronicled instead the persistence of tribalism, to use his word. There can have been little comfort in those researchers for a man whose own value has always been on pushing back the barriers— widening the world of choices instead of shrinking back into clan or sub-clan or sub-sub-clan.

Only HRI knows what remains of his belief in the life of the mind, in the value of clear-eyed understanding and reporting. Something must remain, however battered, I suppose, or else he wouldn't still be doing it. I do know how much he is sustained against outer despair by the strength of those closest, deepest bonds of marriage, family, and friendship. A magic circle, he calls it—a shelter built of love against the storms and emptiness without. All is not perfect serenity inside, as he and I have reason to know. It has not always been easy for me to be his son. Yet we are part of each other and I hope strengthen each other just the same. I am a husband and father myself and have made my own discoveries and formed my styles—not always his. Yet in these matters, as in those of writing and politics, what I have learned I began learning from him.

ARI
May, 1975